CONTENTS

For Arokiya Mary and for Michele

FOREWORD

In the words of a Brazilian woman: 'We are more than half the world's population, and we are the mothers of the other half.' As mothers and carers, as producers and farmers, the work of women supports their families and communities. Yet, throughout the world, the poorest people in the community are predominantly women and [their dependent children. Women, on the whole, often work for no pay at all and, if they are paid, they usually earn far less than men. Two-thirds of the illiterate people in the world are women. Women face increasing levels of violence, because of their gender, and half a million die each year as a direct or indirect result of pregnancy.

The dominant development approach, based on economic growth, reduction of the role of the state and privatisation of public services, far from improving women's lives, often makes them poorer, increases their workloads, and reduces their status. The structural adjustment measures imposed on indebted countries have particularly affected women, with the removal of subsidies, the rise in prices of basic foods, and the reduction of government services; and it is this same model of economic development that has legitimised the exploitation of women through the promotion of the sex tourism industry. Yet women are often excluded at many levels from the decision-making processes which vitally affect their lives.

Oxfam's Gender and Development Unit commissioned this book to explore the ways in which gender inequalities are constructed and the impact of mainstream development on gender relations. The book does not necessarily provide all the answers since gender issues are complex and apply at local, national and international levels. There are many ways of responding to gender needs and there had been questions raised within Oxfam for many years on how best to work with women. The setting up of the Gender and Development Unit (GADU) in 1985 initiated a strategy to integrate gender into all aspects of Oxfam's work and, in a broader context, to define the full implications of gender as a development issue. By redefining 'good' development, and looking at it from the standpoint of poor women in the South, Oxfam set out to revise its existing practices. The function of GADU was to create a culture within the organisation which enabled gender issues to become an integral part of the planning, monitoring and evaluation of projects and programmes.

GADU's strategies include raising awareness of gender issues, providing specialist skills by training Oxfam staff both overseas and in the UK, research, project and programme advice and the development and implementation of a gender policy within the organisation. The work of the Unit is furthered by gender specialist staff who work directly with women at grassroots level, and support workshops and other initiatives with our partner organisations in order to ensure that women's voices are heard and Oxfam can be more responsive to their needs.

Oxfam's partners in the South have played an important part in this process. We have built up contacts and established a fruitful dialogue with women's organisations in the South. A recent initiative combining many of these approaches has been a South-South linking project involving partners from over ten countries aimed at strengthening women's networks and improving Oxfam's field programmes.

Besides its work in the context of the overseas programme, GADU also plays its part in Oxfam's programme of educating and informing the public in the UK and Ireland about the causes of poverty. GADU produces reports, books and newsletters to exchange experiences and increase understanding of gender and development issues. *Half the World, Half a Chance* is part of this wider purpose.

The book looks at the position and condition of women throughout the world. It tries to explain how discrimination actually operates within different societies, the reasons why women are disadvantaged in so many ways, and why development initiatives have so often failed to help women. It provides examples of Oxfam's work with partners in the South who are committed to addressing women's immediate and longer-term needs for cultural and social change. Throughout the book, there are many illustrations of women working together to overcome the obstacles they face. The message is clear: the world can no longer afford to ignore the voices of women. If women have the opportunity to be heard, consulted and involved in planning and implementing development projects the impact and benefit of development on women and the whole community will be greatly enhanced.

If women come together to organise for change and are given the space to use their strengths and talents, a transformation of gender relations can take place enabling women to become equal and valued members of society.

Eugenia Piza Lopez
Co-ordinator
Oxfam Gender and Development Unit

viii

Acknowledgements

I would like to thank Oxfam's Gender and Development Unit for their critical reading of the manuscript and the many helpful insights they have provided. I would particularly like to acknowledge and thank Eugenia Piza-Lopez for her clarity and perception throughout the production of the manuscript. I would also like to thank all the other members of Oxfam's staff in Oxford who took time to discuss the role of gender in their work, and to make case-study material available to me. Thanks, too, to Oxfam's staff in Bangalore, India, for all the friendship and support extended to me at the outset of the project, and to David, Jacob and Oliver for seeing it through to the last page.

Julia Cleves Mosse
Oxford
December 1992

action and play. But when the same baby appeared as a girl and did the same things, the women soothed and comforted it. In other words, at only six months the children were already being responded to according to gender stereotypes.[1]

As adults we tend to believe that we live with a significant degree of freedom, that we are free to choose the way we behave, the way we think, the gender roles that we adopt. We also subscribe to a common-sense view of the world that our way of being feminine or masculine is 'natural' — a direct result of being born biologically male or female. Obviously, a society may have many different scripts, many different costumes, but the core values of a culture, which include gender roles, are passed on from generation to generation like language.

BEN FAWCETT/OXFAM

In Vietnam, women are active in a wide variety of tasks, many of which would be thought of as more typically men's work in other societies.

One of the most interesting things about gender roles is that they change over time, and differ from culture to culture. They are also strongly influenced by social class, age and ethnic background. In nineteenth century Britain it was considered inappropriate for women to work for wages outside the home. But a closer look shows that this only applied to middle- and upper-class women. Working-class women were expected to work as servants for those women who were not supposed to work themselves. Parallel situations exist today in many parts of the developing world. In Bangladesh, for example, many Muslim women would consider it inappropriate to join the paid work force; yet there are plenty of other Muslim women who are forced into work — often as domestic servants — as a matter of economic survival. In other words, class has almost as much to do with deciding appropriate gender roles as has biological sex.

The fact that different societies have a wide range of different ideas about appropriate ways for women and men to behave should make it clear just how far removed gender roles are from their origins in our biological sex. While every society uses biological sex as a starting point for describing gender, no two cultures would agree completely on what distinguishes one gender from another. Some societies are more prescriptive of gender roles than others, who have more scripts or possibilities for acceptable feminine and masculine behaviour. A Sahelian farming woman will have far fewer choices than a middle-class white American woman, who may be presented with a range of gender choices that vary from joining the armed services to training for some profession, to becoming a full-time wife and mother supported financially by her husband. Gender is not a permanent definition of the 'natural' way for women and men to behave, even if it is often presented, or experienced, as such.

Our gender determines the different life experiences we will be exposed to. It may determine our access to education, to work, to the tools and resources needed for industry and craft; it may determine our health, our life expectancy, our freedom of movement. It will almost certainly determine our sexuality, our relationships, and our ability to make decisions and act autonomously. Our gender is perhaps the single most important factor in shaping who we become.

Cross-cultural gender comparisons

In every society that has been studied, men and women have different gender roles. The work they perform in the community is different and their status and power within their society may be different. The way in which gender roles evolve in different societies is due to many different factors, from the natural environment, to the stories and myths used to solve the puzzle of sex differences, why they came about and how the two kinds of people resulting from sex differences can best relate to one another and to the natural resources around them.

Whilst all societies have a gender division of labour, there is an extraordinary variety of work that men and women do. Some societies, such as the Balinese, and the Mbuti from Africa, have considerable overlap of gender roles. Among the Mbuti pygmies, hunting may involve both men and women; men pick mushrooms and nuts when they find them; and both men and women are actively involved in child care. Among the Amhara people, on the other hand, the norm is for fathers rarely to touch their children during the first two years of life, and to expect complete obedience from them thereafter.

A number of studies of work in different societies have been carried out which show that there are very few activities which are almost always performed by men, and even fewer that are always performed by women. In some societies women do the ploughing and men the cooking; in others men make most of the clothes and women build the houses. In one study of 50 different forms of work in 186 societies, only 14 activities were performed strictly by men in nearly all the societies. These were things like smelting ores, metal working, mining and butchering. No one has offered any really convincing explanations as to why these particular roles tend to be reserved for men.[2]

One of the problems about using cross-cultural material on gender roles is that, until comparatively recently, most anthropologists were trained in the West and tended to see all other societies in terms of the patterns of male dominance common in Western societies. Women were seen as subordinate and peripheral, regardless of what they were actually doing; there is far more information about what men do in different cultures because, by definition, the men do the important things, so only men were observed!

How we experience gender

When we are introduced to a stranger, the first thing that we do is to attribute a gender to them on the basis of all sorts of bodily and behavioural clues. We look at their dress, their hair, their way of moving, their beard growth, and the shape of their body, taking the information in and processing it instantaneously and often unconsciously.

This information forms the basis for the way that we will subsequently interact with that person. Communicating gender to others is vitally important; any ambiguity is very disturbing, because it is seen as 'unnatural' — a deviation from the clear-cut sexual message that people are expected to transmit. Just as ambiguity in physical appearance unsettles our assumptions, so also do forms of behaviour which cross traditional gender roles. When men stay at home to look after small children and women become long-distance lorry drivers, there will always be some people who feel uncomfortable with such a reversal of traditional roles. In nineteenth century Britain, women's struggle to enter higher education was seen as so 'unnatural' that eminent scientists predicted that the women's reproductive organs would be destroyed in the process!

Our gender defines us and pre-exists us; we are born into it just as we are born into our families, and it operates at a level beyond our individual intentions. For this reason we tend to experience our gender roles as true, natural and good. The gender roles that we play in everyday life are part of the foundation of our culture, and not easily changed. As one anthropologist has written, 'human beings do not invent new paths for males and females to follow from one generation to the next. Rather, young people are inexorably bound by the sexual life-styles of their parents. No matter how hard they try to be different, young males and females eventually experience the tidal pull of their culture and history.'[3]

Over time, most of us learn to like ourselves in the 'costume' that is considered appropriate to our gender, so that most of us eventually choose acceptable gender roles for ourselves. Things have to change when environmental or political pressures are such that the system would fall apart if gender roles were not modified. A good example of this was the sudden eruption of women into the UK work force during the Second World War, when there were simply not enough men to operate the war-time economy.

Given the significance of our experience of ourselves as female or male, it is not surprising that challenges to traditional gender roles are seen as profoundly threatening. During the twentieth century, in many parts of the world, political, environmental, and social change and upheavals have brought about significant challenges to traditional gender roles. We will look in more detail at gender roles and how they are being challenged later in this book.

Why 'gender' and not 'women'?

Why do we talk about 'gender and development' rather than 'women and development'? Talking about women as a group raises a number of difficulties. The concept of 'women's position' in society suggests that there is some universal position that all women occupy in all societies. The truth is that not only can there be no simple statement of a universal 'position of women' but that even within most societies it is not possible to speak of women as a group sharing common interests. Women share in the stratifications of society. There are rich women and poor women, and the class background of women may be as important in deciding their position in society as their gender. In a multicultural society, a woman's ethnic background may be even more significant than class. Black women in white societies may feel they have far more in common with black men than with their white 'sisters'.

The term gender is also useful because it covers the social roles of both women and men. The relationship between men and women is often crucial in determining the position of both. Equally, the kinds of relationship that can exist between women and men will be the consequence of a society's definition of appropriate gender behaviour. The work that women and men do in a particular society is determined by class, gender and ethnicity. But most women also live in families, and gender relations in the family represent an extremely important aspect of the way in which women experience the world. Decision making, access to resources, division of labour, and relations outside the family may all be decided by the gender relations within the family unit itself. One of the 'discoveries' of the last decade of development is that it is not possible to assume that the interests of everyone in the family are the same. The interests or needs of the women in a family may be quite different from the interests of the men. These interests are not based on the biological roles of women and men but on their social roles and the power and differences of status vested in these social roles. For this reason, such interests are sometimes referred to as 'gender interests'.

Above all, we talk about 'gender and development' because this emphasises the fact that any development initiative will affect the lives of both women and men. It is simply not possible to alter the dynamics of a society in such a way that only men or women are affected. Any development project, whether it be the building of a large dam or the provision of small-scale credit to poor (male) farmers, will affect both women and men. The fact that it may affect them in different ways is a result of the positions they occupy in their society. By being aware of their different interests and roles we will be in a much better position to understand the process of social change. To talk about gender also implies the need for men to become involved in understanding and supporting the changes in gender relations which will be necessary if a more just and equitable balance is to be achieved between the sexes in society.

2

WHY DEVELOPMENT IS A GENDER ISSUE

*The South is a half world of spreading deserts, water deficiency, high popu-
lation, low energy consumption...low employment and industrial output,
high debt and low income. The South owes the North $20 trillion, and bears
the burden of a net outflow to the North of $50 billion a year. In a situation
of such inequity, who is shutting down whom?...Modernism as a whole
[has failed] including the very economic model which the North has urged
and continues to urge upon the disadvantaged South.[1]*

What does 'development' mean?

This chapter tackles some of the many different meanings that the
word 'development' has come to assume, and asks why gender has
become an important issue in development thinking. We start by
looking briefly at the dominant paradigm of development as set out in
the North during the last four decades, and then set this alongside the
analysis by women from the South, as a way of opening up discussion
of different approaches to development. The standpoint of poor
women in the South provides a unique perspective from which to
view the results of orthodox development practice and introduces
alternative views of defining, and practising, good development. A
theme that runs throughout the book is the gender division of labour,
and a later section of this chapter introduces the idea of the gender
division of labour itself as a development issue. The chapter concludes by asking whose voice is in fact listened to in the process of
development, whether for national development plans or small-scale
rural development projects.

In the years since the Second World War, as former colonies became independent and joined the world's economic system of planned economies, banking and credit, development was seen as a process of industrialisation and economic growth, encapsulated in what has come to be termed 'modernisation'. Following the example of the capitalist North, newly emergent nations were encouraged to industrialise as a way of tackling poverty; the rich 'developed' countries of the North offered development assistance, in the form of injections of capital inputs and technical assistance, which was supposed to encourage economies to reach a point from which sustained economic growth could 'take off'. Simultaneously, emphasis was laid on providing the infrastructural facilities and institutions — from schools and hospitals to airports and hotels — to assist the transition towards modern, capitalist, industrialised societies.[2] It was assumed that the benefits that accrued to developing countries through the process of modernisation would gradually 'trickle down', through all the different socio-economic groups that compose society, and that poverty would be slowly eliminated. During the 1950s and 1960s the principal development actors, Northern governments, the World Bank and the United Nations, were joined by a range of smaller, non-governmental organisations (NGOs), such as Oxfam, who tended to finance small-scale infrastructure — schools, wells, clinics and agricultural projects — for the rural and urban poor.

By the beginning of the 1970s, the growing gulf in 'Third World' societies between those who were benefiting from this pattern of economic development, and those — a growing majority — who were not, became increasingly obvious. Modernisation was planted in societies where non-democratic, hierarchical social systems were already established and, far from tackling inequalities, frequently exacerbated them. The introduction of high-yielding varieties in 'green revolution' farming, for example, may have led to massive increases in food production, but the control of the land by a small group of landlords meant that the benefits of such increases did not necessarily go to those who actually produced the food.[3] Looked at on a national level, this disparity can be illustrated by India, a Southern country which has successfully developed a modern capitalist industrial enclave, benefiting a minority, urban elite, but leaving the poverty of the majority of rural people largely untackled.

The first attempt to rethink this dominant model of development planning identified the 'social' dimensions of development as an area of neglect, in an analysis that viewed the major mistake of earlier development practice as missing out on the 'human factor' — the great majority of people who were perceived as having been inadequately incorporated into development efforts to date.[4] These social and human issues were seen as a set of social and cultural constraints that could be overcome by the further extension of technologies (agriculture, training, and education) into rural areas, and by the further penetration of capital into non-capitalist and non-commercial forms of production. The monetisation of economies has, for example, proceeded rapidly, and markets where goods can be sold for cash are found everywhere. The attempt to include the human factor, however, continued to see people as passive recipients of development, planned by outsiders, as 'consumers' of development rather than 'producers'. As a result it failed to perceive that 'people' are in fact women and men, with different needs and interests; it also left out most of the very poor, and failed to perceive that the model itself was adding to their impoverishment.

LIZ CLAYTON/OXFAM

Contrasting lifestyles in the South: New Delhi, India. Modernisation and industrialisation has not brought universal benefits.

In the 1970s, development literature began to express a crisis in confidence in orthodox modernisation approaches, and a search began for alternative analyses and models. Before looking at some of the ideas that have emerged from this process, we need to look further at the results of orthodox development practice, as seen through the eyes of women in the South. While it could be argued that many of these criticisms of development have their roots in reactions to early industrialisation in the North,[5] what is fundamentally new is that, for the first time, it is women from the South who are speaking about the process of development. In the following section we look at some of the writing of women from Africa, India, and Latin America: voices from the South talking about the consequences of development models that have failed to tackle inequalities, and to incorporate all sections of society into development.

Voices from around the world

Over the last decade, a growing number of women — scholars, activists, grassroots workers and journalists — have questioned the 'development' that transfers resources out of their countries, destroys the environment, and adds to inequalities of class within Southern countries. It is not possible here to do justice to the range of voices that have been raised in criticism of the dominant paradigm of development thinking, but we can listen to some of them, and hear what women are saying about the connections between gender, the environment and development. These voices reflect the growing confidence of the global women's movement in its stance against poverty, and injustice, wherever it is found.

Voices from Africa

The Association of African Women for Research and Development (AAWORD) is an NGO that networks among African women researchers who are studying the problems of development in Africa. During the Nairobi World Conference in 1985 they released a manifesto stating their analysis of the crisis affecting Africa, which remains as pertinent today as it did when they wrote it.

> Today the world is in crisis. The impact of this crisis on the
> countries and peoples of the Third World has been very
> severe....Africa is the most affected continent as this economic
> crisis is aggravated by natural disasters such as drought in
> many parts of the continent. However, the major problems faced
> by Africa are external domination and the misplaced priorities
> of existing development strategies resulting in internal misman-

agement. We note the disproportionate bias of the national budget in favour of military expenditure at the expense of basic human needs and services...

In...Africa, the colonial and neo-colonial experience — the major feature of which was external orientation — has mostly benefited the countries of the North at the expense of those of the South. In addition, development strategies which depend on external finance, technology and advice have contributed to such current economic and social crises in Africa as the food crisis, unemployment, massive displacement of populations, political and religious fundamentalism, and very damaging adjustment policies as a result of loan conditionality clauses...

Today most of Africa suffers from one of the worst agricultural and food crises in recorded history. The main feature of this crisis is the lack of adequate food, water and fuel, all of which are vital concerns in women's lives and responsibilities. This crisis is a result of both colonial and post-colonial export-oriented agricultural policies which failed to address the issue of national and regional food self-sufficiency. A concrete result of this policy is the total neglect of local methods of production and food crops that are mostly produced by women...[6]

Voices from India

The themes of colonialism and neo-colonialism, export orientation and misplaced development strategies are also picked up in the following extracts from the influential activist and writer Vandana Shiva, who calls orthodox development thinking a 'new project of Western patriarchy':

The old assumption that with the development process the availability of goods and services will automatically be increased and poverty will be removed, is now under serious challenge from women's ecology movements in the Third World, even while it continues to guide development thinking in centres of patriarchal power. Survival is based on the assumption of the sanctity of life; maldevelopment is based on the assumption of the sacredness of 'development'.

...Reductionist economics assumes that only paid labour produces value. On the one hand this leads to ignoring man's [sic]
dependence on the natural world, while on the other, it provides
the ideology of the gender division of labour such that women's
work in providing sustenance is treated as having no economic
value even while it provides the very basis of survival and well-
being. Since poor Third World women provide water, fodder,
wood from the free commons that nature provides, collecting
them is not considered work by reductionist economics. A gen-
dered dichotomy is created between 'productive' and 'non-pro-
ductive' work on the basis of money and price as the only measure of economic worth and wealth.[7]

Voices from Latin America

In the following extract Ester, a woman from Bolivia, speaks about the
fruits of development after three official 'development decades'.
Bolivia is one of the Latin American countries facing a debt crisis, a
consequence of uncontrolled lending by Northern banks and governments to poor countries in the 1970s. Very little of that money, osten-
sibly to finance national development, reached poor women like
Ester, yet alongside other poor women, she now finds herself paying
back the national debt.

Peasant women are the most affected by the economic situation
because they do not have the financial means to study....As far
as peasant women are concerned nothing has changed in the
last 30 years. They don't have a hospital, for example, or a
health post. They have no light, water, farming tools, none of
that. They still do everything by hand, with ploughs pulled by
oxen. Their lack of education holds them back, they can't make
any progress. The little that they earn from what they sow and
harvest buys a little sugar and rice to subsist on. They badly
need education so as to see to their children's health and learn
the value of different foods... Many housewives can't afford to
buy meat for themselves any more...The crisis affects women
because wages are very low. Of course there's plenty of food,
you can get it anywhere. But there is not any money, the wages
are not enough to buy anything. Households have seven, ten,
twelve, fifteen members. Women have to devote more energy to
finding money whenever they can. Women have to support

their homes on their own when the husband is not working. They sell a few potatoes or onions. They make their small children join in, too. They send them to polish shoes or sell newspapers or sweets while they are selling somewhere else...Women here in Bolivia try to meet their needs in the crisis as best they can, in desperation. But the government doesn't realise, that we women are forgetting our culture, neglecting education and knowledge...[8]

The failure of othodox development

These three extracts provide analytical, first-hand accounts of the failures of orthodox development theory and practice. We can pick out a number of key themes: the international context as an obstacle to development, particularly the export orientation of Southern economies in an unjust global economic order, and the international division of labour which consigns the South to the production of low-value raw materials, and supplying workers for off-shore assembly plants; the local context, particularly the internal mismanagement of Southern economies, and unjust social structures in which local elites have a major interest in co-operating with international development strategies; oppression and repression and the maintenance of relationships of inequality by the exercise of power, whether through in-country repression, external military intervention, or the bias of national budgets in favour of military expenditure; colonialism and neo-colonialism; environmental damage and dislocation; the debt crisis; the failure of governments to invest in productive assets for the poor; and the unequal impacts that development has had on women and men, compounded by the effects of class and ethnicity. Failure to recognise and support the work of women in food production and other non-commercial forms of production is stressed by all three writers.

These voices speak from experience of the crisis in development, and state clearly why development is a gender issue. Many of these themes are developed further in Chapter 6, which looks at issues such as the debt crisis, environmental crisis, and militarism. Let us now look more closely at some of the ideas introduced by AAWORD, Shiva and Ester.

For Shiva, development is an extension of the relationship that most Third World countries originally had with their colonial masters. Colonial rule converted subject territories into sources of cheap labour, raw materials and food. At the same time, colonies became markets for goods produced in the colonising country. In the process, relatively self-sufficient countries and regions were transformed into dependencies, a process which still continues. AAWORD echoes this with its comment on the external domination and the external orientation of African countries, which have benefited countries of the North at the expense of those in the South. Both of these views draw their analysis from one of the most important critiques of modernisation, which has become known as 'dependency theory', and is particularly associated with the writings of Cardoso and Falleto, and Gunder Frank. Dependency theory argues that capitalist forms of development (in particular) inevitably increase the dichotomies within society and between societies. Southern countries are poor because of the subordinate and marginalised role that they have within the world economy, but far from being merely a North/South divide, poverty is created within countries by a process of 'internal colonisation'. According to Gunder Frank, the whole world can be seen as a series of metropolis-satellite constellations, stretching from the board-rooms of New York to the tenant farmer in the remotest Andean valley: 'Each metropolis appropriates part, or even all of the economic surplus of its satellites. Thus, landless labourers may be exploited by small landowners. But they too may have economic surplus appropriated by large landowners or provincial business classes. And so the chain continues until the top of the hierarchy, the world metropolis, is reached and there is nobody above this metropolis to appropriate from it.'[9] Dependency theory does not exclude an industrialisation strategy, but rather suggests an approach which attempts to avoid dependency on the international economy. It looks for 'spaces' in which dependency might best be avoided, such as in rural economies, in agriculture, and in rural industrialisation.[10]

Dependency theory has also highlighted the need for a reinterpretation of the history of colonial expansion, seeing in the 'civilising process' a history of subordination and exploitation still being recreated through contemporary mechanisms, as AAWORD argues. Industrialisation and modernisation still rely on foreign investments; many Southern economies remain geared up to export, rather than to produce for the local economy, just as they were in the colonial past. Some Southern countries remain dependent on the export of a single commodity — such as peanuts from Guinea Bissau — for foreign exchange. This leaves them extremely vulnerable to fluctuations in the world commodity market. Colonialisation served to unite the colonised and colonising in a single, global economic network of

FRANCES RUBIN/OXFAM

Colonial systems of production of raw materials persist in many Southern countries. Cane cutting on sugar plantations in Brazil.

unequal relationships, which in many ways is still in operation today. The power and presence of transnationals, and the development priorities of donor agencies, whether foreign governments or multi-lateral bodies such as the World Bank, can restrict the autonomy of local governments. Southern countries are put at an enormous disadvantage by the way in which the global economy works. The low prices paid for valuable natural resources produced in the South are in part the legacy of colonial systems which began the transfer of raw materials out of the South at terms highly advantageous to the North. The Bruntland Report commented on the way in which Africa has been particularly affected by the gap in power and resources between rich and poor countries:

> Sub-Saharan Africa's economic well-being depends even more than low-income Asia's on developments in the world economy.

Within the past decade, many sub-Saharan countries have been hit by adverse trends in commodity terms of trade and external shocks such as higher oil prices, fluctuating exchange rates and higher interest rates. Over the last ten years, the prices of major commodities such as iron ore, sugar...and cotton have fallen significantly. In 1985, the terms of trade of sub-Saharan countries (except oil-exporting countries) were 10 per cent below 1970 levels.[11]

Coupled to these unfavourable terms of trade, characterised by falling commodity prices, are the rising costs of debt repayment and interest charges. The debt crisis that emerged in the 1980s and the consequent need to raise foreign exchange for debt servicing has speeded up the process whereby huge areas of land, which had either been under forest or used to grow crops to feed local people, are being converted to growing cash crops for export. As a result, local markets and local environments suffer. Ester's account highlights the fact that structural adjustment packages to ensure the payment of debt have led to serious cuts in public services, and real decreases in incomes, which we will look at more fully in Chapter 6.

Another element in the changing analyses of development drawn on by Shiva can be summarised as 'limits to growth' theory which, like dependency theory, looks at the limits of capitalist development. It highlights the environmental costs and consequences of sophisticated technological progress, and the destructive effects of industrialisation. It warns of the non-sustainability of current patterns of economic growth, given the earth's finite resources. This view of the damage that has been caused globally by Northern industrialisation, and the similar environmental consequences of expanding industrial enclaves in the South, goes hand in hand with the need for 'appropriate' development strategies which take account of the individuality of nations and regions. Shiva's narrative also highlights the growing shift towards 'commoditisation', a process in which services and goods tend to gain a commercial value, in response to a process of economic growth and activity which registers only those activities and processes that involve money, credit, and cash transfers. This trend has had a major impact on what might be described loosely as 'subsistence' economies. Subsistence simply means creating enough to support a community (a village or region for example) in a relatively self-sufficient way. Orthodox development thinking has tended to see this form of subsistence economy as 'poverty', because it does not generate surplus that can be sold in the market place. Yet as the African writer R. Bahso explains, we need to make a distinction between poverty as subsistence and poverty as deprivation. Subsistence living may appear to 'richer' outsiders as poverty but it may satisfy local needs adequately. The process of economic development, if not sensitive to local needs, can so damage existing local economies that real poverty (i.e. deprivation) is created as a result.

A well-documented example of this kind of disruption to a local economy in the name of economic development occurred when the nomadic Afars of Ethiopia were displaced from their pasturelands in the Awash valley. The Awash River, the only major river that runs eastwards out of the highlands of Ethiopia , was controlled in the 1960s to provide irrigation for Dutch, Israeli, Italian, and British firms to grow sugar and cotton. As a result the annual flooding of the river which covered the valley with rich soil and provided grazing lands for the Afar people, was disrupted. The Afars went in search of new pastures, and tried to make a living on the ecologically fragile uplands, which were in no way suited to their nomadic lifestyle. The cattle found less and less to eat and the Afars began to starve. When drought struck the Wollo Region in 1972, 25-30 per cent of the Afars died.[12]

The problem lay not in the inadequacies of Afar nomadic life — which had flourished for hundreds of years; the problem lay with the attempt to 'develop' the Afar lands and bring them into the mainstream economy, without regard to the actual needs and requirements of the Afar people. This is not to argue for maintaining indigenous cultures at an arrested stage of development; people from nomadic, tribal, or other indigenous groups and lifestyles, may wish to preserve their way of life, but usually also wish to have access to goods and services which make them less vulnerable and improve the quality of their lives. They often insist on their right to develop their own culture by incorporating elements of external cultures in ways that are compatible with their own structures, traditions and practices. Invariably they have a vision of development and progress which is appropriate to their own cultural traditions, and which offers them opportunity, self-reliance and a stake in the development process.[13]

Rethinking development

Out of a confusing conceptual climate, fresh ideas have begun to emerge, and a view of development which involves the whole of society sharing in the benefits of that development is beginning to emerge. Perhaps surprisingly, these ideas have been rapidly assimilated within development circles, both official and voluntary, though practice lags behind theory, and the political will to implement or facilitate this broader view of development is hindered by powerful vested interests, North and South. A number of elements have become important such as the tackling of poverty; the equitable involvement of all people into the economy; improving the quality of the lives of women and men in terms of access to essential goods and services, together with the information they need to make choices; the creation of a suitable, diversified productive base to satisfy the needs of the population, and to enable countries weather changes in the international economy; the reshaping of the sexual division of labour; the creation of political institutions which safeguard and allow the exercise of basic civil and social rights (including women's rights), and provide the conditions of access to these rights in ways which allow social conflict to be resolved peacefully; respect for cultural values and aspirations of distinct social groups.[14]

This view of development requires a strong re-alignment of interests and a focus on particularly vulnerable sections of national populations, essentially the rural and urban poor; and among them, a specific focus on women. This emergent development 'philosophy' has stressed the 'qualitative and perhaps unmeasurable dimensions of development; values which give a sense of fulfilment. Self-reliance is highlighted in the context of a participatory democracy in which the 'consciousness-gap' between the leaders of society and the masses is closed', and in which people are seen as the subjects of their own worlds, rather than the objects of other people's worlds.[15] The emphasis is on a process of empowerment, in which through organisation, people gain the strength to create a space for themselves, and to build up the material assets to support their own growth and development. The organisation process, in whatever form it takes, such as struggles for justice, social organisation or for access to resources, is not an end in itself (as we shall see), but the means to development.

How does this re-evaluation of development strategies involve gender? To answer this, we can turn to consider development from the standpoint of poor women.

The standpoint of poor women

Panjo is 22 and lives in the village of Jhandra in Gujarat, North India, in the shadow of the huge dam project in the Narmada River Valley. The Narmada Dam is a classic example of a massive development project, partially funded by the World Bank. If the dam is built, Panjo's village will be flooded. She is being asked to move from her village and leave her way of life for the sake of a 'development'. She explains: 'The Government says it is building the dam to provide irrigation for farmers. Here we have no irrigation; we depend on the rains, and yet we do not have to go begging with bowls in our hands. What good is this irrigation if it causes so much suffering to so many people?...People who are uprooted go to the cities but we do not like the air in the city, the water there doesn't taste good...'

This is the standpoint of one poor woman affected by a development project. The World Bank sees things differently. As the Bank President told journalists in Bombay, 'We don't govern your country. Your government has to decide the priorities. We only provide financial assistance.' Another view is that of the State government in Gujarat, who see in the Narmada Valley project an opportunity of provide irrigation to nearly 5 million hectares of land and generate 2,700 MW of power.[16] And it would also be possible to find different standpoints among rural men and women living in different parts of Gujarat, for whom the dam offers different opportunities and costs.

In August 1984 a group of women met in Bangalore, South India, to discuss development issues. They formed themselves into an organisation known as DAWN — Development Alternatives with Women for a New Era. According to DAWN, only by starting with the perspective of poor women such as Panjo can we provide a 'much needed reorientation to development analysis'.[17] For if development is about the well-being of all, it makes sense to start with the world's poorest citizens. The statement issued by the United Nations on declaring 1976-1985 the Decade for Women pointed out that women perform two-thirds of the world's work, receive only 10 per cent of the world's income, and own only 1 per cent of the means of production. When we also consider the enormous gulf between the First and Third World Nations — one quarter of the world's population receive four-fifths of the world's income — the magnitude of the dispossession of the world's poorest women comes more clearly into focus. If the benefits of development are to reach the most vulnerable members of the South, development, DAWN argues, must start by seeing the world from their perspective.

If conventional development projects have by and large failed to reach the poorest of Third World societies, it is doubly the case that they have failed to reach low-income women. 'Male bias' in projects has largely presumed that, because women are members of male-dominated households, their interests are reflected in the interests of their husbands or fathers. As it has become clear that the perception of the 'community' as a unit with some consensual unity is wrong in its failure to understand the distinct socio-economic groups within any geographical area, so too, it has become clear that, even within the disadvantaged groups of a community, women are often hidden from view and forgotten. Consequently, women often suffer harsher extremes of poverty than the low-income men of their communities, especially those women who head their own households. Though poor male farmers, male tenants, and landless men are often geographically, socially, and culturally isolated from development efforts, women of the same socio-economic groups tend to be still worse off, and isolated from the chances of improving the bases of their livelihood. They lack access to resources for development, for example, to credit or to the attention of extension workers; gender inequalities produce barriers to their equal social participation, and the lack of viable organisations to represent their interests prevents them from either developing a voice or having it heard.

HUGH BELSHAW/OXFAM

Women's work in the Third World is vital for the survival of poor families. Here, women tend a vegetable plot in Alayo, Peru.

Another reason for starting with the point of view of poor women is that, after a decade of development which specifically focused on women, there is evidence that suggests that many of the world's women are worse off now than they were in 1975. In Latin America, for example, severe recession has led to lower standards of living and high unemployment. Per capita GDP was at least 10 per cent lower in 1986 than in 1980; seven countries had a loss of more than 15 per cent and four had more than a 20 per cent loss. Nineteen of 23 countries show negative rates of growth in the 16-year period from 1970 to 1986.[18] While recession hits everyone, it is poor women who are hit hardest of all, as they remain the ones responsible for feeding, clothing and educating children, with shrinking resources. When governments struggling with IMF austerity budgets cut back on welfare services, it is women whose work is increased. As long as the task of keeping families together remains a women's responsibility, women will continue to bear a disproportionate share of the costs of failed 'development'. Women's work in the Third World is vital for the survival of poor families, and for the continuance of their whole society. Women are at the centre of the reproduction of life and society, not just in a biological sense, but through their role as food producers and farmers, gatherers of fuel and water, cooks, cultural guardians, teachers of their children, and healers.

This centrality of women to the production and reproduction of social networks and the fabric of society itself is emphasised by Ela Bhatt, one of the founder members of the Self Employed Women's Association of Ahmedabad, India, who has spent many years listening to poor working women and representing their perspective. She wrote:

These women are indeed great, as I learn that they are better fighters against poverty than their men, have more calculative, stable, forward-looking strategies to deal with their own environment. Everywhere in the country, we found that women were the most committed proponents of our future. A concern for the future is strong with them. So the future of the nation lies in the hands of these women. No doubt, they are becoming more aware, education is spreading amongst them, they are making plans for a better future to enter the twenty-first century with steadier steps.[19]

The gender division of labour as a development issue

As we saw in the previous chapter, throughout the world women and men perform different tasks, although the tasks performed by each gender vary. The gender division of labour, and the way it has been perceived by development planners, has had important consequences for the sort of development that has come about.

In some peasant societies in the South, the division of labour by gender is an efficient way of ensuring the survival of the family unit and adapting to a given environment. A division of labour need not necessarily imply a ranking of status; women's work may be seen as equally valuable as men's, though there are also many peasant societies in which the division of labour does involve a ranking of significance along gender lines. At the risk of generalising, it appears that when a money economy is introduced, the balance between women's labour and men's labour begins to shift. There is some debate as to whether colonialism, to give a historical example, increased gender inequalities that already existed, or introduced them. Almost certainly colonial rule changed gender relations in one way or another. According to one argument, colonial rulers took as a model women's roles in their own societies, and therefore assumed that women could not, should not or did not work for gain. European empire builders tended to assume that all human societies were organised into hierarchies dominated by men. As Ruth Bleier, a North American scientist, pointed out, '...the experiences derived from our own society are inappropriately projected onto institutions and behaviours of other societies: dominance hierarchies and sexual stratifications are constructed where they do not exist: women are seen (or, more accurately, not seen) as subordinate and peripheral regardless of what they are doing, since what women do, by definition, is unimportant.' This line of thinking concludes that the export of European ideologies and gender stereotypes — that women work only in the house and not outside it, that men are breadwinners, and that in the family unit everyone benefits equally from a family wage — to the South has had incalculable consequences.[20]

More recent research suggests that to see pre-colonial societies as utopias of gender equality may be rather idealised, and that oppressive forms of patriarchy already existed in some pre-capitalist and pre-colonial societies. Nancy Folbre, for example, argues that the society that the British encountered in Zimbabwe was already marked by patriarchal social relations; elder males controlled the means of production, land and cattle, and reproduction: 'Young men submitted to patriarchal control over part of their life cycle; women never escaped it.'[21] Hierarchies based on age, gender, and other social criteria clearly made receptive ground for the introduction of European views of gender. Women's work has been seen as secondary and a 'natural' part of her biological role, as we shall see in the next chapter, and such views have determined (until very recently) the nature of development planning. The need to counter such negative assumptions about women's gender role is another important reason why gender is a development issue.

The European notion of a male breadwinner and a female 'housewife' was the underpinning of many development projects in the 1960s and 1970s. The family became the last bastion of the trickle-down theory, with the assumption that if the men of a family were targeted and given benefits, these would trickle down to other family members, and the whole unit would be better off. In Africa, where women grow most of the food, the consistent practice of targeting men for access to land and agricultural inputs, and excluding women, has had a major effect on the amount of food being grown (see Chapter 6). Beliefs about women's roles have also affected the process of land reform in many parts of the world. The assumption that men were the farmers led to the granting of formal land rights to men, even when traditionally women had used the land to grow the family's food.

The introduction of industry has involved similar mechanisms. When mining and other industrial processes were introduced in Puerto Rico, Mexico, Argentina, and other Latin American countries women took on industrial work. Within a matter of years, ideas about the appropriate gender division of labour had forced many women out of work by, for example, preventing them from doing night-shifts.

At the risk of over-generalising, a trend has been discernible in the gender division of labour in the last three or four decades of development. If men tend to become involved in the modern cash sector of the economy while women tend to remain in the domestic and subsistence sector, any existing polarisation between the gender roles of men and women will increase. The result can be to undermine the autonomy and self-sufficiency of women within the family, at least in terms of the resources available to them. Women may become dependent on men as controllers of the family cash income, yet there is no reduction in women's responsibility to deliver basic needs to the family. From being independent producers and providers, as their mothers and grandmothers before them may have been, women the world over have found themselves becoming housewives; a process described by Barbara Rogers as the 'domestification of women'. Once confined to the domestic sphere, women have been offered development projects of their own - based on knitting, embroidery or food processing, tasks that women are supposedly more suited for. As the international division of labour shifts again, a number of developing countries are witnessing significant changes in this pattern as women have joined the industrial labour force, particularly in the manufacturing sector. We will look further at the implications of this in Chapter 4.

Whose voice are we listening to?

The patriarchal structure which is predominant in most societies excludes women from the decision-making processes. It is the men who communicate with the outside world. The introduction of new technology, educational programmes, new equipment and various services, are always negotiated primarily with men. This international capitalism (in the form of aid and development) has implicitly institutionalised men's domination over women because knowledge, whatever kind it may be, increases the extent of men's power.
Government Minister, Burkina Faso.[22]

Whose voice makes itself heard in the process of development? How do those responsible for planning and implementing development projects go about listening to the voices of women like Ester and Panjo? However well-intentioned, a development organisation can find it very difficult to listen to the voices of poor women. Imagine the following scenario: a bilateral development organisation plans to spend a large sum of money on an agricultural project in a rural part of Africa. How does it go about listening to the voices of poor women and seeing the proposed project from their viewpoint? A team of consultants visits the area — usually a mixture of people, some from academic institutions in the donor country, and others from institutions in the country concerned. On any official, government-sponsored trip it is extremely difficult for the consultants who are planning, appraising, implementing or evaluating the project to get very close to the people for whom the project is intended. Field visits to project sites may be carried out in a style that is intimidating to village people, especially women. Consultants may not speak the local language and have to rely on interpreters and key informants for their information about the area. Even when the donor organisation makes a real effort to listen to women and get their ideas, there may not be enough time during the visit for consultants to gain the trust of the women concerned and allow them to work out what they themselves need and want. Given these constraints, it is extremely difficult for poor women to make any kind of input into a project designed for their benefit.

This is one problem; a further problem is that many development planners have not considered the women's perspective to be relevant to a project unless it was specifically designed to benefit them. According to a War on Want critique of the British Aid programme, over 80 per cent of the total aid budget was not deemed relevant to women by the ODA. Yet any development initiative will affect both women and men. All aid has effects, whether positive or adverse, on all members of the community to which it is offered. Even for the 20 per cent of projects that were seen as relevant to women, War on Want argue that there was 'no proof that women are taken into account...when these projects...are planned, appraised, implemented or evaluated'.[23] Since the War on Want report was written, the ODA have begun to take the issue of gender more seriously, and there are now deliberate efforts to plan for gender inputs into project design.

It is not only large multilateral or bilateral agencies that find it difficult to listen to women. NGOs have a very mixed record when it comes to thinking about the different gender needs of women and men. An ODI study of 16 projects with a focus on economic development in rural areas of Bangladesh, India, Uganda, and Zimbabwe found that 'contrary to expectations, there was little evidence to suggest that the projects as a whole greatly improved women's economic and social status, or effectively challenged prevailing patterns of discrimination.'[24] Men dominated the leadership in grassroots organisations and NGO alike. Part of the problem is explained by the Minister from Burkina Faso, quoted at the beginning of this section: in many societies, it is only men who communicate with the outside world. There may be cultural constraints on women coming together, and meeting foreign donors or their representatives; but, as we will see in examples later in this book, many women, once given the opportunity, will readily respond to development initiatives.

There is also a difference between consulting women and allowing women to set the agenda (see Chapter 8). Very few funding agencies have even begun to consider the latter as an appropriate way of facilitating development. The simple idea that women are as important to

the process of development as men is relatively new; many development proposals still take the form of a main project for men, plus ten
sewing machines (or embroidery classes) tagged on to the end to
show that the project has considered gender.

In the last decade many development agencies, both large organisations such as UNICEF and the World Bank, and NGOs, have begun
to think about gender and development in relation to the programmes
they fund. Oxfam has set up a Gender and Development Unit
(GADU) to stimulate and advise on a more gender-sensitive approach
within the organisation, and many Oxfam offices around the world
have had workshops on gender issues. The World Bank and other
multi-lateral organisations have published documents outlining their
approach to gender. Listening to the women of the world is gradually
becoming an acceptable way to do development. How far the poor
women of the world are really setting the agenda for their own development, however, remains an open question.

TANVIR/OXFAM

*Listening to women is vital if they are to play their full part in development pro-
grammes. Jahanava, a Samata worker, advising women in a village in
Bangladesh. Samata is an NGO which helps people claim land to which they are
entitled.*

3

MOTHERS AND HOUSEWIVES?:
Gender, reproductive and productive work

Despite differences in family form, kinship structures, marital arrangements, political and economic structures, women are everywhere charged with producing and raising children up to the socially designated end of childhood. They are charged too with the daily upkeep of the household... [1]

Woman of Africa
Sweeper
Smearing floors and walls
with cow dung and black soil
Cook, ayah, the baby on your back
Washer of dishes
Planting, weeding, harvesting
Storekeeper, builder
Runner of errands....
Woman of Africa
What are you not? [2]

Okol B'Pitek's song illuminates the working life of an African woman, and it is the daily lives of women in the South that form the focus of this chapter. Women's work in reproduction, in productive economic work, and in community management has been called the 'triple role of women'.[3] This chapter focuses on women's reproductive and productive work within the household, that part of women's lives that has been apparently 'invisible' to development planners: their work in fuel and fodder collection, in dairying, poultry-keeping and vegetable-gardening, in household craft work, in home-working, and in the family fields; and their work in bearing children and taking primary responsibility for domestic maintenance. The importance of this work has often been obscured by a view of reproductive labour that dismisses it as a 'natural' part of women's biology, instead of seeing it as an aspect of a socially-determined gender role; and by a view of work that is synonymous with formal labour in the full-time, paid workforce. This dichotomy between 'domestic' activity and 'work' simply does not exist for millions of women in the South. The line between reproductive and productive work is a fine one, and unless we understand these complex and multi-faceted gender activities, we cannot appreciate how they have been affected by — and affect — the process of development. The failure to recognise and appreciate women's productive work within the household has prevented a full recognition of women's other work, particularly in the informal sector, which is often an extension of their productive work within the household.

For women the world over, work in the household, whatever form it takes, is an important part of their gender role, an activity in which, particularly if they have children, they invest great energy and commitment. To understand gender and development, we have to understand the work that women actually do.

Is mothering natural?

Nature has equipped women to bear children; it is only women who become pregnant, have babies and breastfeed them. Common-sense tells us that mothering must be 'natural'. But the term 'mother' is itself a social term; as a name — Mama, Mae, Mutter, Moeder, Amma, Mere, Madre, Matka, Makuahine, Ibu, Mamae, Ema, Aiti, Mor, Ame, to name just a fraction of the world's words for mother — it belongs to language, a human construct; as a form of behaviour, mothering varies so much that it is difficult to pin down the essential components of the role. In Matabeleland in Southern Africa, the word 'mother' does not necessarily apply to one's biological mother at all. In India, the mother-in-law, grandmother of the baby, often takes over almost all the early nurturing except breastfeeding. In many parts of the world, wealthy families employ nannies to carry out all the routine, day-to-day care of infants, usually with no ill-effects. So what is mothering and why is it important in any discussion of women and development?

Work in the household, coupled with childcare, are important parts of the gender role of women the world over. In the South, women have little help from technology in carrying out their everyday tasks.
Dehusking rice with a stick, in Bolivia.

SEAN SPRAGUE/OXFAM

Because most of us experienced some form of mothering in our early years — the first and probably most lasting influence on us — we associate mothering with what is best and most natural. Our experience of bonding with a mother figure (not necessarily our biological mother) is reinforced the world over by powerful ideologies about the role of women as mothers, often with religious underpinnings. Catholicism has the Virgin Mary as the ideal, self-sacrificing mother; in India, motherhood is venerated and sons look on their mothers as some form of deity; for some Greek and Russian Orthodox women, motherhood is redemption for having been born a woman. Western socio-biology has also persuaded many people that their common-sense view of the world is rooted in biological fact: that the fluctuating hormones and secondary sex characteristics of women not only make mothering the biologically ordained occupation of women, but in fact almost add up to a separate order of existence.

What are the consequences of seeing the 'real' work of women as mothering? One consequence is that any other work women do is seen as supplementary or secondary, while paradoxically, because pregnancy, giving birth, suckling, and the nurture of children are seen as 'natural', they too do not really qualify as work, and neither, by extension, do all the other productive tasks that women perform in and around their households for the benefit of family members. Defined as non-work, such activities have not until recently been seen as legitimate targets for development assistance; so it is that women farmers in Africa still tend their land with hand-made hoes, and Indian village women dehusk their rice by hand. Another consequence is that the responsibility for childcare, even after children are weaned, is seen as primarily women's.

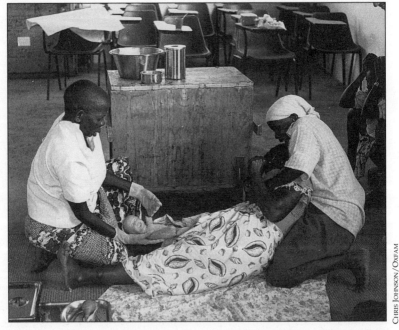

CHRIS JOHNSON/OXFAM

For most women in the South, help in childbirth is given by village midwives rather than trained medical staff. Basic training in hygiene for traditional birth attendants, as seen here in Mozambique, can result in significant improvements in maternal and child health.

Combining childcare with work outside the household places a considerable strain on women, particularly for urban migrants who have left kinship networks behind in their villages. Paulu, whose story is included on page 135 found the responsibility for caring for small children on a hazardous building site in South India particularly difficult. A study among poor working women in Costa Rica found that, as the economic crisis extended women's working day to as much as 17 hours, one of the greatest anxieties shared by the women was their inability to fulfil their roles as mothers and carers as they wanted to; their concern for the well-being of their children permeated every aspect of their lives, and they curtailed involvement in political and community organisations so as to spend time with their children.[4] It is often the poorest, most marginalised women, migrating in search of labour, who have the least support from extended family networks; consequently their children rapidly become part of the informal economy themselves.

A further consequence of seeing motherhood as the natural state for women is that non-motherhood is defined as deviant. Women who are involuntarily childless are seen (and see themselves) in some societies as cursed. The label of 'barren' in many countries around the world carries with it the greatest stigma, and childless women the world over will do almost anything to make themselves fertile, to walking over burning coals in parts of South Asia, to submitting to the trauma of *in vitro* fertilisation in the North. Women who choose not to have children may also be seen as deviant, though in many societies, in most social classes, to choose not to have children is simply not an option.

The work of childbearing has major consequences for the health of millions of women in the South. Every year, at least half a million women die as the result of pregnancy, many as a result of illegal abortion, others in childbirth or in the weeks following the birth. Such deaths are seen as in some way a 'natural' consequence of the role that nature has designed women for. Those most likely to die are very young women, particularly if they have three or more pregnancies close together while they are still under 20, or older women who have given birth many times. A closer look shows that these deaths are not natural at all, but a consequence of social and economic systems in which women have little control over their fertility, and in which their lives, and deaths, are accorded little significance. This view is supported by the fact that the Safe Motherhood Initiative was so very late in joining the development agenda. It was only in 1989 that the right of women not to die as a result of becoming pregnant became a political and development issue, long after advocates had been found in the fight against other epidemics in the South.

To what extent, then, is mothering really 'natural'? Childbirth is not only an event of intellectual and emotional significance for the woman concerned, but every aspect of motherhood is carefully regulated and controlled by a complex system of social customs and rules. Who and when a woman marries; how rapidly she conceives; when, how and where she spends her pregnancy; her experience of giving birth; the *post-partum* period; and the kind of mother she becomes; all of these, far from being 'natural', are socially determined, and a part of her gender role.[5] Biology is just the raw material. The meaning of these events, the way they are experienced by the woman herself, by her family, and by her community, are determined by gender, class and ethnicity, and all the other cultural building blocks with which humans organise their societies. To say that it is 'only natural' for a woman to be a mother is to fail to see the complexity with which we build our social roles. In many countries the 'naturalness' of the mothering role is now under challenge as more fathers become involved in the day-to-day nurture of infants and children.

Motherhood often gives women their only opportunity for power and influence in societies which deny them other chances for autonomy; children are a women's constitution in the narrow political world of the family. Models of development initiated in the North, where attitudes to the centrality of childbearing have changed, may fail to appreciate fully the value of children to their families. In some parts of the South — particularly in Africa — many women will be pregnant and lactating for more than two-thirds of the time between the ages of 17 and 35. Similarly, in the Caribbean, while for historical reasons women may be disinclined to marry, they take pride in having large numbers of children. According to a report by Change, 'the slaving tradition that women bear children persists with new meaning. A woman who does not bear children is "an object of pity, contempt or derision". Childbearing is her "womanship". The social and emotional pressures to prove her fertility are such that a barren woman may even go insane.' Children are a woman's wealth, as well as a burden that she may have to cope with alone.[6] For development workers to look only at women's economic or productive role and ignore her reproductive role, in an attempt to gain for women equality of treatment with men, is as misguided as the opposite view, that of focusing on her reproductive role and ignoring her economic role.

Naturally housewives?

The housewife is a comparatively recent invention. At most she has only been around for about a century and a half, when she made her debut in the drawing-rooms and kitchens of the North. Since then, the housewife has migrated, and housewives are now found all over the world.

Housewives came into being when the process of industrialisation enabled upwardly mobile men to imitate the aristocratic rich and have a wife who did not need to work but who could represent the status and wealth of her husband. Industrialisation meant that households, instead of being the centre of production (making the items needed in the house, such as soap, candles, dairy products, preserves), began to move to their current position as centres of consumption. The tasks that had formerly been supervised and *8* performed by the women of the household were now done in *Young* factories, and goods were bought in shops. In Europe, the gradual disappearance of servants from middle-class households after the First World War meant that women had to learn to do housework themselves, and become domesticated 'housewives', a trend that continued until the 1950s (the exceptions being the two periods of war during which women were encouraged into a wide range of different responsibilities). By the time of the baby boom in the 1950s and 1960s, the model of the modern housewife had emerged: a mother and wife whose feminine propensity to serve leads her to assume responsibility for bringing up the children and caring for the family home, with the necessary cash provided by a male breadwinner. Many men and women still consider that the domestic arrangements of households, including childcare, are primarily the woman's responsibility, even when both partners work.

But why should the history of housewives in the industrialised North be of relevance to the poorer women of the world? Why did the process of domestification of women in the North have a profound influence on women in the South? If we look at the way in which work is organised in a typical rural household it is clear that everyone shares in it, and everyone's contribution is valued. Among the Turkana women and men of North Kenya, studied by Cathy Watson, the work of the household varied from season to season with the dry season as the time of the hardest work. There was a clear gender division of labour, but of all the tasks recorded by Cathy Watson, the men and boys were only involved in herding and watering the animals. The women and girls, besides participating in the herding and watering of the animals, milked them and processed the milk, cooked, fetched water, collected fruits, built the houses and compounds, carried out agriculture, made utensils, carried out some craft work with leather and beads, collected firewood and made charcoal.[7] The study shows how one family divided up the work to form a productive family unit, in which the contribution of women and girls was central. Still part of a pastoralist way of life, and not dependent on money for access to goods and services, Turkana women had not yet become housewives.

JEREMY HARTLEY/OXFAM

Turkana woman in charge of a flock. Women take a full part in the care of animals in many traditional pastoralist systems.

The work of housewives

Housewives around the world do a huge variety of tasks which have one thing in common — a link to the home and its occupants. They tend the children, they obtain the family food supply, whether from the family fields or the local supermarket; they wash the clothes, at the river or in the washing machine, and they may add a little to the family income by poorly paid, part-time work that does not jeopardise their main work, which is caring for the home and the family. The important thing about housewives, however, which links them around the world, is not what they do; it is the conditions and relations under which they do it. Housework is an aspect of a gender division of labour under which men tend to get the paid and women the unpaid work. This is the link between the history of housewives, North and South. The process of industrialisation has, in general (until recently when gender relations within the workforce began to change), tended to lead to a male workforce. In many countries women found themselves squeezed out of formal sector employment by male-dominated trade unions. Other women have tended to carry on doing what they have always done; the difference is that the circumstances under which they do their work have changed in the move from a subsistence to a money-based economy.

If we take the example of the Turkana pastoralists, we can illustrate this process of change more clearly. Imagine that a Turkana community was offered development projects which involved settled agriculture, growing cash crops for export or a local urban centre. If the job opportunities that arose were primarily offered to men, the Turkana women would find themselves on the edge of a cash economy, with no access of their own to the cash. They might carry on raising children, looking after goats and keeping up the vestiges of their former lifestyle, but the basis of their subsistence economy would have been undermined. At the same time, their dependency on their menfolk might grow; whereas once the women and men in the household worked on tasks that were seen as equally important, with the introduction of money, and the access to things that it can buy, the status of the work of each partner changes. The men would gain access to modern institutions, to banks and extension facilities, and the women would be left still further behind.

In other words, we are defining housewives in terms of their access to money and resources. Since in modern economies money, and the goods and services it can buy, are a measure of status and rank, the problem for housewives is not the actual nature of the work they do, though it may be boring and repetitive, but the fact that it is unpaid and has no status attached to it.

Economic actors

There is no work, yet the grind of work is killing me.[8]
(A woman in India, employed in the informal sector.)

In reality, the pattern of a stay-at-home wife and a male breadwinner is inconceivable for the majority of women in the South, because their men are too poor or have left the household. As countries get poorer, the pressure on women to earn intensifies. Because of constraints both on their time and mobility, they are forced to make themselves available at the cheapest rates, whether in agriculture, factories or as home workers (when women take work into their houses). The sexual division of labour means that women are frequently considered as the secondary earner of the family, while the man provides the main wage, regardless of whether or not this is the case. In reality, the work of many poor women in the South is what enables their families to survive, and the poorer the family, the more it depends on the economic productivity of a woman. Most women cannot obtain work in the formal sector, that part of the economy with wages, pensions, regulated conditions of work and an organised labour force. Responsibility for their children and for providing food for the family forces millions of Southern women into just about any kind of work for cash — women work as petty traders, in sweat shops, as domestic servants, on building sites, as road makers, road sweepers, prostitutes, and in many other low-paid occupations in the 'informal' sector.

The majority of women in the Third World work incredibly hard, but the irony of their situation is well summed-up by the quotation at the head of this section. Women are ground down by work, but at the end of the day, what does their work count for? That their work inside the house does not count is illustrated by instructions issued with the 1971 Indian census:

> ...a servant who works as a cook in his or her employer's home for wages will be considered economically active, but a housewife, even if she may work much more than a paid servant, in having to cook for the family or looking after the household will not be treated as economically active...[9]

Such a view has serious consequences for women; their work is overlooked by everyone, by their governments, husbands, families, development planners, and census takers. Women suffer because men do not recognise their work. Real work is by definition what men do, behind the plough, in the factory or in the office. Patricia Jeffrey records the words of one North Indian woman, named Zubeida: 'Cooking roti and stew, collecting fodder and cutting it, removing cattle dung and making dung cakes, sweeping up....Enough! I work the whole day — and even so my husband says 'What do you do with yourself all day?'[10]

To give an idea of the variety of tasks which women undertake, let us look at a typical day's work for a woman in Nepal:

Get up 4.00 am,
Pack up the bedding
Prepare morning tea
Sweep the house and the courtyard clean
Prepare breakfast
Process milk into yoghurt, buttermilk and ghee
Winnow grain; prepare rice, dahls; grind spices
Fetch fuel and water
Clean dishes
Feed, clothe and wash children
Wash and mend clothes
Spread out bedding at night
Mend the house
Care for the cows, chickens and donkeys.

In all this amounts to some 12-16 hours of work a day

Yet work outside the household is undervalued too. In a major study of gender and poverty in India, the World Bank concluded that India invests far less in its women workers than in its working men, and that women's lack of access to the inputs they need for education, training, and other means of growth and change, is profoundly linked to their gender role and the cultural association of women with the 'inside', or the home: 'By contrast, men belong to the 'outside' where livelihoods are earned and political and economic power is exercised.' The failure to see, to invest in and to reward women's roles as economic actors has had major consequences for women's productivity. It is not only society or governments that undervalue women's work. Women themselves find it difficult to see the real value of what they do, as the following case study shows. The study also demonstrates the transformation that can come about when women start to organise to ensure that their work is adequately recognised and rewarded.

CASE STUDY: Organising domestic workers

The following extracts come from a book by a group of women in north-east Brazil called *Why We Should Work with Women* (for a fuller discussion see p.203). These extracts, written by Dulcinea Xavier, describe work with domestic workers in the Recife Metropolitan Region, an example of a local-level initiative which grew into a national movement. She traces how, over time, the need to incorporate a gender analysis into the work became crucial; a more general class analysis was simply not able to address the nature of domestic work and the specific problems of women domestic workers. Many of the issues we have been looking at about women's 'natural' work are illuminated here.

> Organising of maids in Recife began just prior to the military coup of 1964. At that time the urban workers' movement, mainly concentrated in the capital, was very active ... [but] at that time, women's problems were not dealt with as specific issues that needed to be addressed in a different way from the general problems of the working class.
>
> ...Domestic workers, even the most aware, find it difficult to analyse their life and work from a gender perspective, given that up to now their professional identity and place in society were seen through a class analysis. This is because those guiding the church and union workers, never gave much space to analysing gender in theory, let alone in practice.
>
> If we do not incorporate the notion of gender into the question of paid domestic work, we will end up leaving aside the 'feminine identity' which is an important factor in the under-valuing of the job. Society sees this profession as a 'natural' extension of feminine identity. Since this work is seen as 'natural' then it is unnecessary to pay well or assure their basic rights.
>
> Domestic workers themselves are unable to see the value of their work... not recognising their social and economic contribution and repeating the general perception of the 'invisibility' of domestic work. It is as if she were a prisoner in two homes, her own, and where she works. In the case of other working women, the same question is expressed in the conflict between having two possible identities; that of being a mother and wife, and that of having a job.
>
> For the domestic worker the psychological and social attachment to the 'natural identity' of feminine tasks is strong. For her this tension is hidden, and it is when this is expressed openly that change can occur, with a redefining of women's social and political identity.
>
> ...At the local level, the most important result was the

decision to found an association [of domestic workers]... Since 1980 the number of new associations in Recife continues to grow as well as increasing participation of domestic workers in various political events. The association offers, through discussions and meetings, a permanent process for growth in political awareness. In 1987 and 1988 skills training courses were offered which enabled the integration of new members, as well as equipping them better for work.

...The most important issue of the recent past has been, without doubt, the struggle to widen the labour laws under the new constitution. This involved a very intense mobilisation of national dimensions, with demonstrations in various cities, and even in the National Congress in Brasilia. Given that most of the demands were conceded, it can be considered a successful campaign. Another fundamental result of the new constitution is that the associations will be transformed into unions.

Rights guaranteed under the new constitution include:

The right to organise in professional associations or unions
Minimum salary
One paid day off per week
Annual holidays
Maternity leave
Proportional notice of termination of work
Retirement benefits.

The consequences of development

The failure of the development process to understand and support the reproductive and productive role of women within their households, and within the informal economy more generally, has meant that in almost all countries with weak economies and rapidly changing social systems, women, other than a minority of middle-class, educated women, have to struggle to maintain anything like an equal share in the development process. In many cases, more development has meant more subordination. The women of the Bhil tribal people of Western India give a clear recent example of this process. In this instance, the initiators of development were Gandhians who saw much tribal life as backward and primitive. They hoped that by initiating social development they would bring the Bhils into mainstream Indian society.

CASE STUDY: From tribal women to housewives

The Bhils are indigenous people of India. Their traditional tribal society is characterised by subsistence production and a sexual division of labour which is remarkably even-handed. Bhil women enjoy far more freedom then their Hindu sisters. There are no taboos surrounding menstruation and childbirth, and fewer social restrictions. A system of bride-price confers a higher status on the family of the bride and on the bride herself than the more usual dowry system, and Bhil marriage is more contractual than sacramental, with a relatively loose marriage tie. Divorce is common, and often initiated by the woman. Women are key actors in agriculture, and important decision makers in the household, though they are excluded from community decision-making bodies.

Over the last few decades some Bhils communities have started to modernise; encouraged by social development workers, they have gained access to resources and settled. In the process, what were relatively isolated communities have come into contact with the dominant Hindu society, and as they have settled down the process of social change has accelerated. This 'hinduisation' of Bhil tribals has had particular effects on women, weakening their social status. It has brought with it purdah, the banning of widow remarriage, the replacement of brideprice with dowry, and a greater submission of women to their husbands. Divorce is becoming rarer (and male-initiated), and the inferior treatment of girl children seems to be on the increase. What appears to be happening is that these tribal women, particularly in lowland villages, are becoming housewives, dependent on their husbands in a way that was not the case when they lived in a relatively autonomous subsistence economy. The shift from the free and equitable marriage contract that could be terminated by either partner to dowry marriage, turns daughters into a burden rather than an asset. A Bhil woman in purdah could never contemplate divorcing her husband; she would have no other means of support. The new Bhil housewives are being educated in the taboos and restrictions on behaviour that characterise the lives of Hindu women in the area.[11]

This account illustrates the need for development interventions to address the problems women face as a result of changes in their social environment; development agencies must understand the roles and skills of indigenous women and enable them to maintain their cultural identity.

CASE STUDY: Development planning for mothers and wives

Take the following scenario: a European agency wants to fund a development project for women in an urban region of Latin America. The agency works through a local NGO which employs a local consultant who reports that the main role of women is as wives and mothers and their main problem is lack of money. The agency decides that the best way of supporting these women will be to set up a project which will provide them with a steady income. Accordingly, the NGO sets to work to design an income-generating project. After several months of planning, a centre is set up, and supplied with raw materials for embroidering cushion covers. Each woman in the project is given an interest-free loan of $25 with which to buy the raw material from the centre. The centre buys back each embroidered cushion cover at the rate of $5 a cover, and the raw materials for each cover cost the women $1.50. It takes a woman at least eight hours to stich the cover, so a woman can earn at best about $25 a week. The project arranges for a doctor to visit the centre once a week, to provide mother-child health care, ante-natal checks and so on.

Embroidering the cushion covers is tedious, isolating (each woman works in her own home), fails to teach the women any new skills, and has no security, since the women do not know how long the project will last. The money the women earn is very little, and the embroidery adds enormously to their already heavy workload. After a while some of the women begin to drift out of the project. Other women with growing daughters get them either to do a larger share of housework, or to start stitching the covers as well. Meanwhile at the centre, the cushion covers are piling up. No one had really investigated the outlets properly, and those they had originally planned to use cannot sell the covers quickly enough. After two years it is clear that the project is going nowhere, and the funding agency decides not to renew its grant. In its report it comments on the fact that it was 'hard to generate the support and enthusiasm of the target group' — in other words, blaming the women for the project's failure.

There were clearly a lot of things wrong with this project, but we can draw out four points to illustrate the consequences of basing a development project on stereotypical ideas about women as housewives. Firstly, the project was based on what was seen as a typically 'feminine' skill, embroidery. Many development projects for women are based on traditional ideas of what women do best — jam and pickle making, tailoring, knitting, and cake making. While it may be true that many women have skills in these areas, to build a project on them fails to develop new skills. Secondly, the project was managed from the outside without involving the women in the planning of the project. The women were consulted to the extent of identifying their main need as cash, but it was assumed that the women lacked the ability to plan and implement a project. If the women had been able to work together to design the project themselves, producing something that might have met a real need in the community, which only they were qualified to judge — cheap school books or nursery school furniture, to quote just two examples from successful projects — the project might not have collapsed. Projects that assume that women are 'just housewives' fail to take into account the skills of management that women develop through running busy households on very limited resources.

Thirdly, the project failed to recognise how busy the women already were. Most had little extra time to stitch cushion covers. So they roped their daughters in. The error of assuming that women have some sort of household support system that enables them to take part in income-generating projects is as insensitive to their needs as the opposite error of assuming that women are not interested in economic programmes. If the project planners had allowed the women to work out a joint system for solving their problems of domestic responsibilities (through incorporating a creche and mid-day meal into the project, for example) not only would the women have contributed and benefited more, but another gender stereotype would have been challenged: that women need, or prefer, to be confined to their houses. By bringing the women together in one place, the project might have enabled them to discuss their experiences and begin to tackle the problems they had in common. And finally, the project planners assumed that the money earned from the cushion covers was a subsidiary wage, a second income. They were not therefore particularly concerned at the low level of wages generated because it was assumed that there was already a male breadwinner in every household. But this was not the case for several women and represented another gender stereotype.

Projects like this one do nothing to challenge the view that women are primarily housewives, passive, dependent, and without real work (i.e. they can take on additional activities). With more thought and imagination, the project could have challenged all these stereotypes, and enabled the women to set up and take control of a successful project.

N. Cooper and J. Hammond/Oxfam

Women meeting together to work on traditional embroidery, in Ethiopia. This project combines craft production with literacy and numeracy training.

Women-maintained households

Using the term 'women-maintained' instead of the more usual 'women-headed' emphasises the fact that, although many women take sole responsibility for supporting their families, they are seldom accorded the same recognition, rights, and powers as male household heads. A growing number of the world's households are maintained by women: twenty to thirty per cent of households in the Caribbean and Central America; 27 per cent in Sub-Saharan Africa; 16 per cent in North America; 15 per cent in South America and 11.7 per cent in India. Among refugee families in one area of Central America as many as 90 per cent of families are supported by women. Among refugees from Sri Lanka flooding into India, it was not unusual to find households headed by young women of 15 or 16, suddenly responsible for three or four younger siblings.

Why are women-maintained households on the increase? Different factors are responsible in different parts of the world; in Asia widowhood is a primary cause, whereas in Southern and Northern Africa and the Middle East, migration is more often the reason.[12] In many parts of rural Africa, husbands are very commonly absent for long periods. Internal migration (where men leave to find work in cities) and migration across national borders is the main cause. In Botswana, Lesotho, Mozambique, and Swaziland women support households while their men migrate to the South African mines, often for periods of 12 to 15 months. In Lesotho, almost 60 per cent of male workers have seasonal jobs in South African mines, and in the Transkei, the percentage of women-maintained households has been recorded at 67 per cent.[13] South African law specifically prohibits the wives and children of migrant labourers from accompanying their husbands. Migration has profound effects on the women left behind. They are left with the sole responsibility for farming, but given the absence of male labour and the low resourcing of subsistence agriculture, productivity is very low; consequently women have had to increase their workloads taking on more trading, marketing, brewing beer, casual labour on other, larger farms, or even migrating to local urban centres themselves. According to a Minority Rights Group Report, despite the increase in decision-making powers within the household and the management of food production, women remain subordinate to their husbands because of dependence on his cash earnings (which he may or may not send home) and his rights to the land. Some family units do not survive the migration; cash remittances cease altogether, and women are left to support themselves and their children.[14]

In Latin America migration is also a factor, but there are other social dynamics at work. A Minority Rights Group report on women in Latin America suggests that the increase in women-maintained households could be interpreted as an indication that women are beginning to free themselves from more repressive and restricting aspects of *machista* culture. Paradoxically, women who support their own households and have more power over their own decision making are also the poorest, and have very little economic security. Similarly, in the Caribbean many women choose to live with their children, and have short-term visiting relationships rather than a permanent, resident partner, though this pattern is reinforced by migration.[15]

The world over, North and South, women-maintained households are disproportionately represented among the poorest sectors of society. Since economic activities have to be combined with childcare responsibilities, the income produced is usually substantially lower than that produced by men in the same class, exacerbated by the fact that women still receive less money than men for the same job in many parts of the world. Janet Henshall Momsen points out that development has been accompanied by a decline in kinship obligation and co-operation within the extended family group; consequently, women whose partnerships break down are much more likely to have to struggle alone.[16] Increasing poverty also means that kinship groups simply do not have the resources to support additional family members.

Despite the growing number of households maintained by a woman, development initiatives frequently ignore or discriminate against them. There are well-documented examples of project benefits being offered to the heads of households, but missing out the women. In refugee camps, for example, agricultural implements and seeds are still more readily offered to men, to grow food for their families, than to women. The world is organised in numerous ways designed to make the existence of female-maintained households invisible. Census takers in some countries are instructed to name the oldest son, even if he is a young boy, in preference to the woman who is actually keeping the household together. Clearly, the myth that the male breadwinner and the female housewife is the normal or best arrangement for human beings still clings tenaciously, despite overwhelming evidence to the contrary.

The undervaluation of women's work

Women's work, the world over, is undervalued. If census takers are told not to include women's household work on their census forms, the message is clearly: 'Do not count women's work, because women's work does not count.' If housework were added into figures for global GNP, it has been estimated that the latter figure would go up by at least one-third. The work that women do is sometimes described as 'invisible' because it goes statistically unrecorded. Women's work is all about making a living, rather than earning a living; throughout the world, but particularly for low-income women in the South, it is this multiplicity of daily acts, this making a living, which keeps countless households alive.

4

UPHOLDING AND CHALLENGING GENDER SUBORDINATION

For all societies the common denominator of gender is female subordination, mediated by class and race.[1]

This chapter provides an introductory overview of the ways in which gender subordination is upheld in societies throughout the world. It looks at some of the social, political, and economic institutions which divide resources, opportunity, and power differently between the two genders. It cannot hope to provide anything more than pointers, since in each society, North and South, different political, cultural and democratic traditions dictate how gender relations will be structured. It begins by arguing that gender subordination on such a broad scale can only be understood if we view it as a structural problem, beyond individual intentions, and shaping thought and action through the social institutions we occupy, and the political, cultural, and economic institutions that shape our social worlds. The chapter starts by looking at the family, giving as examples of its impact the questions of son preference and sexuality, both of which have become important issues to women's movements around the world. It then moves on to look at the related issues of access to property, ritual, tradition, and cultural taboo. Violence against women is one of the most potent weapons to ensure their compliance with gender norms, while religion has been used to legitimise subordination in every tradition. The chapter looks at both. Turning to the issue of women's work, the nature of subordination within working culture is discussed, particularly in the informal sector and within manufacturing for export. This section also discusses two related forms of work in South-East Asia, tourism and prostitution, seeing in this particular nexus an intensification of many of the themes developed in this book — North/South exploitation, sexuality, class, and gender subordination. The chapter concludes by looking at legal systems and education. Throughout the chapter, it becomes clear that each of these institutionalised forms of sexism is under attack. Case studies of the work of women's groups in the South illustrate the imaginative and committed ways in which women are beginning to challenge these foundations of gender subordination.

A structural problem

Most people who are born and grow up in those countries in the North with liberal democratic traditions share certain assumptions about behaviour. Put simply, we believe that we do what we do because we want to, and behave in certain ways because we have chosen them. If we were to stop and consider how much of our behaviour is conditioned by our gender, and how much of that gender role we have not in fact chosen for ourselves, we might be surprised. In order to understand how gender affects us, our belief in the self-sufficient individual needs to be modified by another one — that people are fundamentally social beings. The young Karl Marx made the point with telling bluntness when he said 'It is society which thinks in me'. Obviously this does not mean that we cannot, up to a point, arrange our thoughts in our own way and have original ideas. But, while there is indeed 'a person, an individual and unique experience, ... it is in large part made up of common elements'. If we were to tear from ourselves our social material, we would as Louis Dumont expressed it, have little left other than the 'potentiality for personal organisation'.[2]

The social institutions that we enter as individuals, from our arrival in our families at birth, through our education, youth culture, and into the worlds of work and leisure, marriage and starting families of our own, give us clear messages about how 'normal' people behave, according to their gender. We learn the options open to us. Although, for example, a white middle-class professional woman will be offered more life chances and choices than the young black woman who cleans her office, nonetheless, for both women, the choices will be limited by appropriate gender behaviour.

In theory, for women in the North, every walk of life is open; at the same time, they are constantly reminded that their primary role should be that of wife and mother. The dominant gender message built into all the social institutions they inhabit is that whatever else they do, from becoming bus-conductors to mountaineers, they should be attractive and desirable to men, and that, ideally, one man will become the partner to whom all their emotional energy is directed, in the institution of marriage. This message is reinforced in fairy stories and nursery rhymes, in teenage and women's magazines, in advertising, on television, in the cinema, by religious institutions and, in some countries, by tax and social security legislation. And the arrangement is portrayed as freely chosen by self-determining individuals.

When we look at societies outside the industrialised North, where the ideology of individuality and the belief in an individual's freedom do not hold so much power, the fact that gender roles do not rest on individual inclination but on the very structure of society becomes much clearer. Women writing in the dossier *Women living under Muslim laws* write that '... many ... women have no choice at all in the direction their adult lives take — they are directed first by their fathers and mothers, and then by their husbands and mothers-in-law'. Religion dictates particular ways of behaving, tradition others. To an outsider from another culture, the fact that a woman is expected to restrict her freedom of movement during menstruation may appear highly unnatural and unacceptably restrictive. For the society which insists on this seclusion, the practice will appear a natural and normal part of being a woman. Such practices show that nothing in the human world is 'natural', least of all the way in which we perceive bodily events such as menstruation.

We need a theory of gender which goes beyond our individual intentions. By seeing it as an ideological, social, and structural issue, built into our lives with the same force and firmness as the fact that we are born into families, we can understand it as preexisting us and defining us, rather than the other way round. The reason why it is often so hard to challenge gender roles is because most societies in the world are patriarchal, and through this power structure, traditional gender roles in which women are subordinate are upheld and perpetuated.

Why people talk about 'patriarchy'

The word 'patriarchy' originally had a narrow meaning, referring to the system, historically derived from Greek and Roman law, in which the male head of household had absolute legal and economic power over his dependent female and male family members and his male and female slaves. It is sometimes argued that patriarchy, in this sense of the word, came to an end in most of Western Europe in the nine-teenth century with the granting of civil rights to women, particularly married women. More recently, the term 'patriarchy' has come to be used around the world to describe the situation of male dominance over women and children within the family and the extension of this into male dominance in all other areas of society. 'Patriarchy' is the concept that men hold power in all the important roles in societies — in government, the military, education, industry, business, health care, advertising, religion — and that women are, in the main, deprived of access to that power. It does not imply that women are totally powerless, or totally deprived of rights, influences, and resources; rather, that the balance of power is in men's favour.

This has important implications when we consider why traditional gender roles are difficult to alter. It is a basic feature of societies organised along patriarchal lines that the gender relations between women and men are unequal. Challenging gender inequality is threat-ening because it challenges the whole social structure. Patriarchy per-meates all aspects of society and social systems; and we will now look at some of these and see how their structures, which give men privi-leges at the expense of women, uphold gender differences.

The family

The 'nuclear family' unit, consisting of a mother, a father and two or three children, is the perfect unit for an industrial society because it means that the demand for products will go on expanding indefinite-ly as nuclear families reproduce themselves. The nuclear family is only one form of household grouping, however. Different societies around the world organise themselves in other ways. For a typical Ashanti girl growing up in Ghana the immediate family group con-sists of her mother, grandmother, mother's brothers, and mother's sis-ters and their children. She calls all the women in the household 'mother' and, when she visits her father's house where he lives with his mother and siblings, she calls everyone in the household 'father'. In many parts of South Asia, people live in extended families — grandparents live with sons, their wives and their children, under one roof.

Despite the variations in family structure, and despite a growing number of woman-headed households, many societies expect women to be subordinate in marriage to a male head of household. This has important implications for women in the control of their reproductive lives, in a preference for male children, and in the autonomy they have over household affairs. In the rural community in north India, studied by Patricia Jeffrey and her colleagues, brides were referred to as 'someone else's property', and after marriage, young women had to adopt forms of behaviour that demonstrate their subordinate status: a young bride would rarely initiate a conversation with her father-in-law, but would use a child as a go-between.[3] Daughters-in-law cannot go far from their homes, and can go nowhere without permission. Husbands expect obedient wives and may enforce their authority with physical violence. Her own parents will be very reluctant to interfere, even if they suspect their daughter is being ill-treated. Only when a woman has daughters-in-law of her own, or if she and her husband set up their own household, will she experience any power and influence over the running of her life. Rural north India is not an isolated, though an extreme, example of the subordinate position of married women in their husband's households.

Within a patriarchal family unit, the interests, needs and power of the various family members will be different, which is why gender-sensitive development planners argue that taking the family as a unit in development planning cannot guarantee the distribution of benefits equally to all the members of the family. Yet the family unit remains a dominant focus in much development planning, particularly among some agencies with a Christian agenda and an ideological commitment to upholding the integrity of the family. Considering the income of family members separately reveals how increases in income affect both family dynamics and patterns of consumption. It has been shown, for example, that increases in the mother's income tend to improve both the quality and quantity of food available for her children, whereas increases in men's income tend to go in 'productive investments, consumer goods and entertainment'.[4]

Son preference

> Raising a daughter is like watering a shady tree in someone else's courtyard.

(Indian proverb)

One consequence of the subordinate position of women is the development of son-preference, a preference so advanced in India, Pakistan, and Bangladesh that it has had a significant effect on the sex-ratio in the population. Currently in India there are only 929 women to every 1,000 men; in the UK there are 1,060 women per 1,000 men. It is not difficult to see why women prefer sons; daughters will one day leave home, taking a significant proportion of the family's wealth in the form of dowry, whereas sons offer the promise of future autonomy and authority over daughters-in-law and grandchildren. Women who produce sons are treated better than women who only give birth to daughters. And this preferential treatment is passed on to their children. There is widespread evidence that boys are breast-fed more often and for longer than their sisters; boys are taken to doctors more promptly than are girls; boys are fed before girls, and educated more seriously. Among middle-class Indians son-preference expresses itself in the growth of clinics which offer amniocentesis for sex-testing, and the abortion of unwanted female foetuses. In some villages in Tamil Nadu and Rajisthan, infanticide of baby girls is still practised.

By bearing in mind our description of gender subordination as a structural problem, these extreme forms of discrimination are more understandable. If the social definition and value of maleness and femaleness is extremely polarised, it is not surprising if we find people acting in accordance with these definitions.

In the early 1980s the use of amniocentesis for determining the sex of foetuses gained considerable popularity in urban centres in India. Advertised as a 'humane service for women who do not want any more daughters', an estimated 78,000 female foetuses were aborted between 1978 and 1982. The women's movement in India was quick to respond, seeing in the growing trend — presented as an expansion of women's reproductive choices — a serious threat to the status of Indian women. They began to talk back in the media, arguing that sex-choice was another form of oppression, and that 'under the guise of a choice we may indeed exacerbate our own oppression'. The analysis that grew out of the women's movement linked together class, race and sex in its challenge to the growing institutionalisation of son-preference. Journalists, women's organisations, and voluntary health organisations, lawyers and doctors, formed the 'Forum Against Sex Determination and Sex-preselection Techniques' and organised an effective campaign using films, exhibitions, public meetings and television coverage, to convey the social implications of the tests. They organised pickets in front of hospitals carrying out the tests and put up thousands of posters. Some of the most successful actiions were the demonstrations by parents with daughters, and activities undertaken by school-girls, challenging the view of girls as less valuable than boys. As pressure mounted, the Government of Maharashtra was forced to make the practice illegal in the State.[5]

Sexuality

They are born of our womb. We keep them in the womb for nine months and nourish them with our blood, but the man claims them, saying that after all they are born of his seed.

Woman from Madhya Pradesh, India.

Sexuality is another area in which women in patriarchal societies find themselves highly controlled. The use of language often makes explicit the idea of a husband's rights over his wife's childbearing capacity. He alone plants seeds in her. Many women throughout the world believe that the husband's seed contains all that is needed for the baby to start growing; the mother simply provides the nourishment to make it grow. All over north and central India the process of reproduction is referred to by the metaphorical use of the two terms the 'seed' and the 'earth'. Men provide the seed and the essence, and since the seed determines the kind of child, a child's identity is fundamentally derived from the father. (Curiously enough, the inherent contradiction between the belief that men determine the nature of the child and the blame attached to women who fail to bear sons, is not appreciated.) The mother's role — as the nourisher — is continued through breastfeeding once the baby is born.

This sexual asymmetry is clearly expressed in the Hindu marriage rituals. The bride goes through the ritual of 'consecration of the field', aimed at purifying her womb ready to receive the seed. The metaphor is taken further, and a woman is expected to bear pain; just as the earth is ploughed, furrowed, dug into, a woman, too, is pierced and ploughed (sexual intercourse is sometimes referred to as 'ploughing'). Just as a man has rights over his field and its produce, so, too, he has rights over his wife's sexuality, her reproductive capacity andwhat her womb produces. He also has rights over her productive capacity and labour power and these two rights — over her productive and reproductive work — are not unrelated. Just as women's work in reproduction is undermined and undervalued by an ideology that sees the real inputs as male, so, too, is their contribution to the household economy ignored or grossly under-recognised. Women under patriarchy stand alienated from their productive and reproductive labour; the fruits of both belong to someone else.

Women's groups around the world have begun the process of reclaiming sexuality as an area in which women can challenge their oppression. They are looking at received understandings of women's sexuality, linking women's economic and social subordination with their sexual subordination. At the same time, this 'politics of sexism' has been linked to the 'politics of desire',[6] as women have looked at the positive possibilities of sexual freedom; at questions of pleasure as well as of power, of choice as well as subordination. In the process the idea of sexuality itself as a social construction, rather than a biologically innate, unchanging entity has become important; sexuality is seen as the 'intricate and multiple ways in which our emotions, desires and relationships are shaped by the society we live in'.[7] Understanding these social forces is the first step towards changing them, by ensuring that women have an opportunity to think through the place and meaning of sexuality in their lives and in their relationships. In the process, questions of identity, obligation, power, pleasure, choice, and consent are raised, and the opportunity women have for autonomy in this intimate area of their lives.

CASE STUDY: The work of CIDHAL

Oxfam works with one of the oldest organisations in Latin America, CIDHAL, which was started in the mid-1960s by Betty Hollands, a Belgian feminist living in Mexico. CIDHAL started as a centre for research analysis and documentation on women in Latin America, and later evolved into a more active group committed to promoting education and organisation of Mexican women, both urban and rural. CIDHAL has long experience of preparing materials for women, and their publications are widely circulated and read. The extract below comes from a book called *Cuerpo de Mujer* — a woman's body — and it reflects a growing demand by women around the world for information on their bodies, their sexuality and their relationships.

> For four or five years we have felt the need for a clear book to work with women. They tell us of the need to break with ignorance about our bodies and sexuality... Why did we come up with the title *A Woman's Body*, if our original idea was for it to be on sexuality? Because [we] see the need for a new view of sexuality, embracing our whole body, all our feelings and not only, as we had been taught, to have children or for the pleasure of the man.

> Sexuality was relegated to the night, in the dark, after the day's work... an obligation which must be met and not a need of life and feeling... Sexuality is something natural, something we all need. Sexuality is necessary for communication; it is a pleasure for most men and women. It has to do with what we think about our body and about people, with our feelings, thoughts and actions....

People's sexuality is expressed in the desire to give and receive words, looks, laughs, caresses, attention, and understanding, which means that the meeting between bodies will be deeply human... Our body will be able to feel pleasure if there is communication between partners. However, this is not the experience most of us have of sexuality.

We have been taught to think that sexuality is a part of life which has only to do with genital contact, that it is something private, secret and almost shameful. We think it has nothing to do with social relations, with history, with our work or with the economic system... The sexuality we experience is repressed and limited... it has remained a private matter which is talked about very little.

We have been led to believe that there are some characteristics which go with female sexuality and others which go with masculine sexuality. For example we think that masculine sexuality means that the man is aggressive, uncontrollable, impulsive, strong, active and the possessor of the woman. And we think that feminine sexuality means the woman is passive, patient, obedient, weak, dependent on the man, and she is only fulfilled by having children and she is always ready to give to others without caring what happens to her... However, men and women do not have to be like this.

Access to property

In much of the South, property, usually in the form of land, is the key to survival, and access and control are intimately related to kinship patterns and marriage. As such, land and property rights are an extension of familial control over its members. Not surprisingly therefore, the world over, women do not have the same access to land as do men, and very few women have full control over their land by acquiring it in their own right. At the same time there is a huge diversity of inheritance patterns practised, dictated by local tribal, religious, and customary and statutory law. In many societies, property is inherited through the patrilineal line, but even in the minority of societies in which inheritance is matrilineal (such as the Asante of Ghana, and the Rembau of Malaysia) control over property and land tends to remain vested in men, the difference being that in matrilineal systems the men are the maternal uncles, the brothers, and sons of women.[8] In many countries in Sub-Saharan Africa; in Peru, Bolivia and Paraguay; and in Islamic countries, women do not have the same inheritance rights as men. Under the Islamic code, a daughter's inheritance is limited to half that of a son's share (because daughters are expected to marry and have their needs provided for by their husbands, still leaving them dependent on a man, of course). In some societies the process of Islamisation has had a detrimental effect on inheritance patterns. Among the people of Mafia Island on the Tanzanian cost studied by Patricia Caplan, historically access to property was egalitarian. As indigenous ideologies are being influenced by Islam it is becoming more difficult for women to gain access to productive assets such as coconut trees.[9]

In Sub-Saharan Africa customary laws discriminate against women; land rights often devolve to men on the assumption that there is always a male head of household, even though this may mean that women members of the family may lose their status as independent farmers. Governments have tended to replicate this attitude towards women farmers through land reform programmes or co-operative developments.[10] According to a Minority Rights report, under the laws of many African countries land rights continue to be given to the male head of household, despite the fact that the majority of men migrate to the urban centres for work.[11] This has enormous significance for the women who are left behind to farm the land. The failure to gain land rights has been accompanied by a failure to gain rights to a range of other resources such as information, technology, credit, training, and agricultural inputs such as fertilizers, pesticides and seeds. Women are forced to remain dependent on men simply to ensure access to the land they need to grow food for their own and their children's survival. Consequently, many women, in Africa and in other parts of the world remain in their marital home despite maltreatment and violence, for fear of loosing access to the few resources they have, land and children.

Many women's organisations are addressing land and property rights. In Zimbabwe, for example, women have attained equal rights to land on the resettled co-operative farms. Co-operative members have obtained usufruct rights although the land itself remains the property of the State. Housing projects in many parts of the world have responded to pressure from women's groups to grant housing rights in the woman's name. The importance to women in gaining access to and control over key productive assets cannot be overstated. Productive assets offer security; loans can be secured against them; dependency on violent or coercive relationships can be lessened; and women gain status from possessing their own means of production.

JOHN BAGULEY/OXFAM

Women working on a co–operative farm, Zimbabwe.

Securing a more equitable share for women is not easy. The key has often been seen to lie in land reform. According to one Oxfam report, almost every developing country has already introduced a programme described as 'land reform' but most of these have produced negligible results because they have not really been designed to change the power structure. Most have not even considered the question of gender. Laws alone are not sufficient to ensure a change in attitudes, though good and equitable laws remain an essential starting point. In Zimbabwe, an Age of Majority Act was passed in 1981, formally granting women the right to own property; despite this, land in rural areas is still reserved for a woman's father, husband or son. The majority of rural women simply do not know about the laws passed in their favour, or how to use them.[13] Women's groups around the world are trying to address gaps of this nature, through training programmes and workshops, as the case study below demonstrates.

CASE STUDY: A workshop on women, law, and development

In September 1989 a workshop was held in Kenya, with Oxfam project partners working with women, to facilitate their work through training, teaching materials, and legal resources. A focus of discussion was inheritance and property rights under the complexities of customary law and civil law, in relation to marriage, separation and divorce. Participants at the workshop were given specially written handbooks on the law, designed for lay people, and two women lawyers from the Law Reform Commission were invited to prepare materials and help present the workshop.

Among the many case studies presented at the workshop was one given by Zambian participants, about a campaign to change inheritance laws; an alliance of educated and grassroots women had been formed to campaign against an unjust law. In 1986 the Law Development Commission in Zambia had presented a draft inheritance bill to the Attorney General, designed to prevent the property 'grabbing' that was leaving families homeless. Unfortunately the bill lay dormant in the AG's office until the Decade for Women prompted its revival. The Zambian Women's League and an NGO Coordinating Committee, along with other women's groups, were responsible for lobbying for its ratification. They set up opinion polls; organised a march-past for the President in which women wore T-shirts with the slogan 'Protect the Widow'; lobbied sympathetic MPs; used the mass media and held seminars at which widows who had lost all their property told their stories. At a women's prayer day, the President instructed that the bill should be passed, and while some legal clarification remains, the children and widow of the deceased now receive a significant degree of legal protection safeguarding their access to the property of the marriage.[14]

Violence against women

There is a link between the varieties of violence done to women all over the world — rape and battering, dowry deaths in India, female genital mutilation or circumcision in Africa, the creation of pornography. The link is in women being seen as objects to be owned and exchanged by men, rather than as individuals with rights over their bodies and their lives. As such, freedom from violence has become a key issue for women's groups the world over. Recent figures document the staggering toll of domestic violence. In the US, battery is the leading cause of injury to adult women and a rape is committed every six minutes; in Peru 70 per cent of all crimes reported to police concern women beaten by their partners. In Lima, a city of 7 million, 168,970 rapes were reported in 1987 alone. In India, 8 out of 10 wives can expect violence in their households. The most dangerous place for women, the world over, is at home.[15]

Violence humiliates and intimidates women; fear of violence prevents many women from taking initiatives and organising their lives as they would choose. Fear of violence is a key factor preventing women from participation in development; it may prevent a woman from going to a family-planning clinic, for example, or attending literacy classes. Womankind Worldwide— an NGO set up to look particularly at the needs and potential of Third World women — published a report on violence against women which documents some of the reasons why violence may be on the increase: new methods of production have led to changes in relationships between the sexes, which in turn may have heightened domestic tensions in societies where men believe that it is their right to control their partners. Wives have been beaten for their 'inability, or refusal, to accept the extra work involved in cash crop production'; women who are not so highly dependent on their husband or partner's support may be less vulnerable to abuse, though unemployed men may equally take their frustrations out on their women.[16]

Sexual violence is linked to other forms of violence; in the last two decades attitudes towards rape have shifted significantly, led by women's movements around the world. From seeing rape as a crime committed by abnormal men unable to control their lust, rape is now seen as an act of violence committed by 'normal' men against women: it is primarily a mechanism of control and intimidation. Interestingly, rape laws in many countries of the world retain the idea of rape as an act against property — the property of another man, either the father of an unmarried girl or the husband of a married woman. This idea of women as property, women as objects of exchange, is fundamental to understanding acts of violence committed against women in all parts of the world.

Maria Mies sees the idea of women as property underlying the increase in the number of rapes carried out against rebellious peasants in rural areas in India. Not content with burning houses, and beating up the men, landlords and henchmen rape women. According to Mies, 'These acts have nothing to do with sexuality but...women are seen as the only property which pauperised men still possess. The rape of their women teaches poor men the lesson that their status is one of absolute powerlessness...Class rule and the oppression of women are here closely interwoven. He who owns the land, owns the women of the land.' The same rationale — women as property — underlies the violence that such women often receive from their own husbands. According to the women's movement in India, it is seeing women as objects of exchange between the men of two families that is the root of the problem of dowry death. Police records show a high death rate among young women, due to burning, usually in accidents in the kitchen. In Delhi alone, 690 women died of burning in 1983, and of these 270 were between the ages of 18 and 25. Although only a handful were alleged to be 'dowry burnings' (the deliberate burning of a young bride by her in-laws as a way of getting rid of her on the pretext that she did not bring enough dowry to her marriage), women's groups argue that most if not all such deaths are not accidental. Some may be suicide, but many are murder. Yet very few of these deaths are ever investigated and even fewer result in convictions. The women's movement in India has spoken out strongly against dowry and dowry deaths. On many occasions women have taken to the streets in rage and grief at a suspected dowry death. Yet the deaths continue.

ALISON BARRETT/OXFAM

Women taking part in a demonstration in Bangladesh, organised by a local NGO, to protest against the increasing level of violence against women.

In parts of Africa women are also speaking out against female circumcision; at the same time they recognise that it is a practice so deeply rooted in the construction of gender roles in Africa that it will be very difficult to eradicate. An account of female circumcision in Kenya by a Kenyan woman points out that it is part of a rite of passage, a turning point from childhood to adulthood; without the rite, a woman would be regarded as childish, outcast, irresponsible, and importantly, impure. Female circumcision is an extremely difficult practice for outsiders to comment on. One approach which was adopted by the World Health Organisation in 1975 is that female circumcision can only be tackled by the women of the countries in which it is happening, when they feel ready. How they tackle it will be up to them. Another approach argues that the morbidity and suffering that result from circumcision places it in a similar category to maternal mortality — equally a result of social and cultural circumstances. As such it is a legitimate issue on which women (and men) outside the countries concerned could take an advocacy role — though the agenda must be set by the women affected. The majority of women who are circumcised do not protest; as circumcision is usually carried out on very young girls, refusal is not an option. Religion and family tradition are implacable, and revolt would be tantamount to social suicide. To refuse excision and infibulation would mean condemning oneself to be outcast from society.

But we should remember that social surgery is not restricted to Africa. Northern women undergo social surgery voluntarily in the form of cosmetic surgery, again in the interests of retaining and reinforcing a gender role, this time to remain attractive and young-looking. The parallels are certainly there: cosmetic surgery to cut away wrinkles and bags, to smooth out cheeks and necks, to alter bosoms and bottoms, and even to tighten vaginas is seen as a reasonable if extravagant way of spending one's money. Yet the women who undergo such operations are doing so in pursuit of a gender role that insists that whatever else women do in life, their primary purpose is to be attractive to men. Cutting out parts of one's body for the sake of 'beauty' and desirability is also a form of sexual mutilation.

Pornography is another form of violence against women which upholds gender differences. Discussions of pornography have been bedevilled by ideas of liberation, freedom of expression, and questions of morality and censorship. Susanne Kappeler argues that the content of pornography is not the issue: the issue is representation and what it means to turn a person into an object. Pornography conditions male arousal to female subordination, humiliation, pain, rape and mutilation: whether 'soft' or 'hard', the pornographer, the person who creates the images, always starts by reducing his 'subject' to an object, an object that can then be sold to men as property.[18]

CASE STUDY: 'A Centre for Women in Need'

Domestic violence is growing in Zambia. That is the conclusion reached by a network of NGOs and the National Commission for Development and Planning. In a series of meetings in Lusaka the YWCA was chosen to spearhead a process of building support structures for abused women. The YWCA consider that the apparent increase in domestic violence is linked to social and economic change in Zambia. Traditionally such issues would have been dealt with within the family; a woman could go to her uncle for support, and if necessary would return to her own nuclear family. As the economic climate in Zambia continues to deteriorate families may not have the resources to absorb more people, and women suffering from violence have very few options open to them. Growing poverty itself brings a host of social problems, and the YWCA believe that the despair people feel increases incidents of family violence, with women and children being the primary victims. More positively, Zambian women are becoming more aware of their rights as equal citizens, and are starting to demand that society finds positive methods of dealing with violence against women, instead of pretending that it is not an issue.

The YWCA is working on a series of interlinked support structures; a safe house to provide short-term shelter; an expansion of the Drop-in Centre they already run, where women can come for advice, counselling and information; mobile support services which could visit rural areas on a regular basis; a public education campaign; and the training of women throughout the country to counsel abuse victims. The 'Women in Need' project will provide a valuable resource for Zambian women. Just as important is the insistence that the issue becomes one for public recognition.[19]

CASE STUDY: Confronting violence to women

Confronting rape and other violence to women has become an important part of women's health projects around the world. The following extract comes from an inaugural speech by the director of CIDEM (The Centre for Information and Women's Development, La Paz, Peru) at the start of a campaign against violence to women.

> For us, (rape) is the crudest expression of the relations established in society between men and women... As an institution identified with women, and particularly with poor women, we have been disturbed to see the alarming increase over recent months in physi-

cal aggression against women...Precisely because in the context of social relations, men and women do not occupy the same place in the social hierarchy, there is a structural form of discrimination which is expressed in labour relations, and above all in the family environment. There is a lack of appreciation of women's contribution to society through domestic work and in bringing up boys and girls. What we see is a permanent forum in which the man expresses his strength, his virility, and his machismo in relation to women. This means we should not be surprised that we are currently witnessing an increase in the number of rapes because what is occurring is simply a sign of men's appropriation of women's sexuality.

Certain common expressions in our language such as to 'make her mine' or to 'possess' a woman reflect exactly the macho and dominant attitude of men to women. 'I became his', 'he made me his' are expressions for the carnal act of possessing a woman which are used in different ways, different circumstances, and different environments...So when we speak of rape, we do not refer simply to those sexual actions where the violence is obvious, but to all types of rape, all types of non-consensual sexual relations, whether within marriage or outside it.

It is our aim today to hear the voices of those who are linked to this theme by their activities, experience or profession and can illuminate for us what is actually happening in our society with respect to this problem...with the aim of initiating a campaign of reflection and education to change attitudes.

Ritual, tradition, and cultural taboos

Traditionally held ideas about correct gender behaviour can have profound effects on women's lives, providing a strong reinforcement of gender patterns in society. An understanding of gender differences in the ownership and control of property, in the sexual division of labour and in the value of women's economic labour needs to be balanced with another view, since women's lives are equally determined by the way in which childbearing and other events — puberty, widowhood — are perceived and organised by their society. Some anthropologists have argued that gender is the basis for a dual social system; the whole structure of society, beliefs, and behaviour hinge on the idea of a fundamental opposition between the two sexes.

In a study of Kabylia, Algeria, the French social anthropologist

Pierre Bourdieu shows how social and physical spaces are divided up according to perceptions of male and female roles. Houses are divided into two halves by a low wall; one half, which is slightly higher, is the place of 'male' cultural activities, cooking and weaving. The lower, darker half is the place of 'female' natural things, the household animals, the water pots, the green fodder and wood, and also natural activities, such as sleep, sex and birth. But this opposition between the female and male places within the house is mirrored in a larger opposition between the house and the rest of the social space, the male world of places of assembly, the fields and the market. The Algerian proverb 'Man is the lamp of the outside, women the lamp of the inside' expresses this.

In Kabylia women are defined by their childbearing status; unmarried adult women are seen as 'bad wood' or 'twisted wood', akin to fallow ground. Sterile women are not allowed to plant in gardens or carry seeds. During menstruation women are not allowed to prepare meals, work in the garden, plant, pray or fast. Women are charged with all the tasks involving the protection of things that grow and shoot, that are green and tender, whether of humans and animals, 'things in the morning of life'. Women hoe, gather herbs and vegetables from the garden, and look after cows. As in India, procreation is perceived as a male act of opening and sowing, akin to ploughing. A bride's arrival at her new house is marked by almost the same ritual as that for the start of a new agricultural cycle, when the ox, plough and seed set out for the fields. She is welcomed at the doorway by a basket of fritters, eggs, wheat, dates, nuts and pomegranates, and she breaks eggs in a gesture symbolising fertility. Such tightly organised patterns of behaviour are described by Bourdieu as a 'book' from which children learn their society's vision of the world.[20]

Most societies have particular rituals, marking puberty, marriage and childbirth, related to an underlying belief system, and these practices hold communities together and enrich the social fabric of people's lives. The tension arises when these beliefs and actions discriminate against women, or infringe their human rights. Such tension demands that we are cautious in our attitudes to other cultures and their traditions, taking our lead from women within the society concerned. Recently, for example, taboos surrounding menstruation have come to be seen as a positive aspect of women's lives, since they give women a chance to have a much-needed rest. (Presumably such periods of rest always were interpreted positively by the women concerned; the shift is in the attitude of outside observers.)

The approach to this nexus of issues must be one of immense sensitivity, which insists that discussion be led by women from the community under consideration. Just as Australian aborigines now reject the efforts of white Australians to interpret their culture and art for them, so women of the South reject the attempt of Northern feminists, however well-meaning, to set the agenda in terms of challenging cultural practices that are perceived in the North as inimical to the well-being of Southern women.

Religion

Religion is a foundation stone of gender difference. Under most of the world's religious traditions, women have been given a secondary and subordinate role. Christian tradition is hostile to the idea of women taking a leadership role, though there is evidence that throughout Christian history there have been communities in which women have played a leadership role. The debate over women priests has produced all sorts of reasons why women should not be ordained, many of which refer to women's fundamental biological difference, and her childbearing role, as well as to history and to tradition.

Women living under Muslim laws face different kinds of constraints, though a statement in the dossier 'Women Living Under Muslim Laws' should alert us to the dangers of generalisations: 'Our different realities range from being strictly closeted, isolated and voiceless within four walls, subjected to public flogging and condemned to death for presumed adultery (which is considered a crime against the state) and forcibly given in marriage as a child, to situations where women have a far greater degree of freedom of movement and interaction, the right to work, to participate in public affairs and also exercise a far greater control over their own lives.'[21] Nonetheless, many Muslim women feel (as indeed do women in many religious traditions) that their lives are 'shaped, conditioned and governed by laws, both written and unwritten, drawn up from interpretations of the Koran tied up with local traditions' and that 'generally speaking men and the state use these against women, and they have done so under various political regimes'.[22]

For Hindu women, there is a history of negative and critical writings about their sex. Manu the Law-giver's much quoted dictum 'From the cradle to the grave a woman is dependent on a male: in childhood on her father, in youth on her husband, in old age on her son' is not so very far from the truth for millions of Hindu women.

Most religious traditions have, in the last three decades, attracted feminist scholars who have argued that it is not the texts of religions which have caused the problems but their interpretation. Christian, Jewish, and Muslim feminists have re-examined their scriptures and come to the conclusion that their religions offered the possibility of liberation and improvement in the position of women, but that tradition and history have subverted this potential and used religion to repress women. Other scholars have pointed to the fact that almost all religions have at some point offered opportunities to women to exercise power, usually through the mystical tradition. In Islam women made a significant contribution to Sufism, and there have been several notable women Christian mystics.

The questions of religious teachings, textual interpretation, and traditions are not simple ones, and while most religions have developed liberal movements, there is an equally strong pull towards fundamentalism, which tends to stress women's difference and, whether in the churches of the US or in the mosques of Iran, claim a divine sanction for polarised gender roles.

Religion may be used to repress women, but women the world over have used religion as an opportunity to come together, and as a source of solidarity with other women. The story of Rigoberta Menchu, an Indian Guatemalan peasant woman, offers an example of the role of Christianity in one woman's fight for social justice against an oppressive military regime. By the age of 23 she had already become famous in her country as a national leader, and her life-story reflects vividly the experiences common to so many Indian communities in Latin America.

> At the end of 1977, I decided to join a more formal group — a group of peasants in Heuhuetenango...and yet, I still hadn't reached the rewarding stage of participating fully, as an Indian first, and then as a woman, a peasant, a Christian, in the struggle of all my people. That's when I started to get more involved...I began travelling to different areas, discussing everything...Why do they reject us? Why is the Indian not accepted? Why is it that the land used to belong to us?...Why don't outsiders accept Indian ways...I started to work as an organiser. No one taught me to organise because, having been a catechist, I already knew. We began forming groups of women who wanted to join the struggle...Our main weapon...is the Bible. We began to study the Bible as a text through which to educate our village...We began looking for texts which represented each one of us. We tried to relate them to our Indian

culture. We took the example of Moses for the men, and we have the example of Judith, who was a very famous woman in her times. She fought very hard for her people...we feel it is the duty of Christians to create the kingdom of God on earth...This kingdom will exist only when we all have enough to eat, when our children, brothers, parents don't have to die from hunger and malnutrition.[23]

Working culture

Gender discrimination in working culture is not only about male bosses and female secretaries within the formal sector. Gender discrimination in the division of labour outside of the household context touches almost all the economically productive work that women in the South perform. In this section we look at women in the manufacturing sector, where the large-scale employment of women is an aspect of the changing international division of labour; in the informal sector; and in tourism and prostitution as it has developed particularly in South-East Asia in the last two decades.

A theme running throughout this section is the paradox at the heart of much of women's economic activity: it both liberates women, and subordinates them; it gives them an income, but, when carried out in poor and unregulated conditions, can be deeply exploitative of their time and labour.

Women in manufacturing industries

There is growing evidence that a 'new international division of labour' has developed, in which countries in the North are increasingly specialising in research and development, finance and administration, while in Southern countries, manufacturing is beginning to replace their former role in the supply of raw materials. Within this international division, Southern countries become the global production line, and women operate the machinery.[24] In order to attract foreign capital into their countries, Southern governments have set up free-trade zones. These come with large incentives — the promise of a cheap, docile, and unorganised work force (predominantly female); help with loans; subsidised factory space. A preference for female workers has become an important part of the international division of labour. A study done of the selection of workers for Mexico's electronic factories found that employers were looking for women who were unmarried and preferably under 20.

Female labour is preferred because it is inexperienced, unlikely to unionise, perceived to be docile, dependent, and easily managed.

Above all, it is cheap. Many of the women employed are taken on as trainees at minimal rates, and laid off once they are qualified. In one study it was found that an electronics plant had a staff turnover of 100 per cent in an 18-month period. Women working in such factories have little job security since they can be laid off whenever demand is slack and then re-employed again on temporary contracts when demand picks up. The nature of much assembly-line work, particularly in electronics and in the manufacture of professional and medical equipment such as heart pace-makers, demands stamina and good eyesight, and many women resign voluntarily from the electronics sector when they are aware that they can no longer reach the production level required because of deteriorating eye-sight and other problems. The hierarchy in these plants reflects that of the rest of society: the executives, production managers, quality control and personnel managers are always men. The department supervisors are usually men, and the line heads are preferably men. The operatives are always women.

PHILIP WOLMUTH/PANOS PICTURES

La Romana Free Trade Zone in the Dominican Republic. This factory employs 140 workers at an average wage of 3 dollars a day making electronic circuits for Ford and Chrysler. Most of the workers are young women.

While it is obvious that women have benefited from new job opportunities, and for many of them incomes have risen from zero to the minimum wage, it is also true that women have gained the available jobs because it is easier to pay them less, sack them without compensation and control them in the factory, although, increasingly, women workers are organising to press for better pay and conditions. The rapid incorporation of large numbers of women into the work force is sometimes presented as an example of women being 'integrated into development'. What is actually being created is sex-hierarchies that echo the division of power between women and men in the family.

Women in the informal sector

The informal sector is the workplace of most working women. Unregulated and unorganised, it is often even more exploitative of the labour of poor women than it is of poor men. In the paddy fields of South Asia, women may be paid as much as a third less than men for the same work, may face sexual harassment, work throughout pregnancy until the day they give birth, and have no provision for childcare afterwards. In the Bogata region of Colombia women work in flower production, growing carnations and other exotic flowers for European and US markets; they work seeding and transplanting in humid greenhouses; they fumigate seedlings, weed the beds and care for the flowers, working in factory-like conditions under a blazing sun; finally they pick and package and refrigerate the blooms. Well over half the workers suffer from occupational illnesses, such as pain, poisoning from chemicals, and muscular paralysis due to abrubt, and extreme changes of temperature.[25] Women in the flower industry suffer from a form of gender bias common to a number of jobs in the informal sector, which can be summed up as the 'nimble finger' syndrome. Women predominate in a range of both informal and formal sector occupations, from *beedi* rolling and the match industry in India, to the electronics industry in off-shore plants throughout the South, on the grounds that they are more manually dextrous. In practice, manual dexterity is not rewarded as a special skill, and is instead an excuse for employing extremely young women, and children, who are seen as a particularly docile workforce.

The World Bank report *Poverty and Gender in India* makes the point that India is one of the few countries in Asia where women's share of employment in the formal sector has fallen in the last decades, accompanied by a 'vigorous growth' in the informal sector, which has become the major source of employment for urban women.[26] It highlights many of the problems common to all women making their living on the margins of the formal economy. Among poor urban households, almost all women are employed in occupations that range from rag picking, to construction work, to home-based production, all carried out under conditions that offer little job security, extremely long hours, little chance of a growing personal income, and hard or unhealthy working conditions. Unfortunately, attempts to regulate and improve conditions within the informal sector can, if not carried out with the full participation of the women concerned, have detrimental effects on opportunities for women. The World Bank argues that 'Even if it were possible to enforce existing labour regulations throughout the informal sector, this would probably have the same effect that it had in the formal sector: a shift to more capital-intensive production, labour shedding where possible, and yet more elaborate manoeuvres to obtain a flexible, low-wage work force.'[27]

CAROLINE PENN/OXFAM

The world over, women are a vital part of the informal economy, contributing to household income by their work as traders. This market is in Cambodia.

Clearly, if women are not in control of the process, they will lose out. Only by enabling poor women to create their own jobs, either individually or in co-operatives, by providing better access to land, credit, raw materials, technology and markets, will they be able to benefit from changes within the informal sector. That this is possible is well illustrated by the case study of rag-pickers from Ahmedabad (see pages 162). The market women of Ahmedabad offer a similarly

clear example of competition for resources within the informal sector
along gender lines, and the way in which, if they are well-organised,
they can resist developments inimical to their own economic well-being.

Women vegetable vendors have sold in the same market spots in
Ahmedabad for years. As urban land prices have soared, their spaces
have become much sought after by larger, male, merchants and town
planners, who have pressurised the police into arresting and fining
vendors for carrying out their business. The Self Employed Women's
Association of Ahmedabad (SEWA), a large umbrella organisation for
women in the informal sector, organised the vendors into demanding
licenses, a process that has taken them both to the Gujarat High Court
and the Indian Supreme Court. Now 329 women who sit in the
crowded area of Manek Chowk have a legal right to sell their vegetables, and cannot be moved on. SEWA also extends financial and a
wide range of other services to self-employed women.

CASE STUDY: **Women and work in the Lebanon**

*The courage of Lebanese women in the face of adversity has never failed.
The hope of renewal is in the hands of the women who, throughout this
war, have sustained life.*

Irene Lorfing

A study of women's activities in the war-torn economy of the
Lebanon highlights some of the gender issues involved in the study of
women and work. Despite the war and the enormous social disruption that accompanied it, traditional values 'hang on tenaciously', particularly those that concern the role of married women in the workforce. When displaced Shiite and Christian women of rural backgrounds were asked if they would like to work to help their families,
they consistently replied: 'To leave home in order to work outside is
not conceivable. Our presence near our children and our old, sick parents is more important than the little bit of money we could earn...for
us married women it is too late, but we ask for better for our daughters.' Even among university students, traditional values were being
questioned but not necessarily rejected. Such values have a restrictive
effect on the entry of women into the employment market, affecting
professional training, conditions of work, and the kind of employment that is open to women; professional training, for example, is
largely limited to secretarial work, dressmaking, beauty specialisms,
nursing and hairdressing. With the exception of a few managers of

businesses, some doctors and engineers, the majority of women workers are paid less than men. Moreover, a large proportion of women workers in the service sector, in industry and in agriculture are employed on a casual basis, and do not benefit from social service provisions, or the protection of the code of employment.

According to a study done in West Bekaar in 1981, only 5-25 per cent of family income comes from women's work. However, this figure may well illustrate the problem we came across in Chapter 3, in under-representing the true value of women's work: most rural women who work within the context of their family receive no monetary compensation, and are not considered as workers. Yet Lebanese women produce all sorts of goods as part of their role as wives and mothers — foodstuffs to sell in the market, sewing and needlework — and it is this ability to make ends meet on extremely limited resources that has kept families together, often in disastrous conditions.[28]

Tourism and prostitution

Among many of the countries of South-East and East Asia, economic development has been based on tourism. The forms of tourism that have become most prevalent have upheld strongly polarised gender roles. In order to earn a living from the economic opportunities available, many women sell sexual services. Tourism in this context highlights many of the facets that determine gender roles: biological sex, ethnic identity, class, and the relationship between rich North and poor South.

In order to understand the phenomenal growth of tourism in the last 40 years and its impact on women, we have to look at some of the conditions that led to its development. The growth of Third World tourism was a carefully promoted activity. At the end of the Second World War the aviation industry found itself with the capacity to produce large numbers of planes but nothing for them to do. This, combined with the post-war boom which led to increased wages and increased leisure time in industrialised countries, and growing attempts by the US to exert its influence over South-East and East Asia, were all factors that came together and encouraged the concept of the 'package tour' to 'exotic' countries. Tourism also received massive World Bank funding, through a special department set up in 1970, known as the Tourism Projects Department.

The growth of tourism was not something that was initiated by the countries of the South; they were persuaded by economic arguments: tourism as a foreign exchange earner, tourism as a job creator and booster of national income. To this day, Southern tourism is firmly controlled by the countries from which the tourists come. Third World countries have virtually no control over the information produced about its societies in the North. Advertising turns the 'natural' resources of the Third World — 'sun, sea, sand, and sex' — into commodities which can be bought. Tourism has grown to be one of the largest items of world trade, and the major foreign exchange earner for many small island countries such as Fiji, Jamaica, Seychelles, and Cyprus, and either first or second earner in countries such as Thailand, South Korea, Kenya, Colombia, Lesotho, and Tanzania.

Sex tourism in parts of South-East Asia was largely a consequence of American foreign policy — to contain the spread of communism in the region after the Korean War. In 1967, a treaty was signed between the US military and the Thai government allowing the US soldiers stationed in Vietnam to come on 'rest and recreation' leave in Thailand. The resulting expansion in hotels and places of entertainment was spectacular. By 1970, spending by the US military was equivalent to one-quarter of the total value of rice exports. Much of the money was spent on 'personal services' — in other words, the sexual services of Thai women. Inevitably it was not the Thai women themselves who reaped the benefits but the owners of the entertainment industry, often members of the Thai military. Once the US pulled out, the rest and recreation market was widened to appeal to a more international clientele. This was done by the systematic incorporation of sexual services into tourism in Thailand. Such tours were promoted energetically in Europe in the 1970s, less flamboyantly in the 1980s.

The growth of sex-tourism has received explicit government backing in many of the countries in which it is occurring. In South Korea in the 1970s the women 'servicing' Japanese businessmen were instructed to 'make sacrifices to get foreign money ... this self-sacrifice is a matter of pride for them and for the nation'. Similarly, government officials in the Philippines under the Marcos regime made explicit their view that female sexuality was to be regarded as an economic asset in their tourist ventures for national development.[29] Sex tourism is sometimes justified by pointing to the poverty of the countries in which it occurs. Sex tourists may be told about the need of individuals to earn a family wage, and encouraged to believe that prostitution is an expression of women's autonomy to make decisions about their own lives and sexual conduct. Many visitors to South-East Asia assuage their guilt by persuading themselves that they are visiting cultures which have different moral and sexual mores — that sex is an accepted and traditional part of hospitality.

But what of the women who are providing the 'personal services'? Estimates of the number of women in Thailand earning their living from prostitution vary, but somewhere in the region of 6.2 to 8.7 per cent of women between the ages of 15 and 34 are reckoned to be involved in selling various forms of sexual services. For women working as prostitutes the issue is less a moral one than an economic one. Any discussion of the moral issues involved would need to start with questioning the right of the First World to turn parts of the Third World into its battleground and playground. There is no doubt that the profits from prostitutes' labour has national and international linkages, and that prostitutes are as abused and exploited as any other female workers in the Third World. Thanh-Dam Truong, from whose excellent study of prostitution and tourism many of the details in this section have come, makes the point that 'behind the glossy view of sexual attraction and temptation for which prostitutes are disciplined and trained lies a world of exploitation, violence, and cruelty'.[30]

CASE STUDY: Working with prostitutes in Rio de Janeiro, Brazil

To see prostitution as an economic issue, and prostitutes as abused and exploited as any other female workers in the South, opens up the way to work with prostitutes that takes account of their special needs. In Rio de Janeiro, one project with prostitutes takes as its starting point the view that prostitution is work like any other, albeit under difficult circumstances. Prostitutes have particular requirements: access to education that takes account of their work and lifestyles; basic information on women's health, especially HIV and AIDS, together with access to contraceptives and STD clinics; access to information and counselling in relation to legal rights; the need for security and safety on the streets.

In order to address these issues, prostitutes in Rio de Janeiro set up a network in 1986 to create space in which to share their experience. The First National Prostitutes' Conference grew out of the network, and was held in 1987. Networking is only one aspect of the work; their supporting organisation, ISER (Instituto de Estudos da Religiao: Institute of Religious Studies), has set up a number of other projects, designed to explore beyond the specific issue of prostitution to look at the lives of all those living 'outside' mainstream society, under the umbrella heading 'Self-esteem in marginalised groups'. This overall concern translates into five project areas; prostitution and civil rights; a prison project; a school for street children; a health project; and a newspaper called 'A Kiss from the Street'.

The prostitution and civil rights project has taken up an imaginative range of activities, from television debates on the human rights of prostitutes to street parties in downtown Rio de Janeiro to publicise the project among prostitutes. A 'photo-novel' giving information about AIDS, and condoms, were distributed at the party. The project also carries out research, for example, documentation work on the 'social memory' of prostitution in the city in the first half of this century, and a study of prostitution and religion.

The need for self-esteem, for education, for good health and for other initiatives that offer dignity are vital for women working as prostitutes. The work of ISER in looking at both the immediate needs of the women, and at the broader picture of social and economic conditions in which women become prostitutes, or marginalised in other ways, seems to be particularly fruitful.[31]

Legal systems

Legal systems around the world sanction and reinforce gender differences. Part 3 of the Indian Constitution, for example, lays down certain fundamental rights. Every citizen is guaranteed equality before the law, and discrimination is prohibited. But the Constitution contains a sting in its tail as far as women are concerned. This comes in the form of 'Freedom of Religion', under Article 25, which says 'Subject to public order, morality and health ... all persons are equally entitled to freedom of conscience and the right freely to profess, practise and propagate religion'. This part of the Constitution means that Hindu, Muslim, Parsi, Christian, Jewish, and tribal women are subject to the personal law of their own communities, and personal law is the area which affects women most significantly, touching on issues such as rights to property, maintenance, divorce, adoption, child custody and polygamy. It is as if the law says to women, 'We grant you the right to equality, but if your religion says otherwise, we cannot interfere.'

Women living in Islamic countries have different rights under Muslim personal law to those enjoyed by men, even while criminal law offers them similar treatment. Gender differences are maintained and perpetuated by the personal or family law of a country, which may offer quite different rights to men and to women. Pakistan offers a good example of the process of the Islamisation of a legal code that was originally a British colonial legacy. The Constitutional provision granting complete equality to women no longer operates, and a number of new laws have been enacted which have relegated women to an inferior status. One example is the Hudood Ordinance of 1979, a statute that governs the laws of sexual violations. Originally the maximum punishment for rape was stoning to death, though this has now been reduced to 25 years imprisonment and 100 stripes with a whip. This seems like strong protection for women, but in order for the maximum sentence to be passed against a rapist, four men have to have seen it taking place, or the accused has to admit to the crime. The raped woman's testimony has little value; even to admit to an alleged rape can be highly risky for a woman since she might find herself accused instead, and the case might be converted to *zina*. *Zina* is any sex outside of marriage, and is an offence punishable with four to ten years of rigorous imprisonment and 30 lashes. Women activists in Pakistan cite the case of Safia Bibi, a blind 18-year-old woman who was raped by her employer and his son and became pregnant. Her father filed a complaint of rape, but the court convicted Safia Bibi of *zina* and would have punished her, were it not for the immense pressure from women in Pakistan who campaigned on her behalf.[32]

In Algeria, a new 'Law on Personal Status' has recently been introduced, despite being rigorously campaigned against by Algerian women, which has diminished women's status within the family. For example, the new code explicitly states that the aim of marriage is reproduction, which means that a woman can be divorced or 'repudiated' on the grounds of infertility. 'Repudiation' means that a man can simply send his wife away; she is no longer married to him, but she is also not divorced and so not free to marry anyone else. Other changes mean that women in Algeria have lost their right to work without first getting the permission of their fathers or husbands.

Women can suffer under legal systems in several ways. The actual content of the law may affect women, particularly laws on marriage and divorce, custody of children, land and employment. In addition, the structure of the administration of law often makes it difficult for women to gain access to the courts, to get legal advice and to even discover their rights under the law. Customary law is a powerful force in many countries, even when there is a legal system in place. It tends to be women who are most discriminated against under customary law, since such laws deal with things like family relations, marriage, divorce and custody — often central issues in women's lives.[33]

Legal attitudes to the crime of rape in many countries of the North show similar assumptions about gender. In a detailed study of rape cases in Canada, the authors came to the conclusion that rape victims were only considered to be 'real' if they conformed to some stereotype of a respectable woman, either monogamously married, or virgin. Women who had broken free of their parent's home, and marriage, and who had tried to be autonomous, sexually and otherwise, were not seen as 'credible' rape victims. In the perception of the law, such women had put themselves at risk and forfeited their rights to either protection or redress. Rape was originally perceived as an offence against a form of property, owned by men, not against the person on whom the act was perpetrated; current rape laws still echo these historical origins.[34]

ROSHINI KEMPADOO/OXFAM

A seminar in St Vincent for women community workers and community group members on women's roles and workers' rights. The subject of discussion here was the extent to which existing laws entitled women to their full rights as workers.

CASE STUDY: An alternative vision of the law

Santo Domingo, Dominican Republic; a group of 25 women gather in the shanty-town area of Capotillo. Some are women with children, a few are women in work; many are young women about to leave school. It is the final afternoon of a course designed to demystify the law for poor women, to present a version that they can use to their own advantage. The subject this afternoon is the Labour Code, and the women lawyers presenting the session explain the ways in which certain Articles discriminate against women, and others which might benefit women are not effectively applied. One Article says that if, because of pregnancy, women are unable to do their existing job they should be offered alternative, more suitable employment. Another that lactating mothers should be given three extra rest periods of 20 minutes during the day. A discussion is generated; how can employers be made to fulfil these legal obligations? And anyway what use is provision for breastfeeding time if there is no workplace creche at which to leave the baby?

This class is just one part of a programme run by CENSEL (Centro de Servicios Legales para la Mujer), one of the few organisations offering legal assistance to women in the Dominican Republic. Legal aid is offered through personal counselling, a weekly radio programme, and regular popular bulletins that are published and distributed in the *barrios*. An Oxfam field worker writes that 'CENSEL has been successful in presenting an alternative vision of the law, demystifying the patriarchal and *machista* character and sexual discrimination it often implies.' The education with women's groups is complemented by research and counselling on violence against women, and the enforcement of child support on fathers who have left women with children. By training networks of women to work with other women, CENSEL hope that in time this activity will be 'translated into a wider use of legal mechanisms for the defence of women's rights (hardly ever used because of lack of knowledge) as well as in an increase in women's participation in advocacy and activities to improve their present situation'.[35]

Education

... not enough ... and not the right sort.

Kate Young

How does education uphold gender differences in the South? We can look in two directions for an answer; firstly at the quantity of education that girls get, and secondly at the content of the education they receive. The amount of education girls receive differs from country to country. At primary level, in Sub-Saharan Africa, 93 per cent of boys are enrolled but only 77 per cent of girls. This contrasts strongly with Latin America and the Caribbean where almost all girls are enrolled in primary school. At secondary school levels only 22 per cent of girls receive a secondary education in Sub-Saharan Africa, in comparison with 36 per cent of boys. But contrast this with Latin America and the Caribbean where slightly more girls receive secondary education than boys — 53 per cent to 51 per cent.[36] Figures for much of the Asian sub-continent reflect a similar pattern to that of Sub-Saharan Africa. With the exception of Latin America and the Caribbean, the girls of the world are less likely to receive an education than their brothers; not surprisingly, therefore, two-thirds of the world's non-literate people are women.

Learning to read and write can open up great opportunities for women who missed out on education as children. Literacy scheme in Bolivia.

Girls who receive little or no education suffer a massive disadvantage in facing the modern world. They lack resources that might enable them to tackle their poverty more effectively; without basic education, most subsequent training is closed to them, and economic opportunities are therefore limited to the informal sector only. Women who were not given an education themselves speak poignantly about what they feel they missed: ' Without education, you are nothing in this world. I wish that I could be born again. I wouldn't get married so young, and I would learn and learn until I died.'[37]

The NGO Womankind identifies three barriers to women's education: the economic climate, social attitudes and the school environment. Until the 1980s, school enrolment figures for girls throughout the world rose, suggesting that the dream of universal primary education might one day be achievable. However, in the last decade economic deterioration throughout the South has led to cuts in public expenditure on education. School fees have become more common, and the costs of school uniforms, books, pencils and so on may deter families from educating all their children. If there is a choice to be made, boys usually receive preference. These social attitudes are, as we have seen, deeply ingrained. A farmer may need assistance during busy times of the year, and is more likely to take her daughters out of school than her sons; she expects her daughters to share her domestic burden. Additionally girls may miss school during their monthly periods, either because social custom demands it, or for simple practical reasons. Early marriage and rapid motherhood may be another social factor preventing a girl from finishing her education. Two-thirds of girls born in Bangladesh in the late 1950s were married by the time they were 15; among Muslims in India, leaving school for early marriage is not uncommon. For those girls who do go to school, the school environment will determine what kind of education they receive; this is a major factor in the ways education may uphold gender inequalities rather than challenging them.

Much education offered to girls is a 'double-edged sword', in that it reinforces and heightens their sense of inadequacy as girls. Available literature suggests that while there is much that is inadequate or inappropriate about curricula in general, the effects of this on girls may be more damaging than on boys. Kate Young explains that this is because of the stereotyping of women's and men's activities found in school literature; 'The expectations and models that are built into the curricula seem to be more prejudicial to girls than they are to boys.'[38] Additionally, girls are often offered a restricted curriculum, emphasising domestic science and other 'feminine' skills, rather than science and technical subjects. When these biases inherent in curricula are added to the problems of lack of adequate role models for girls beyond a certain level of education and the generally lower expectations of girls held by parents, teachers and girls themselves, it is not difficult to see why education may reinforce gender roles rather than challenging them. Many teachers are not themselves conscious of the discrimination that women as a gender face, and they are not able to challenge damaging stereotypes in educational material, career options available to girls, and school environments that may discriminate, simply because they do not perceive them.

One of the consequence of the way in which conventional schooling tends to reinforce social stereotypes is the steady drop-out of girls as they move upwards through the educational system. In Papua New Guinea in 1985 there were roughly equal numbers of boys and girls at the primary level; by secondary school age only 35 per cent of the pupils were girls, and at university level in the same year, women students were only 15 per cent of the total. Clearly, this kind of education is failing women; it fails to prepare them for anything other than their role as wife and mother and, while there is evidence that education does make a difference to the health and the likelihood of the survival of their children, most women in the South are also traders, factory workers, farmers — workers of all varieties. Literacy is important, but if women are to gain from economic opportunities in a rapidly changing world they need other skills as well — numeracy, accounting ability, and technical skills.[39]

For millions of women around the world the opportunity of going to school never came, and they married and had children without any formal education. Yet for these women, non-formal programmes offered by local church groups, trade unions and NGOs can offer both practical skills and a chance to increase their confidence and self-esteem, a basis from which to challenge the apparent rigidity of social structures. One woman who had participated in a non-formal education project in Delhi said that learning to read and write had opened her eyes. 'Even though I was an old lady I was a baby; now I am like my grandchildren, and life is starting again.' Non-formal education programmes are, like conventional schooling for girls, fraught with problems; inadequate follow up, poor teaching materials, badly-trained teachers. Yet people working in development around the world are working to challenge even these problems, as the following case study shows.

CASE STUDY: Producing adult literacy materials

'I only want to learn how to read and write my name, and I will do anything to learn.' These were the words of a woman in Kimsaraman, Kenya, after her child's health card was mixed up with another child's at a visit to a clinic; neither mother was able to identify her own child's card. Few women in the Baringo district of Kenya can read and write; 72 per cent of women and 35 per cent of men are non-literate. The keen desire of the women of Kipsaraman to read and write prompted community health-workers together with Oxfam staff to begin a literacy programme in the community. They saw the programme as a process which 'empowers women and men to read and write their own reality. The process assumes from the beginning that learners are creative and that learning is not a matter of memorising and repeating given syllables, words and phrases but rather of reflecting critically on the reading process itself and on the profound significance of language. The process must include the relationship of men and women to their world. It must be a process that questions the reality that deprives them of their right to live a full human life....The literacy process must be a cultural act of freedom.' This view of literacy insists that the materials used in adult education must come from the hopes and worries of the community for which it is intended.

Surveys among the community to identify the key or 'generative' themes showed gender to be a clear priority. Who provides food for the family? Who does most of the harvesting: women or men and why? What is the relationship between men and women? Who makes decisions in the family? What are the traditional structures for decision making in the community? A materials production workshop was held, and different groups put down their findings to such questions, from which key themes were identified. The second step was to study the structure of the *kalenjin* language to identify the most commonly used sounds. These sounds were then linked up to the key themes. One of the first key sounds to be identified was *'kame'* meaning mother. This was linked to the theme of women and illiteracy, the problems they face and task of teaching them to learn to read. For the first ten lessons, ten key words were chosen, and linked to the most common concerns of the community. These ten words included the most commonly used consonants used in the *kalenjin* language. This process of developing key themes, words and consonants continued until a full programme was developed — a programme in which the relationship between men and women is seen as central. In time, the women and men of Kipsaraman will be able to read and write about their own lives; in the process of learning they will have challenged many of the forces that previously kept them from literacy.[40]

Public man: private woman

One of the most powerful ideologies underpinning gender differences is the division of the world into the realms of public and private. The public realm, comprising of public institutions, the state, government, education, the media, the worlds of business, corporate activity, banking, religion, and culture are in almost all societies in the world dominated by men. Certainly there are individual women who enter and may eventually lead such institutions, but nowhere do women as a group exercise power and influence in the public domain in the same way that men do. Ethnicity, class, and religion may play a large part in deciding which men exercise power, but women's access to power is always less than that of men from the same background. This has important implications for the practice of development and for the ability of development planners to ensure that development is equitable and benefits both women and men. Because women are poorly represented in the public sphere they are less able to exercise power and influence for the well-being of their gender. The ideology of public and private tends to mean that women's sphere of influence is the house, whether this is a council high-rise tenement block, a large home in a wealthy middle-class suburb or a shack in a shanty town. In the last 20 years there has been a growing recognition of the importance of this sphere in the sustenance of communities and families, and the centrality of the household in determining gender roles and inequalities.

Throughout the world women are reclaiming, or claiming for the first time, public spaces; women's access to the media, to education, the formation of international networks of women, and the gradual entry of women into public life are beginning to challenge the ideology of public and private. As the testimony of the stories and case studies presented in this book make clear, inequality based on gender is under increasing attack.

5

'A TRIPLE YOKE OF OPPRESSION':
Gender, class and caste in a
post-colonial world

For many women, problems of nationality, class, and race are inextricably linked to their specific oppression as women. Defining feminism to include the struggle against all forms of oppression is both legitimate and necessary. In many instances gender equality must be accompanied by changes on these other fronts. But at the same time, the struggle against gender subordination cannot be compromised during the struggle against other forms of oppression, or be relegated to a future when they may be wiped out.[1]

Most movements for self-determination among colonial nations have been far from advocating the liberation of women. On the contrary, women's resistance to male oppression is generally relegated to the margins, separated from class and national struggles and subordinated to the wider and 'higher' cause of national liberation. The issue is often treated as a divisive and distracting self-indulgence, rather than the result of social structures and relations. Thus, it is assumed that women can liberate themselves only after liberating all other oppressed sectors of society...Reconstruction in both men's and women's roles always manages to remain part of an unrealised future agenda.[2]

One woman, all women?

Since the issue of 'women' became important to the global political and social agenda in the 1960s, the question of whether we can legitimately speak about women as a group has been an important one. Within any one country, the differences between individual women are determined by their social background, their class, education, ethnicity, and age. The experiences and expectations of a black, single mother living in an inner-city area may have little in common with those of the wife of a wealthy white suburban banker. How can the term 'sisters' be used with anything other than irony in the face of the hierarchical structures that exist between different women?

But, even if women are 'positioned' differently in their societies on account of their class and ethnicity, there are factors which unite women as a gender, some of which were discussed in the previous chapter. This chapter takes a different perspective, and looks at the oppression of women within racially segregated societies, within oppressive class and caste systems and as members of indigenous populations, setting these oppressions within a historical context.

The chapter argues that women are oppressed not only by their gender but by their class, race, caste, and colour, sharing these oppressions with men from similar social groupings. But if poor men are doubly oppressed by their colour and class, poor women experience a 'triple yoke of oppression'. According to a document put out by the African National Congress, women's triple oppression lies in their position as members of an oppressed nation within the land of their birth, as members of the working class or landless peasantry, and as women, subjected to discrimination in marriage, property rights and access to services. While nationalist movements, and popular movements to tackle racism, class and caste have taken root all over the world, the specific oppression that women face, even within their own communities and families because they are female, has not been addressed by liberation movements. Indeed, when women have tried to insist that gender inequalities are tackled at the same time as nationalist or class struggles, they have been accused of being divisive. Gender equality is usually set aside until 'after the revolution'. A number of socialist-inspired revolutions this century have initially supported some degree of equality for women, but later, when established in power, have promoted a stable social order based on nuclear-type family structures and male dominance. In recent years, however, the growing confidence of the women's movement has enabled women to insist that they are listened to, even while they have taken a full part in class or apartheid struggles, arguing, as DAWN puts it, that 'the struggle against gender subordination cannot be compromised during the struggle against other forms of oppression, or be relegated to a future when they may be wiped out.' On the contrary, the analysis of the women's movement argues that problems of nationality, class and race are deeply bound to women's specific oppression as a gender.

The first half of this chapter briefly sets out the context in which to understand the oppressions of class, race, caste, and colour that women and men experience as a legacy of both colonial and post-colonial economics, and highlights the ways in which throughout this process women have been further oppressed by their gender. The second half of the chapter looks at popular struggles, and the role that gender issues have come to play in these movements, as women have insisted that their specific oppression as a gender is considered within the context of the broader struggle. It starts by looking at gender issues in the Latin American context, both in the struggle against the Junta in Argentina, and in the rise of the women's movement in Brazil. The role of gender in the Apartheid struggle highlights many of the linkages that are the focus of this chapter. Finally the chapter looks at the specific oppressions of indigenous women and of women within caste systems.

In order to understand gender in the context of struggles against other forms of oppression in the South, we have first to understand more about the legacy of hierarchy and inequality left by colonisation and some of the post-colonial institutions that structure relations — including gender relations — in the modern world. Class, nationalism and ethnic struggles have dominated the post-colonial history of many Southern nations. How has gender been dealt with in the context of these other issues, and how has the women's movement fared in insisting that gender equality becomes a fundamental part of newly-independent societies? First we turn to look briefly at colonialism and post-colonialism.

A colonial legacy

Many parts of the South are the ex-colonial territories of Northern industrial countries and have experienced long periods of direct control by another power. In Latin America direct colonial rule by Spain and Portugal lasted for roughly three centuries, ending in the early or late nineteenth century. India experienced a colonial history of 250 years, and in Africa and many parts of South-East Asia, colonialism lasted for at least a century. An enormous amount has been written about the psychology, political economy, and history of colonialism, and more recently about the effects of colonialism on gender relations. One theme that has attracted the interests of feminist scholars is the extent to which the colonies, their raw materials and their populations, were seen as natural resources to be exploited. In 1908, a historian wrote about the Dutch colonisation of Sri Lanka:

> It has already been seen how native life was subjected to all sorts of economic shocks, how native industry was cynically cramped or crushed in order to assure the profit of a closed monopoly. The Dutch came without question, to regard the native as simply one of the factors entering into the making of money, a factor to be treated in the same objective way as water, soil, or any non-sentient or inanimate element.[3]

'Natural' is here an economic category, a category of everything which did not have to be paid for, or which should be as cheap as possible. The idea of colonial labour as a natural resource to be exploited as fully as possible meant that appalling conditions and minimal wages could be justified on the grounds that 'natives', both male and female, were of a different (lower) form of being, 'naturally' inferior; in short, they **were** nature. A journalist in Sri Lanka at the turn of the century noted that while plantation workers did not 'enjoy the luxury of much space...their ideas of comfort are not ours, and they are better pleased to live huddled together upon the mud floors of these tiny hovels than to occupy superior apartments.'[4] Countless examples of this sort exist in print, including very recent ones. (This author was in a meeting at which tribal people in India were described as a 'natural resource' by forestry officials.)

These arguments sound familiar, since we have already heard them used about women; women's labour as 'natural', woman as 'naturally' inferior, woman as nature. The writer Claudia von Werlhof takes this sequence to a logical conclusion, and argues that black women are doubly exploited in this process: '...each individual man, including black men — even when treated as "nature" — is given a mini-monopoly over a woman. Like the great white man, even the small white man is permitted to dominate a piece of "nature" as if it were "natural" property or his "colony". Even black men receive the "nature of their nature". Even where land, implements, a house, let alone capital, have been denied, one thing has been guaranteed — a woman.'[5] This law of 'male sex-right' subordinates women in all cultures, but doubly so in subordinated cultures.

ROSHINI KEMPADOO/OXFAM

In the Caribbean, the descendants of slaves still work on plantations as an exploited labour force, poorly paid and often given inadequate protection when using pesticides or fertiliser.

Another important issue is the extent to which the colonial legacy manifests itself in the persistence of highly stratified societies. If we take the example of the Spanish and Portuguese-speaking countries of Latin America we can see how the intensely segregated nature of pre-industrial Spain and Portugal left their mark after three centuries of colonisation. When the Spanish colonised Latin America they took with them, and implanted in Latin American soil, forms of hierarchy based on race, religion and class. The oppression of indigenous Indians and the development of slavery that swept through Latin America added to the racial mix and the racial segregation of society. In the Caribbean, the development of slavery and the sexual exploitation of women slaves by white slave owners led to a series of complex social divisions based on colour, ranked according to a 'fairness' (of skin colour) principle.

Colonial economics

Colonisation was about economic expansion; colonising powers were in search of raw materials and new markets. As industrialisation and capitalism took hold in Europe, the colonies became essential sources of cheap commodities, food, and labour, and markets for products manufactured in the ruling country. The process of colonisation drained wealth and resources to the colonising power and transformed formerly self-sufficient communities into highly dependent ones. Different colonists established different patterns; in Southern and Eastern Africa the bulk of the land was taken over by settlers, while the indigenous populations were forced on to small tracts of poor quality land. In Latin America, colonialism brought the rapid destruction of local populations, through war and disease, followed by the creation of huge plantations owned by white colonists and serviced by slave labour. In Asia, the bulk of the land remained in local hands, but systems of private property and special taxes put money into the hands of the colonisers.

With the gradual ending of colonialism, Third World countries had an opportunity to reverse the damage done. Few were able to make the kind of massive structural changes required to bring about more equitable societies, and most bear all the marks of the ex-colonised. Colonial rulers have been replaced by local elites whose financial and social interests are best served by maintaining the status quo in partnership with their ex-colonial masters. Sri Lanka, for example, remains dependent upon international capital investments and market forces beyond its control; its population is divided along communal lines that match the different positions they occupy in the island's economy, a situation with roots deeply embedded in Sri Lanka's colonial past. The following case study of the colonial process in Sri Lanka provides details of how a relatively self-sufficient island economy was transformed into an export-oriented plantation economy. it also looks at the effects of colonialism on gender relations. The study is adapted from Jean Grossholtz's book, *Forging Capitalist Patriarchy*.

CASE STUDY: The colonial history of Sri Lanka

Sri Lanka's colonial history began in 1505 when the Portuguese stumbled on the island during a monsoon storm. The islanders were already trading with other Asian countries, exporting cinnamon, gems, elephants, and areca nuts, and importing salt, fish, rice, and cloth. The Tamil kingdom in the north formed a discrete entity, sharing many cultural aspects with South India. The pattern of land use varied from place to place but land ownership in the usual sense of the word was non-existent. Villagers cultivated land for their subsistence needs, and as populations grew, land was cleared from the jungle and new villages were established. The Portuguese ambition of dominating the spice trade was well served by their arrival in Sri Lanka; they offered to protect the country from foreign invaders in exchange for elephants, trading rights, and cinnamon. Instead, they built forts, rapidly took over the sea lanes and came to control the worldwide cinnamon trade, reaping huge profits. Most of the island's trade goods were commandeered by the Portuguese and the profits shipped home to the Portuguese ruling class, leaving little left to barter for the rice and cloth of India, essential commodities in the lives of the local population.

The arrival of the Dutch furthered the exploitation of the island. If islanders refused to provide the spices, they took them with military force; if they found crops growing independently, they burned them, and often the whole village as well. The burning of nutmeg and cinnamon trees which take years to grow to maturity destroyed the livelihood of local people to whom the trees belonged. Dutch control of the trade in nutmeg often resulted in profits to Holland of 5,000 per cent. In the end, their greed destroyed the trade. The price of cinnamon was kept so high that would-be purchasers looked for substitutes elsewhere. As the spice trade gradually slipped away from Sri Lanka the island was left with neither an adequate food supply, nor the means to continue its international trade to purchase the food it needed.

The British period in Sri Lanka began in 1796 and continued until Independence in 1947. The British take-over was marked with a Charter of Justice, stating that the British were to 'preserve inviolate to the natives of this Island, their local habitats, their ancient tenures, distinctions and religious observances, and to secure to all classes of people the protection of the laws'. Sinhalese and Tamil resistance to British rule rumbled on throughout the period of colonisation, but the British policy of creating an aspirant, native bourgeoisie, committed to European culture and ideas with an education like their rulers, did the job of creating a group of local leaders who could help control their own people, and whose vested interest in the development of capitalism in Sri Lanka eased the way for the British. To complement the Charter, the development of capitalism in Sri Lanka was accompanied by the creation of a legal system and a political structure which created the ideology of democracy, and the idea of rule by consent. The fact that the law was imposed on the population by military conquest was conveniently lost sight of, as was the fact that the demands of the British home economy directed the way that the colony was developed. The British began by pursuing what little there was of the spice trade, but on its demise initiated the transformation of Sri Lanka into an island of plantations — tea, coffee and rubber — for export. In the process, they profoundly changed patterns of land use throughout the island.

Sri Lanka's first British governor, Frederick North, stated that 'the establishment of private property is the object of all my institutions', and this is more or less what happened to huge tracts of Sri Lankan land, which, originally 'acquired' by the government was sold off to Europeans after 1833, for coffee plantations. When demand outstripped supply with a clear title, the government passed the Crown Lands Ordinance which stated that 'all forest, waste or uncultivated land was to be presumed to be the property of the Crown until the contrary is proven'. Areas of forest cleared by local people for gardens and farms were also declared to belong to the Crown unless the claimant could show proof of having paid taxes on it for a period of 20 years, clearly impossible for most people. The government posted its intention to sell land in the Gazette, in English, again excluding the vast majority of people from preserving their land. The Ordinance had the effect of opening up vast stretches of land, and effectively dispossessed native people of all but their houses and paddy fields. Grossholtz argues that 'this ordinance stole the land of Ceylon from those who, by local custom, law, and authority, had the right to use it...it effectively destroyed the last vestiges of communal land and it restricted most native ownership to subsistence paddy lands and house lots.'[6] Without the use of forest land, villages became less self-sufficient, and peasant agriculture was impoverished throughout the island.

With the growth of the plantations, the need for labour became urgent, so the British instituted compulsory labour in various guises. A letter to the Ceylon National Review in 1906 showed that the British still had not finished scheming up ways of sufficiently beggaring the local population to force it into work:

Nearly every family of villages has a large enough paddy field to keep them in idleness for six months out of the year. In what other country of the world is this possible?...And what is the remedy?..Only one, that is, a higher rate of taxation...The result of the higher tax would be that the Sinhalese would have to turn out to work whether they liked it or not and the only work they could get would be on the estates...

In the end, the problem of labour was solved by encouraging large numbers of Tamils from South India to migrate to the plantations. By 1917 some 358,000 Indian immigrant workers were employed over 2,000 tea gardens. The tea grown was almost pure profit. Women tea pickers were paid 25 cents — 4d sterling — a day, and picked over 14 pounds of tea a day, which was sold in London for between £10 and £35 a pound. None of the profit was spent on the health and welfare of those who laboured to pick it. As far as raising taxes was concerned, the British introduced a land tax on the 'expected' yields of land, whether it yielded it or not, and drove people off their lands when they were forced to default. They also encouraged the sale of arrack and opium, just so that they could tax it.

At the same time as the feudal and subsistence economy was being destroyed, the British were building a substantial infrastructure which included the creation of a new class structure. Impoverishment was not confined to rural areas, and a new urban proletariat was created. Sinhalese middle and professional classes, dependent on the British for their positions and success, and therefore very loyal, eventually formed the backbone of a governing elite at Independence. By the time of Independence, vast amounts of capital had been extracted from the island, and the foundations laid for a future of continued impoverishment and inequality. Colonialism set the priorities for the island in the London markets — and the price of land, the price of tea, coffee and rubber were set in London. The colony capitalism of Sri Lanka was only intended to benefit a few, and that is exactly what it did.

How were gender relations affected by the process of colonisation? Patriarchy preceded colonialism, but with the growth of capitalism women's autonomy decreased. Colonial policy had a detrimental effect on the access of all but a few Sinhalese women to land, and usufruct rights were diminished by the growth of private ownership; for poor women, growing land scarcity forced them into the labour market where they ended up in the poorer-paid sectors. Plantations made use of women, both as prostitutes and labourers; on the coffee plantations women worked alongside their men, but received no wages. Only when women began to work on the tea and rubber plantations was their labour paid, but, seen as subordinate to men, they were paid less.

Obviously the position of women cannot be studied in isolation from men, and changes under colonialism affected both genders. British rule has been described as a 'subtle mix of control and opportunity', which highlights the growth of opportunities in the civil service, in medicine and law. More men were encouraged to compete for these resources, and in the process were manoeuvred into a stronger position within their families. For women of local elites, missionaries had a strong influence, and schooling for girls was established along the same lines as that for middle-class girls in England. By the 1850s middle-class women had adopted European clothes and European habits of music, drawing, dressmaking, and fine needlework, skills seen as valuable in the marriage market. In other words, colonialism introduced and perpetuated the ideology of women as housewives and mothers, and maintained a polarity between different classes of women, those who worked on the plantations or as agricultural workers, and those who acquired lady-like skills in elite urban enclaves. As in other colonies, however, the effect of offering education to women was to make them demand more of it and more equality. As a result, Sri Lanka achieved high female literacy very quickly. In 1921 some 21 per cent of the female population were literate, and in 1981, 83 per cent. Similarly, the westernised elite among Sri Lankan women fought for and won the right to vote much earlier than women in other colonies, achieving the franchise in 1931.

Post-colonialism

Most Southern countries are characterised by an economic gulf between the rich and the poor, partly as a result of being an ex-colony and the positioning of ex-colonies in the current world economy. The characteristics of colonialism, which were an emphasis on private property, commercial production and export orientation, have continued to characterise the economies of most Southern countries. The result has been the maintenance of a small, wealthy elite who have a strong interest in preserving an 'open' export-oriented economy, while large sections of the population are alienated from adequate and stable resources, income, and employment. We have already seen how the economic relations between developed and developing countries work in the interests of the former — the fall of the prices of major commodities such as copper, iron ore, sugar, ground nuts, rubber, and timber in the last decade is one example. In 1983-4, as drought and hunger were taking hold of the Sahel region of Africa, five Sahelian countries (Burkina Faso, Chad, Niger, Mali and Senegal) produced record amounts of cotton for export, although the price of cotton was already falling. Growing cotton for export, instead of food for local markets, was an attractive option for some farmers. Too much export-orientation in an economy means that an internal elite, benefiting from the foreign exchange earned from exports, maintains its life-style and prosperity, while the rest of the population tends to have to over-use lands which may be ecologically fragile and unable to produce the quantities of food needed to compensate for the land taken out of food production.

In most ex-colonies, internal pressures from rich sections of the population demanding an open economy are coupled with pressures from bilateral aid donors, multilateral institutions and transnational corporations to open the economy to foreign capital and divert resources to exports. We can see the process at work, whether in growing strawberries in Mexico or in the clear-felling of tropical rain forests for ranching and the fattening up of beef for export. Lloyd Timberlake describes the plight of the Hadendawa people of north-eastern Sudan, who in 1985 faced extinction from starvation and dispersal. The Sudanese government, with finance from the North, the World Bank and Arab countries, established huge sugar and cotton plantations on the best land along the Nile, ignoring the fact that other land in the Sudan is slowly dying from mis-use. Instead of investing in smallholder farming — women's farming — or in dryland farming on lands where the Hadendawa live, the government put its money into expensive cash crops, which have not paid the nation's way through drought. When drought came in 1985, pastoralists and peasants had 'no irrigated settlements in which to take temporary refuge, no government agencies to buy their livestock, no sources of drought-resistant sorghum seeds ready for planting when the rains resumed'.[7] Timberlake makes the contrast with the US where, in the 1890s and 1910s, farming families faced starvation when drought devastated the Great Plains. The areas are still prone to drought, but programmes of soil and water conservation, rural credit, and agricultural education and advice make it possible for rural people to survive natural disasters.[8]

The results of these policies and pressures are not neutral as far as gender relations are concerned, but tend to have specific and different effects on women and men. In agriculture the development of legislation on private property invariably led to women losing out when land titles were put in their husband's name. Women predominate in the landless, seasonal labour force, even though they may well be the primary breadwinner and head of their household. Maria Mies, in an attempt to explain the declining sex ratio in India, has documented the way in which women have systematically lost out in all areas of employment since the beginning of this century, with the rise of capitalism, rapid industrialisation, and urbanisation. She argues that post-colonial capitalism as pursued in countries like India has created an ever-growing number of people who cannot be absorbed into the formal wage-labour pool, and therefore have to survive as best they can in what is often called the informal sector. Many of these are women.[9]

In India census figures suggest that women farmers are loosing control of their land more rapidly than men: in 1961, the census showed 33,156,000 women cultivators (that is women who owned and controlled their own land); in 1971 the figure had dropped to 15,976,000. The fact that these were the years in which the Green Revolution began to take hold of Indian agriculture suggests that this is another post-colonial development which has not had neutral affects on the two genders. This shift continues a trend evident as long ago as 1911. A brochure by the Indian Council of Social Science Research documents the steady process of the 'marginalisation' of women:

> In the 40 years between 1911 and 1951, the gap between men and women in the population increased by 27 per cent. During the same period, women's proportion [of] the total work force declined from 525 per 100 males (1911) to 408 per 1000 males (1951). In the 20 years between 1951 and 1971, the gap between men and women in the population rose from 8.9 million to 19.9 million. In the same period the number of women workers in agriculture declined from 31 to 25 million.[10]

Women have not dropped out of the workforce in order to enjoy a more idle, luxurious life. They have simply disappeared from the statistics, out of the measurable, paid, and recognised work-sector, and into the subsistence, part-time and far more vulnerable sector.

Agribusiness, or agro-industry (the corporate control of food production and food processing as opposed to food grown or processed by individual farmers) is another example of a process with colonial roots extending its influence in ways which have had different effects on women and men. Agribusiness is often controlled by multinational corporations, and a similar pattern is shown in many countries. Companies buy up vast tracts of fertile land and convert it to plantations for a cash crop, such as bananas, invariably for export. Agribusiness frequently employs local men, giving them technical know-how and access to equipment. Women are left to continue with subsistence farming to supply the family with food, in far more difficult circumstances than before, and without the help of men's labour. Women are also employed in agribusiness, usually as cheap seasonal labour for weeding and harvesting and in the processing of food once it has been harvested, working, as the following case study shows, under poor conditions and for lower wages than men. The study illustrates the way that agribusiness may appear to be generating employment opportunities, but only by exploiting local resources and labour, particularly the labour of women. It also illustrates ways in which women are organising to tackle such forms of 'development'.

CASE STUDY: The Brazil-nut workers of Para, Brazil

Para, in Eastern Amazonia, is a state in which large-scale agro-industry has been progressively introduced, often with devastating effects on the environment and the lives of the local population, who become a source of cheap labour. The women of Para have been particularly affected because they make up the bulk of the labour force in the processing stage of agricultural production, working under appalling conditions; they also receive lower wages then men. Rapid, unplanned urbanisation has led to very difficult living conditions; women have borne the brunt of inadequate services, poor health care and lack of education.

Oxfam began supporting the Movimento de Mulheres do Campo e Cidade (MMCC) (Rural and Urban Women's Movement) of Para in 1985; one of the first ventures was a joint project between MMCC and its partner NGO, CIPES (Centro de Intercambio de Pesquisas e Estudos Economicos e Sociais: Centre for the Exchange of Economic and Social Research and Studies), which focused primarily on education and awareness-raising among the women employed in the Brazil-nut breaking factories in Belem. Meetings and educational courses resulted in a rapid growth of organisational skills among the women workers. Closely supported by MMCC, they secured a number of improvements in their working conditions; it is hoped that women will soon be elected to leadership positions in the trade union for workers in the food-processing industry.

Members of the newly–formed organisation for rural women workers in Pariaba, Brazil, taking part in the International Women's Day march.

MMCC are now starting to work with rural women employees in the agro-industry to encourage them, too, to organise for better working conditions. MMCC are providing leadership training and are working to stimulate awareness about the relationship between current patterns of development (under which women arguably suffer most acutely) and the deteriorating environment — in order to heighten understanding of the need to preserve the natural resources of Amazonia.[11]

The role of multinationals

Multinationals are in some ways the sons and heirs of colonial rule, in that they exist to create profits from the labour and raw materials of the ex-colony, which are then repatriated to the home country. Many multinational companies have greater power and wealth than the countries in which they operate. In 1984, no African state had an annual turnover as large as Exxon, and only South Africa, Nigeria, Egypt, Morocco and the Ivory Coast had GNPs large enough to earn them a place on the list of the world's 100 largest corporations.[12] As we saw in the previous chapter, they tend to show a global division of labour, with the high-technology, research-based part of their operations located in the North and the labour-intensive processes carried out in the South. The importance of multinationals in the development of the South should not be underestimated, since with their enormous size and wealth they are capable of imposing their own model of development — one based on growth and profit maximisation, rather than an equitable distribution of benefits. The existence of multinationals in a developing country may have significant effects on that country, though not always in the way that the host country had planned. Nonetheless, the promise of employment and foreign exchange has been a sufficiently tempting carrot to persuade many countries to set up free trade zones for multinationals, offering benefits such as no foreign exchange controls, unlimited profit repatriation, cheap labour, anti-strike laws and 100 per cent foreign ownership.

Multinational companies have been particularly active in electronics, textiles and agribusiness. The components of computers, calculators, digital watches and other consumer electronics are put together in spotless, modern assembly lines, usually by young unmarried women, particularly in Latin America and South-East Asia. As we saw in the previous chapter, the effect of multinationals on the role and status of women is a complex one. Working for a multinational is often an unpleasant experience for the women concerned; low pay, unhealthy conditions, short breaks, no leave, exposure to sexual harassment. Peering through a microscope all day to attach hundreds of minute wires to silicon chips may have a significant effect on eyesight after a few years. On the other hand, multinationals offer women a chance of regular paid employment; a welcome alternative to petty trading and other self-employment in the informal sector.

Multinationals also perpetuate gender stereotypes, largely through advertising. They also perpetuate the idea that white, Northern culture is the end point to which all other cultures are slowly evolving. Some multinationals bring with them a whole (Western) cultural package, offering employees opportunities to buy Western cosmetics and clothes via the company. In the process multinationals

cal, indigenous products and impoverish the local cultures
they operate. This cultural 'imperialism' is another echo of
colo..... sm. Just as the local middle-class elites in the colonies rapidly
adopted Western clothes and habits, so now they acquire washing
machines, electric rice cookers, and jeans. The impact of multinational
culture is not gender neutral; advertising restates the colonial ethos:
women are decorative, domestic consumers, housewives and
mothers.

Clearly, multinationals are not single-handedly responsible for
multiplying poverty in the world, but in their filial relationship to the
colonial process and in their effects on local economics they can play
an important part in supporting local class and power structures,
reinforcing existing patterns of male dominance The fly-by-night,
uncommitted nature of the multinational enterprise means that even
though they employ women, they do little to improve the long-term
status of women.

Gender, class and colour

The rise of popular protest

Racism, class and sexism generate popular protest the world over. In
North America the Black Power movement grew out of the Civil
Rights Movement, and some social historians see the contemporary
feminist movement as growing out of anti-racism, claiming that
'without black sisterhood, there would not have been sisterhood';[13]
though feminism has many other roots – in the nineteenth-century
women's movement, in the ideals of the French Revolution, and the
work of writers such as Mary Woolstonecroft. In different parts of the
world, popular and revolutionary movements have prioritised
different aspects of social justice. In Latin America, revolutionary
movements with a socialist ideology have been the most successful
popular movements, in opposition to militaristic, repressive regimes.
In South Africa, the struggle has been against apartheid and racism; in
India there have been popular protests against the caste system and
the exploitation of the scheduled castes and tribes. Nationalist
struggles have occurred the world over.

Many of the popular movements of this century have been about
human rights. Very few, with the exception of one or two specific
movements in support of women's suffrage, have been about
women's rights. This raises questions as to how popular movements
have dealt with the issue of gender, and how women's movements

have tackled issues of class, colour and human rights. To answer these questions we will look at examples of different patterns of protest in which women have been involved.

Class, gender and human rights in Latin America
CASE STUDY: A popular protest based on women's 'traditional' gender role, in Argentina

In 1976 a military Junta took over power in Argentina and imposed a repressive social order and a series of radical economic changes. Social services were cut, free health services stopped, and working-class people suffered a sharp decline in their incomes and standard of living. As the Junta tightened its grip, people began to 'disappear', either imprisoned or killed by the military. In April 1977, 14 women aged between 40 and 62 gathered in the Plaza de Mayo, in a silent protest for their lost children. The women had met while on the trail of the disappeared, and from April onwards they staged a daily protest, processing around the Plaza carrying white handkerchiefs. They rapidly became known as the Madres of Plaza de Mayo. Their protest was a uniquely 'women's protest' against the terrorism of the regime, and it was rooted in their traditional gender role as wives and mothers. One of their slogans was 'We are life'; as mothers, the traditional nurturers and defenders of 'life', this principle was their political stand against a government that disregarded the value of human life. This radicalisation of the feminine left no place for a questioning of traditional gender roles, which were the very basis of the protest itself. Women as mothers had suddenly taken the centre of the political stage.

The National Movement of Housewives was another movement established against the Junta. 'Our policy is that of our husband's pocketbook' was a safe but useful political slogan that allowed women to mobilise publicly on the basis of their traditional role. Other Argentinian women mobilised on a more feminist platform, and the coming together of the traditional, 'feminine' politics with the more overtly feminist ones meant that women's gender interests could not be ignored in the transition to democracy in 1983. Women's issues now have a place in the State structure, and matters that were formerly considered private have been open to public debate. According to one commentator on the women's movement in Argentina, 'Little by little, a new consciousness is being created that changes women's role from the invisible one of performing tasks recognised as "naturally" feminine to the active one of ensuring family survival in conditions of severe economic stress... women are mobilised in the struggle for better housing conditions, for water, and for basic services.'[14]

CASE STUDY: 'Feminine' and 'feminist' protest in Brazil

Brazil has developed one of the largest and most successful women's movements of Latin America, and in doing so has managed to confront the questions of gender and class in a unique way. A number of circumstances came together to forge the Brazilian women's movement. One was the enormous increase in the number of educated and working women in the 1960s and 1970s, accompanied by the fact that white women found themselves earning 35 per cent less than their white male counterparts, and black women professionals earned, on average, 48 per cent less than white women professionals in similar jobs. At the same time, the Brazilian Catholic Church gradually turned against the military regime and towards the poor, raising important class issues as it began to create new 'communities of equals'. Under the protection of the Church, thousands of young women militants were drawn into work in Brazil's urban neighbourhoods, and thousands of working-class women's groups were formed, many of which sprang from the women's sections of the Christian base communities, but rapidly took on a social dynamic of their own. They began to organise around their immediate survival needs, because their gender interests were overlooked in mixed groups. As in Argentina, motherhood was radicalised, and became a point of departure for a whole range of activities as women participated in community politics for the first time and gender needs became the basis of political action.

A third factor was the reawakening of the militant left after severe government repression in the late 1960s and 1970s. Many young women were active in militant left-wing organisations and student groups where the issue of gender was ignored or subordinated to the struggle against the old order; when revolutionary women gave birth, and raised children 'underground' they received very little support, either material or moral, from their male colleagues. Moreover, despite the rhetoric of gender sameness, women played all the 'normal' female gender roles. They ran safe houses, worked as messengers, cooked meals, and looked after the sick and wounded. Many women resented their subordinate feminine role but, as Sonia Alvarez explains, they 'lacked a language, an analysis which would enable them to understand their resentment in political terms'.[15] Although the groups espoused democratic principles, in practice this translated into hierarchies in which women always wound up in inferior positions.

All these strands came together in the 1970s, coupled with the return of many women from political exile, bringing with them the feminist ideas they had encountered in France, Italy and Chile. The Brazilian women's movement was adamant in working for a 'legitimate' Brazilian feminism which would deal with sex discrimination in the context of a larger class struggle, and in rejecting American feminism. The newspaper *Brasil Mulher*, launched in 1975, wanted to 'speak of the problems that are common to all the women of the world ...[and] solutions which have been found both here and in distant places; nevertheless, we want to discuss them in the context of our Brazilian ... reality'.[16]

The problem lay in developing strategies that would support both the class and gender struggle equally. There were those who believed that the specific gender issues should wait until after the revolution; others who argued that gender issues could not wait, especially as women began to talk about and politicise issues that had earlier been seen as wholly private: their marriages, sexual lives, desire for fertility control. Slowly the movement began to formulate the idea that women suffer specific oppression simply by virtue of being women.

A National Council was set up in 1985 with advisory powers, and has had an impact on state policy in areas such as family planning, anti-sexist education, agrarian reform, and day-care provision. Brazil demonstrates the extent to which gender and class can be seen as equally important aspects of the struggle for social justice. Other women in Brazil have expressed concern that issues of race have not so far been highlighted in the same way.

CASE STUDY: **The growth of feminism among peasant women in Brazil**

> *Feminism provides insights into the forms that gender relations take within class relations and enriches our understanding of the meaning of struggle. It goes beyond dignifying women; it means a transformation of men as well...*

Ines, one of the leaders of MMTBP

The impact of the women's movement among peasant and rural women in Brazil has been remarkable. The following case study documents the work of Movimento das Mulheres Trabalhadores do Brejo Paraibano (MMTBP) (Working Women's Organisation), an organisation working in the Brejo of Paraiba, a region in north-east Brazil. It has received funding from Oxfam since 1986.

Machismo culture determines relationships between women and men throughout Brazil. The rural area of Brejo in the state of Paraiba is no different, except that here women are beginning to organise to establish their right to a more equal participation in the affairs which govern and affect their lives. The lands of Brejo are fertile and well-watered, suitable for many different crops, and for small-scale farming as well as mechanised, large-scale sugar production. As a result, land conflicts have grown in recent years. MMTBP began its work in support of rural women wanting equal participation in the trade unions of the area; initially concentrating on issues such as equal pay for women, the right to join trade unions as individuals rather than spouses, and meaningful participation in trade union affairs. As a result, Brejo has seen the emergence of a strong rural worker's trade union movement with a significant involvement of women.

Paraiba, Brazil. Women workers' organisation committee meeting to plan forthcoming activities.

As it grew, the movement became increasingly attractive to other groups of workers, particularly teachers and domestic workers and in 1986 MMTBP was able to organise the first Congress of Women

Workers in the district. Timed to coincide with International Women's Day, it brought together 140 women, domestic servants, washerwomen, factory workers, teachers and rural workers, with the principle objective of drawing up a document on the rights of women to equal opportunities within basic labour rights. The Congress also made proposals for inclusion in the new Brazilian constitution, such as pensions for women at 65 and the full recognition of women as workers by the provision of basic rights such as minimum salary and maternity leave. Despite the eventual, relative failure of the negotiations for the new constitution, the process enabled women to raise these issues at the heart of the union movement. It offered them a broader canvas on which to interpret their rights as workers. One member of MMTBP stated her views clearly:

> As a peasant, I think that maternity leave is a basic right. We bring so many children into this world; we bring them up. We can't give birth tonight and come back to the *roza* [farm]at dawn. I've been working since I was seven, always so poor, so little food at home...I can't describe the fear I have every time I leave my children alone. What if something happens and I'm not there? We need a creche. That is also a basic right! How are we going to make the unions understand it?

As the movement grew in numbers and confidence, it broadened its analysis of the issues affecting women, using gender as its focus. A woman leader of MMTBP explained:

> Our experiences in the movement have shown that women's needs for understanding their own bodies, affection, relationships with their husbands, children, protection from sexual harassment, representation in the unions, equal pay, are very much their priorities. In meetings with their partners they have raised many of these issues and the need to recognise these issues as political.

MMTBP has found imaginative and varied ways of looking at these other gender needs. One initiative involved the partners of women activists. A meeting was held for 70 couples during which family relationships were discussed, leading to a perceptible change of attitude among the men who attended. In a small village not far from Paraiba, a health workshop was organized for 40 agricultural workers by a health team and an experienced nurse. An informal survey was carried out amongst prospective participants and, as a result, the workshop focused on their key concerns: pelvic inflammation, vaginal infections, migraine, anxiety, domestic violence, and sterilisation. In a follow-up visit by a member of Oxfam's Gender and Development Unit, one woman described some of her gains from the workshop:

> I have learned what self-respect is, and how a friendship with my husband is not a dream. In the health workshop I learned about myself and how I can say 'no' in bed. I also know what an orgasm and *coitus interruptus* are, and I have started to discuss the use of contraceptives with my husband. Sexual life depends on two people, and not only one; so I can also expect respect and consideration from my partner.

MMTBP now touches the lives of, and offers support to, over 2,000 women. It has grown into a movement for social change embracing all of women's experience; class struggles and labour rights have been linked to the personal sphere by focusing on gender as an all-embracing context.[17]

Race and gender in South Africa

> *There is no longer any question of accepting excuses for disregarding these problems, least of all the excuse that is most frequently put forward: that the liberation of Black people in general is far and away more important than the liberation of women ... our wish to stand up as a race, with our own specific characteristics, confronting all other races, does not in any way involve brushing aside the problems of African woman's deplorable situation. We go beyond the racial problem, since we are taking our stance, not only as Black women, African women, but also as members of the human race, without regard for ethnic considerations ... this human race consists of social classes and two categories of individuals: men and women, whose relationship to each other is that of dominating to dominated.* [18]

> *Let the walls open their ears and hear that we are sick and tired of our oppression. This inferiority complex has been incarcerated in us women. When a baby is born it does not know if it is a woman or a man. A woman is not born inferior, but is made inferior. We cannot expect Mandela to take this inferiority out for us. We have to do that ourselves...* [19]

In South Africa, women have played a significant part in the fight against apartheid. Meeting organised by the United Democratic Front (UDF) in a sports stadium, in support of democratic rights.

PHILIP LITTLETON/OXFAM

The document referred to at the beginning of this chapter put out by the African National Congress (ANC) about women in the National liberation struggle speaks of black South African women's 'triple yoke of oppression' : 'oppressed as members of an oppressed nation denied all political power or rights in the land of their birth; oppressed as members of the working class and landless peasantry, having been forced into wage employment at derisory rates of pay under highly exploitative conditions; and thirdly, oppressed as women, subject to discrimination in laws they have not made regarding the ownership of property, rights in marriage, and access to health care.'[20] This triple oppression that black South African women face, as women, as workers, and as victims of apartheid, has produced a vibrant women's movement that is clear in its analysis of the politics of gender and race in the country, and is currently working to ensure that in the struggle for a new democratic South Africa 'the fight against sexism [is taken] as seriously as the fight against racism'.[21]

Throughout the twentieth century, women have played a major role in anti-apartheid protest. By the 1980s, women's organisations existed all over South Africa, protesting and organising on a range of issues, from the presence of troops in townships, to nationwide township rent boycotts, and self-help classes in first aid for treating people injured on the streets. People's committees, largely composed of women members, have been set up, which combine local action with trade union activity, and local and countrywide issues.

The ANC, in the document referred to above, describes this work of women in the struggle, but makes its own position on the issue of gender quite explicit:

> While it is the task of women to assert themselves more strongly and to resist all forms of sex discrimination, the winning of national liberation for the entire South African nation is an absolute precondition for any change in the social status of women as a whole. Women's oppression cannot be fully liquidated in isolation. Any attempt to deal with the emancipation of women as a separate issue from the overall struggle is self-defeating.[22]

The message is clear: gender is relegated to an issue of sex discrimination which it is women's job to fight by becoming more assertive. Secondly, the achievement of women's liberation will not be possible until 'after the revolution'. Thirdly, the final phrase sounds a warning to anyone who would wish to prioritise the gender issue within the liberation struggle as a whole. With the unbanning of political parties, the return of political exiles and the attempt to work out a new democratic structure for South Africa, many women's groups are anxious that the issue of gender is not treated in the way the ANC document suggests. One organisation, SPEAK, publishes a magazine dedicated to raising awareness that 'gender differentiation affects all aspects of the lives of the people in South Africa. Unless such an understanding infuses the analysis and action of significant political and development organisations women will not be liberated from their special bondage.'[23]

Looking at the issues SPEAK magazine published in 1990 shows how one indigenous women's group deals with the issue of gender in the broader context of liberalisation. One issue led with the words 'Women's liberation must be part of a new South Africa' and contained an article about the implications of the unbanning of the ANC for women. It also described the International Women's Day meeting in Johannesburg in 1990, when speaker after speaker demanded that 'women must be present at the negotiating table'. SPEAK is very aware of the danger of deferring women's liberation until 'after the revolution'. SPEAK quotes an ANC woman recently returned from exile: 'When we look at other countries we see clearly that if we don't address all problems now, then no way can we address them afterwards. The task then will be to defend the revolution. If you raise an issue that was not raised before it will be seen as divisive. Women's issues must be taken up now, not later.'[24]

In a report of a conference held in the Netherlands for South African women in exile, SPEAK drew attention to the problems of black women who work outside their homes — perhaps the most oppressed of all women in South Africa. It is difficult for working women to join trade unions because they go home after work and do another shift at home. Families themselves further the oppression of women. Delegates at the conference called for housework and child care to be shared by men and women, since 'only when men take equal responsibility for their homes will women be able to take part fully in organisations'.[25]

This marrying of the personal and the political is an essential part of an analysis which perceives gender to be as important as race and class. Without it, all that is left is a call for women to assert and liberate themselves while men concentrate on the liberation struggle. SPEAK's policy of seeing the personal as political is reflected in its concern for women's health, and its willingness to address problems such as violence against women. One issue printed boldly on its cover: 'Breaking the silence: Women say our men must stop beating us.' Violence against women, and women's health, are gender issues rooted in the family which SPEAK and other women's organisations insist must be part of the agenda in designing a new South Africa. Laws are not enough, but they are an important starting point. Changing a society's perception of women is a more difficult task but one to which the South African's women's movement is deeply committed:

> The ANC must be asked what is happening to a non-sexist South Africa. It is not the men who are going to make it happen for us. It is us who are going to make it happen, not only for us, but also for them. Plunge, swim and get to that liberated South Africa.
> Delegate at International Women's Day meeting in Johannesburg, 1990.

Indigenous women

We don't want your development.[26]

As environmental issues have gained a higher profile, the focus has shifted to the people who live in the areas of land, previously isolated from the mainstream, but now under threat from deforestation, agricultural, water and mining projects, and other development initiatives. Such people are often the descendants of the original inhabitants of the territory, which has, at some point, been overcome by conquest,[27] and who have avoided dominant society by their geographical isolation. People such as the Yanomami who live in the Amazonian rain forest have highlighted the issue of the survival of indigenous cultures when their resource base is destroyed. It is not possible in a short section to do any more than sketch a highly generalised picture of indigenous people, and the particular gender needs of indigenous women, since there are an estimated 200,000 million people loosely classified in this way, or 4 per cent of the world's population. Peoples classified as indigenous vary enormously in geographical location, their socio-economic development, their cultural traditions, their kinship patterns and their relationship with mainstream society. Even within a region, or within a single indigenous community, there may be substantial differences. In a seminar held in the Dominican Republic in 1987, one workshop underlined the difficulties of generalising about the problems and needs of the jungle Indians, given their different cultural and historical backgrounds.[28]

At the same time, there are certain features that characterise the life-style of many indigenous people. They may be nomadic, or semi-nomadic, such as shifting cultivators, herders or hunter-gatherers; they may have a world view that consists of a 'custodial and non-materialistic attitude to land and natural resources', seeing in land a sacred quality which is largely lacking in Northern thinking; they may have decentralised political institutions and make decisions on a consensus basis;[29] they may have strong kinship networks, a gender division of labour, and a considerable vulnerability to outside influences. These cultures, though ancient, are at the same time fragile and easily destroyed. One of the reasons that many indigenous people have managed to retain their distinctive cultures for so long is that they live in frontier land; land that until recently, nobody else claimed, owned or exploited. In the twentieth century, growing populations have brought marginal land into agricultural production, and the search for timber and minerals has led to the annexation of large areas of land that was originally inhabited by indigenous peoples.

OXFAM

Group of Brazilian Indian women lobbying congressmen in Brasilia, the capital of Brazil, for Indian rights to land to be stated in the new constitution.

The process of development (as outlined in Chapter 2), has affected indigenous people in many different, frequently negative ways and it has often been the case that women are affected still more adversely than men. Coming into contact with the male-dominated structures of mainstream society can have an immediate impact on the way in which indigenous women are perceived. Access to a money economy has tended to lead to a concentration of money in the hands of men; as money becomes a status symbol, women's lack of access to it underlines their loss of status and, as more aspects of the culture become commoditised, women find it less easy to provide for their families. Poverty contributes to poor health. In Guatemala, Indians have a life expectancy about 11 years shorter than the *ladinos*, or non-indigenous population; and in Paraguay, infant mortality among some Indian communities is as high as 50 per cent (and 10 per cent for the rest of the population).[30] Women in their reproductive role bear responsibility for their family's health, and are doubly burdened when ill-health strikes, especially the epidemics that have threatened indigenous peoples when they have come into contact with mainstream society.

If commercial agriculture is introduced on their lands, or if they are resettled to agricultural areas, men have tended to be the ones to whom the benefits and inputs have been offered, yet women are still expected to maintain subsistence agriculture and offer their unpaid labour to men on the land where cash crops are being grown. At the same time, development on the lands of indigenous people can rapidly destroy all the things needed for the survival of their own social and cultural practices: materials for food, medicine and craft disappear as 'nature' is improved on. Dams, roads and other large-scale projects leave impoverished environments, out of which women must still provide for their families. Men can migrate more easily; the brunt of coping with ecological damage falls on women. In Brazil, forest clearance and the establishment of ranches has had appalling consequences for indigenous Indians, men and women, but specific effects for women. For example, Brazilian journalist Gilberto Dimenstein discovered that young Indian girls, often as young as 12 or 13, are lured with promises of jobs in restaurants, or hotels, and then sent to brothels in remote places, such as goldmining camps deep in the jungle; attempts at escape are severely punished.[31]

The attempt of governments to settle indigenous people can be profoundly disruptive for women. They may find themselves relocated in towns, isolated from their communities with no support other than welfare provision. Resettled families can easily become the poorest and most vulnerable members of their societies, which is what happened in the Gascoigne district of Western Australia when Aboriginal families were interspersed among white Australians in a housing project. Older men simply refused to settle, using the towns as places to drink and not much else. Women were isolated with their children and suffered all the consequences of dislocation from their earlier lives.

Many indigenous people want to share in the benefits of modern societies, but on their own terms; they want access to health care and education, but they also want to strengthen their own ethnic identities, preserve their ancestral lands, and decide their own development priorities. The workshop in the Dominican Republic stressed that Indian women wanted more access to and control over resources that might improve their lives; they wanted more access to appropriate education and more opportunities for learning Spanish; they wanted more control in decisions over childbearing; more say in how money is spent; more self-organisation to defend their territory and opportunities to expand their own self-management. Externally-conceived development projects were seen as putting pressure on communities, being potentially divisive, and as encouraging dependency. It was this development that they did not want.

Women of a different caste

One of the most highly stratified social systems is the caste system, found in India. The caste system allocates everyone a place, whether at the top as a Brahman, or at the very bottom. In India, those at the bottom of the social hierarchy are termed a 'scheduled caste', the post-Independence name for people who were formerly known as untouchables. Mahatma Gandhi called them *'harijans'*, meaning 'people of God' and the Indian Constitution abolished untouchability, at least on paper. In some States, the *harijan* population is as high as one in four, though in other States *harijans* are a tiny minority.

Harijans remain the poorest and most exploited group in India, and it is the women of the *harijan* communities who bear the greatest burden of discrimination, by caste, by class and by gender. This triple oppression is not unlike that suffered by black South African women, in the structurally 'lowest' position they occupy in society. *Harijan* women invariably earn less for their labour than men, often derisory sums under Rs10 a day. In rural areas *harijan* women are regarded as legitimate sexual prey by their landlords and, since most *harijans* are landless, they are entirely dependent on the good will of landlords. As we saw in the previous chapter, when landlords and their henchmen wish to assert themselves against rebellious peasants, invariably *harijans*, it is the women who suffer, as the 'only property which pauperised men still possess'.[32] In some parts of India, until well into this century, *harijan* women had to bare their breasts in front of higher caste men, an indication of their complete sexual subordination. Many rural *harijan* families experience the disruption of migration, when the men of the family leave in search of waged work during the dry season when there is no agricultural work available. Migration can put huge strains on families and particularly on women who are left to hold the family together with virtually no resources.

A global issue

It would be a mistake to look at the case studies in this chapter and conclude that the problems of racism, classism and sexism are only an issue in the developing world. Britain, for example, remains a highly stratified society. When we consider that women-maintained households, and Black and Asian families are disproportionately represented among the poorer households in Britain, a picture starts to emerge of a society that is very much segregated along class, racial and gender lines.

This chapter has argued that one of the legacies of colonialism is societies highly stratified along class, race and gender lines, and that in the post-colonial world the relationship between former colonies and their erstwhile masters remains one of domination. It has also argued that poverty and oppression are a consequence of stratification within societies, and the process of popular protest highlights or prioritises questions of gender and race in different ways. In the next chapter we turn back to one of the questions with which we started, and look at the nature of development and underdevelopment again. Why is it that, at the close of the twentieth century, there are still one billion people in the world struggling to survive on less that $370 a year? We need to explain why life expectancy in Sub-Saharan Africa is still only 50 years while in Japan it has risen to almost 80; and why at least 170 children in every 1000 in South Asia will die before their fifth birthday, but fewer than 10 per 1000 in Sweden. And in the context of this book we need to see why gender is so crucial a factor in answering these questions.

6

DEVELOPMENT AT THE CROSSROADS

Crisis

The word 'crisis' occurs frequently in development literature, particularly that published in the last decade, to describe the situation in the South. The word crisis comes from a Greek word meaning 'a time of decision'. In this sense the word usefully describes both the acute problems facing the world, North and South, and also the urgent necessity of taking decisions that will alter the disaster course on which the world seems set.

Why, after four decades of development, should the South still be described in terms of crisis? Has nothing improved? Development thinking in the 1950s and 1960s saw economic growth as the solution to the problem of world poverty. In the 1970s it became increasingly clear that growth was not solving the problems of the poorer sections of society; the emphasis in development switched to the direct provision of health, nutritional and educational services. Taken as a whole, according to the World Bank the past four decades have seen substantial economic progress; between 1965 and 1985 consumption per capita in the South went up by almost 70 per cent.[1] The problem is one of distribution; for the world's poorest citizens, and particularly its poor women, any wealth being generated goes to others, not to them.

The magnitude of the crisis in the Third World is very real; in 1990 World Bank estimates put the number of people living in severe poverty at more than a billion. Many of the world's poorest countries, particularly those in Sub-Saharan Africa, are seeing their economies collapse, their social services disappear and their populations go hungry. Events in the late 1970s and 1980s have massively contributed to the crisis confronting the world, and the 1980s have been described as the 'lost decade'.[2]

The feminisation of poverty

Poverty has a female face. This is the conclusion of much of the development literature that looks at the way in which women are disproportionately represented among the poor and powerless of the world, as a direct result of the dominant development model that has been promoted throughout the South. The devastation of Southern economies brought about by unwisely invested and unrepayable loans, the ensuing economic crisis and the structural adjustment programmes which have followed have greatly added to the burden of reproductive and productive work for millions of poor women. As a result, many issues that were originally seen as private and domestic concerns, such as health, education, family income and nutrition, have become public and political issues, as women have formed and joined new forms of organisation to tackle the crisis which confronts them. Consequently, the feminisation of poverty also has a more public face, as these new organisations have come into conflict with male-dominated institutions. (See Chapter 8.)

Economic crisis and structural adjustment are one facet of the global crisis impoverishing women. Another is the process of commoditisation and the development of cash economies, which have tended to marginalise women's work. This process is clearly visible in the crisis in food production, particularly as it affects much of Africa. This chapter looks at the consequences of the dominant models of agricultural development for the food supply in Africa. As Southern economies have geared themselves up for export-orientation and the supply of goods and services to urban enclaves, the environmental costs have become increasingly evident. We look at the way in which women have become impoverished through this process of environmental depletion, using examples from India; we also look at the growing problems of cities, as impoverished people leave the countryside where they are no longer able to make a living.

The failure of development policies to address the inequities within and between countries, and the consequent inequitable distribution of resources, has contributed to a heightening of tensions and an increase in spending on armaments both for internal repression and regional, national and international conflict. This chapter looks at how such conflicts have also contributed to the increasing feminisation of poverty and to other social dislocations with specific and different effects on the two genders.

An economic crisis

The economies of the world are interdependent. While the 'levers for change' do not all lie in the North, and internal domestic policies of Third World countries determine the way in which poverty is addressed, the vagaries of world trade, growth of international debt, and the variation in quantity and quality of aid to developing countries have had a huge impact on the economic position of poor countries.

In 1973 the price of oil quadrupled. Oil-exporting countries put their rapidly accumulating 'petrodollars' into European and American banks, who promptly lent it out to developing countries, who needed it to pay the increased oil prices, and for industrial and infrastructural projects. This sudden influx of money was seen by many as an opportunity for Third World countries to develop further on the Western model. Roads, airports, military hardware, and luxurious imports swallowed up much of the capital. But towards the end of the 1970s, the global economic climate changed dramatically. A new rise in oil prices had a crippling effect on the industrialised countries and marked the beginning of a massive recession. This in turn reduced demand for commodities from the Third World, and commodity prices tumbled, in some cases to their lowest level since the Second World War. For countries dependent on single exports, for example, Zambia on copper, the effect was devastating. In one year alone, Africa lost about $19 billion of income because of the fall in commodity prices. The world recession led to industrialised countries enforcing a whole series of tariffs, taxes and quotas designed to protect home industries by stopping imports. On top of this, at the end of the 1980s interest rates soared to 18-20 per cent. Private lending to Third World countries dried up and bilateral aid either stagnated or was cut back.

The combination of these factors devastated many Southern economies; they could no longer afford to pay back the loans they had received, and could not even meet the interest payments on those loans without further borrowing, so going deeper into debt. The crisis was dramatised in 1982 when Mexico called its creditors together and told them that Mexico had only enough reserves left in its central Bank to pay for 12 minutes' worth of imports.[3] Western banks could not afford to let debtor countries default, since they had often lent out more than their own capital — sometimes almost twice as much.

Debts were 'rescheduled', and more money lent to pay the interest on earlier loans. Debtor countries were forced to go to the only lender who was still prepared to lend to them, the International Monetary Fund, whose loans were invariably accompanied by a demand for a package of reforms, designed to trim down the budgets of the countries concerned to make more money available for debt repayment. The result was a staggering reversal in the movement of capital: a flow of $38 billion into the capital accounts of developing countries in 1979 was transformed by 1986 into a flow in the opposite direction of $50 billion. (Asked what was the best joke he had heard in the past year, Ben Elton, a leading British comic, replied, 'Well, it was actually told to me by Oxfam — that for every pound we gave in famine relief in Africa, two pounds came back in debt repayments. That is the best joke I have heard this year.')[4]

Latin America and Sub-Saharan Africa are the areas suffering under the biggest debt burden. There is mounting evidence that the suffering caused by debt repayment has fallen on those least qualified to pay, and least 'guilty' of the debt: the poorest people in the countries concerned. And among the poorest it is women who have suffered most.

CASE STUDY: Crisis in Bolivia: A workshop presentation by CIDEM

CIDEM is the Centre for Information and Development of Women, in La Paz, Bolivia. This is an extract from a presentation at a workshop held for poor women in Bolivia, as part of a Popular Education Programme with groups of mothers, organised around food aid:

Today the word crisis is on everybody's lips; unemployment increases every day, and at the same time the number of women seeking the support which unemployed husbands, brothers and fathers cannot offer their families is on the increase...There are more street sellers, washerwomen and servants; more working women from the suburbs have formed groups to receive food aid, more women are offering all kinds of services; in sum, women's participation continues to grow to meet the survival needs of their families.

The crisis has social consequences; the poverty of the working class is growing, and the consequences of the so-called economic crisis are felt in widespread poverty. But what are the origins of the crisis?....

Bolivia is a mining country, that is, it maintains itself by the sale of its minerals, namely tin, petrol and others. However, they have dropped in price and consequently the Bolivian State receives less money that in previous years...Instead of getting good prices for its minerals, Bolivia is loosing money by producing them. It is as if we owned a house which had become uninhabitable due to the wear and tear of the years and our own neglect...The State, which is selling less and less minerals, no longer has the means to pay its debts to the rich countries, or the famous Foreign Debt which we have all heard about. As the State no longer gets any money from mineral production, it is turning to the budget of the families which is already so low. So it has created a new Tax Law, reduced wages, increased the price of petrol and transport etc...

The downturn in the world economy closed tin–mines in Bolivia, and brought destitution to miners and their families. The women of this mining community built simple greenhouses, of mud bricks and polythene sheeting, in which they can grow vegetables to feed their family. Selling surplus produce brings in some income.

The effects of the crisis are increasing: even before the crisis, the basic needs of the marginal suburbs were not met, such as light, water, medical services etc., but since the crisis they have received no help at all. Everything affects the majority of the population through lack of money — scarcely enough to eat, still less to build dwellings and fit them out, or to by clothes, go to the doctor etc.; so the number of bricklayers, masons, mechanics, cobblers, plumbers and so on facing unemployment will increase...In 1975, 80 per cent of the population...could be considered poor, because their income was insufficient to cover 70 per cent of basic family requirements; they could not even buy the most urgent things needed to survive. Between 1980 and 1983 every one of the families considered poor reduced its consumption by a quarter, so that for example a family which used to buy eight loaves of bread was now able to buy only six...

Structural adjustment

And we, the housewives, ask ourselves: What have we done to incur this foreign debt? Is it possible that our children have eaten too much? ... Or do they wear the best clothes? Have we improved our standard of living? Have our wages become so great? Together we say: No, no, we have not eaten too much. No, we have not dressed any better. We do not have better medical assistance ... Then to whom have the benefits gone? Why are we the ones who have to pay for this debt?

Dominga de Velasquez, speaking on behalf of the women of the Amas de Casa of La Paz, Bolivia.[5]

The package of structural adjustment measures that many countries have submitted to in order to reschedule their loans has varied from country to country, but the basic idea behind each package has been to 'fix' the economy of the debtor country in such a way that it can repay its loan. Adjustment usually called for cuts in consumption and government spending, particularly on imports and social services, but little or no attempt was made to safeguard the interests of the very poor. The most immediate result was, as the Bruntland report noted, 'growing poverty and deteriorating environmental conditions...clearly visible in every major Latin American country'.[6] Adjustment policies have meant huge cuts in wages; in Ghana, for example, whereas in the 1970s one wage-earner could support a family, it is now necessary for two adults and at least one child to work to earn the same amount of money. Public sector employment, often the highest status employment open to women, has suffered as salaries have been cut and payrolls trimmed through redundancies. As the need for social services grows with rising poverty, it is precisely these services that are being cut back. Where medicines were free for the poor, they may now have to be paid for, or may have become unavailable, particularly in countries which import most of their drugs. Education services, public transport, food subsidies, and social housing have been drastically reduced in many countries, and it is the poor who feel the effects of such cuts. More precisely, it is poor women, since they are responsible for the well-being of their families. We need to return to the theme of women's role as managers of households to understand why it is that the debt crisis has placed such a burden on poor women.

Governments, in trimming state expenditure and increasing the role of the market, may appear to be becoming more efficient. What is really happening, however, is a shifting of costs from the paid to the unpaid economy, which is largely run by women. Diane Elson gives the example of reductions in the time patients spend in hospital. While to economists this may appear as an increase in the efficiency of the hospital, it is actually a transfer of the cost of caring for the sick. 'The money costs of the hospital per patient fall but the unpaid work of women in the household rises. This is not a genuine increase of efficiency; it is simply a transfer of costs from hospital to the home.'[7]

This pattern is reflected over and over again in other sectors. If transport services are cut, it is women who still have to find ways of getting to markets; if water supplies are cut, it is invariably women or children who have to queue extra hours to wait for the water. When food is in short supply, men and boys may suffer less than women and girls in the same household, because gender relations demand that the women provide for the males of the household before meeting their own needs. Girls are more likely to be taken out of school than boys, to help their mothers in the task of providing for the family.

In a Lagos maternity hospital, more than a quarter of babies delivered between January and June 1988 weighed less than 2kg, which is a sharp increase in the number of low-birth-weight babies. A study sponsored by UNICEF suggests that 40 per cent of the babies currently born in Nigeria are unhealthy at birth. The commonest cause of low birth-weight is a hungry and stressed mother. In times of hardship there is considerable pressure on women to limit their food consumption, even when they are pregnant. The cost of cuts in food subsidies shows up in the statistics on the health and nutritional status of women, who are paying the price of the debt crisis, and in the well-being of their children.

In the last few years there have been a number of new initiatives to ensure Southern countries cope with the effects of the debt crisis, ranging from the concept of 'debt forgiveness' to other schemes allowing for adjustment to take place over a much longer period of time. The World Bank in its 1990 World Development Report focuses on the problems of poverty and structural adjustment: 'When structural adjustment issues came to the fore, little attention was paid to the effects on the poor... By the end of the decade the issue had become important for all agencies, and it is now reviewed in all adjustment programmes financed by the World Bank. As UNICEF advocated, attention is focused both on how adjustment policies affect the poor and on the specific measures that can be taken to cushion the short term costs.'[8]

How the new patterns of adjustment that are emerging will affect women's gender role is not yet clear. A call for 'Adjustment with Gender Equity' has been made by those most concerned to see the issue of gender given a central place in the development of new models of adjustment. The 'Women's Alternative Economic Summit' that met in New York in 1990 for a conference called 'Beyond the Debt Crisis: Structural Transformation' included the following statement in its final declaration:

Women are by no means passive victims who are unaware of our situation. Women have developed multiple, complex and innovative responses to the global economic crisis, both individually and collectively.

We propose an alternative approach: economic democracy. Economic democracy means that all women must have access to all resources; that women must be active shapers in decisions at every level of society — within the family, in our communities, and in the political process, nationally and internationally. Poor women in particular must be included at the negotiating table in setting funding priorities and development policies.'
(Final Declaration, points 7 and 8).

In order to illustrate the nature of the debt crisis and structural adjustment packages, we will take a case study from the Philippines, using material from a Primer put together by an umbrella group of women's NGOs to educate local women on the nature of the adjustment programme

CASE STUDY: Debt and structural adjustment in the Philippines

In May 1988 the Philippines owed $28.9 billion dollars to 483 foreign banks, and the World Bank and the IMF. The cost of paying the interest and principal payments in the six years between 1987 and 1992 was worked out to be $207 million a day, and this at a time when more than half the population live below the poverty threshold. In the 1989 budget, 44 per cent was allocated to the foreign debt, only 10.9 per cent to education and 19 and 18 per cent to economic and social services respectively. The flow of money into the Philippines will be considerably less than the flow of debt repayments leaving the country. It has been estimated that from 1987 to 1992 a total of $21.4 billion will be paid out, but only $4.2 billion is likely to be received in the form of overseas development aid, a net outflow of $16.2 billion — foreign aid in reverse.

Where did the debts come from? In 1972 the Philippines foreign debt was only $2.2 billion. It rose rapidly during the martial law years, as Marcos encouraged his friends and colleagues to start business empires, for example the National Power Corporation, which eventually led to debts of $795 million which were assumed by the government. Another explanation is the reckless lending policy of the big banks in America, Europe and Japan that lent — arguably pressured — Third World countries to borrow beyond their capacity to repay.

GABRIELA asks, 'Did we benefit from the loans?'; and argues that ordinary people in the Philippines saw few benefits at all. Some of the debts were private debts, subsequently assumed by the government. Millions of dollars never arrived in the country at all, but were siphoned off as commissions and interest rates, while millions more were smuggled into secret bank accounts overseas.

Instead of benefits, ordinary Filipinos are bearing the weight of paying back the loans through a variety of means. One is higher taxes, mainly in the form of indirect taxes that cost people every time they buy petrol, cook a meal, or go to a film. Indirect taxes on basic goods and services mean that the poor contribute disproportionately, both because they are the biggest consuming group, and because they can much less afford the burden of indirect taxes than better-off people. Among the poor, women form the majority, particularly in women-maintained households, and this rise in prices directly impoverishes them and those they care for. Another means of paying the debt is the skewing of the economy to export-oriented industries, garments, electronics and food processing, where Filipino women receive wages only 5 to 15 per cent of those earned by their counterparts in the West and Japan; moreover they frequently work in difficult and stressful conditions. Women in the public sector (781,000 women) who work as teachers, nurses and clerks are overworked and badly underpaid, with no possibility of rises in salaries. Indeed, one estimate of the real cost to the Philippines of its debt claimed that the amount the IMF proposed to cut from the national budget for the period 1989-92 was the equivalent of the salaries of 204,000 elementary and highschool teachers, 15,000 extension workers and 11,500 military personnel, plus government subsidies to 489 health institutions and 602 kilos of seeds.

Removal of government subsidies for rice, and control over its price, another IMF condition, has resulted in a steep price rise. Rice is a staple food for poor families, so the nutritional consequences for poor women in particular will be significant. Estimates suggest that 70 per cent of the population is already suffering from some degree of malnutrition, 22 per cent severely and that 25 per cent of the population suffer from anaemia, particularly lactating and pregnant women.

Cutbacks in social services and government expenditure have particularly affected women and children, because cutbacks means that investment in human capital — education, health, nutrition — simply cannot take place. Women and children suffer because their requirements from the health and social services infrastructure are greater; women care for the sick and elderly family members, for example, and for their children whatever their state of health. These tasks do not go away because of structural adjustment. Women simply have to bear more of the burden through a lengthening of their working day.

As in Latin America, NGOs are working with women to launch self-help programmes such as communal kitchens and childcare, making issues such as the working day of women, once considered a private domestic matter, the basis of a new public agenda.

A crisis in food

Especially in Africa... women are responsible for between 60 and 90 per cent of the food production, processing and marketing. No one can really address the food crisis in Africa or many of the other crises that seem to exist here without addressing the question of women, and really seeing that women are participants in decision making processes at the very basic [and] all the way up to the highest level.

Mrs. King, World Commission on Environment and Development, Public Hearing, Nairobi, 23 September 1986[9]

In many parts of Africa, women grow much if not all their family's food. Farmers winnowing rice, Chad.

JAN LANCASTER/OXFAM

In 1985 the farmers of the world grew more than they ever had before; 500kg of cereal and food crops per head for every person in the world. In the same year, more than 700 million people went hungry. A growing food mountain hides considerable variation in food production. In Africa in particular, there has been a steady drop in the per capita food output since the beginning of the 1970s, and it is becoming clear that there is a long term crisis in agricultural production in many African countries, particularly in the Sub-Saharan region. In the 1930s, Africa was a net exporter of food; by the 1960s 10 per cent of its food had to be imported, and by 1980 Africa was growing only 86 per cent of its own food. By 1980 the cost of food imports was equal to Sub-Saharan Africa's agricultural export earnings, and although there are regional variations, rapidly growing populations have outpaced the growth of food in all but a handful of countries.[10] The crisis in food is linked to a growing environmental crisis; after 20 years of drought and deforestation many villages of the Sahel have lost as much as half of their cultivable land. The roots of Africa's hunger are complex and a detailed analysis is beyond the scope of this book. Factors such as political instability and a failure of long-term planning, misplaced development priorities, the economic crisis and falling commodity prices, national and international conflict, the breakdown of indigenous systems of agriculture such as shifting cultivation in the context of severe and prolonged drought have led to the current crisis. Another crucial factor in Africa's inability to feed itself lies in the failure to understand the gender dimensions of food production.

Women grow at least half the food crops around the world, and in parts of Africa as much as three-quarters. Yet it has taken the rest of the world, particularly the Western world with its deep-seated image of a male farmer sitting behind the wheel of a tractor, a very long time indeed to recognise women's essential work in growing the world's food. National surveys significantly underestimate women's agricultural work. In the 1970 Census, national figures for women's agricultural work in Egypt were 3.6 per cent. A more accurate report showed that in the south of the country half the women worked at levelling and ploughing the land, and between 35 and 70 per cent were planting, tilling and harvesting.[11] The reason women's agricultural work is overlooked is because, like their housework, it is unpaid and sometimes 'invisible' because it takes place in gardens, or with livestock in and around the homestead. Analyses of time-use data from village studies demonstrate that the demands made on women's time are very heavy; their working days are long — sometimes longer than men's by as much as 43 per cent. Women contribute two-thirds of all hours spent in traditional African agriculture, and three-fifths of hours spent in marketing. One study of the work of African women farmers found that they also worked for an average of 56 more days a year than men.[12] The table below gives some indication of the extent of women's labour in five African countries.[13]

This failure to perceive the real extent of the work of women farmers has meant that rural projects tend to work with a conceptual model of the African farming family — a male farmer who provides food for his wife and children — which bears little resemblance to reality. Ann Whitehead describes just how different the domestic organisation of Sub-Saharan African families is from this: 'Most African women have always done, and still do, independent work. They are not expected to rely economically on their husbands or families but to have a separate sphere of work of their own.' In the past, there were many parts of Africa where women grew almost all the food crops, for consumption by their immediate and extended families.[14]

How has this failure to understand the importance of women to food production contributed to the food crisis? In the first instance, it has meant that women's independent farming work has remained

Percentage of Labour Contributed for Production by Sex and Age *(Various sources)*

Country	Crop	Women	Men	Children
Swaziland	Maize (local)	55*	31	9.2
	(hybrid)	49	36	7
	Sorghum	88*	9	1
	Beans	40*	4	2
	Tobacco	35	46	8
Malawi	Maize	54	25	21**
	Cotton	47	46	8
	Tobacco	47	40	13
Rwanda	Root crops	80	20	-***
	Coffee	70	30	-
Sierra Leone	Rice, Upland	55	45	-***
	Rice, Swamp	40	60	-
	Coffee	20	80	-
	Cocoa	20	80	-
Zaire	Root crops	62	9	29

* persons over 64, communal and hired labour not included in table
** includes hired labour considered together
*** no separate figures for children

Source: *Women in Agriculture, 1: Women in agricultural production*, Rome: FAO, 1984, p. 6

unmodernised; women still irrigate their crops with buckets from wells they have dug themselves, in fields with fences they have built themselves to keep out goats and sheep. They weed and harvest and hoe by hand, or with digging sticks, methods that have changed little in centuries. And they grind and pound their crops by hand. The development inputs into African agriculture have not been given to such women. They have been consistently concerned with cash crops, such as coffee, rice, cotton and cattle ranching, and ignored the needs of local food production. A farmer growing coffee has a marketing board to offer advice on fertilisers and pesticides, and to buy the crop when it is harvested. A poor farmer growing food for her, or his, family has no such support. At the risk of generalising, it also seems to have been the case that it is men who have gained the benefits of cash cropping, both for export and burgeoning urban markets within Africa, while women have continued to grow food for local and family consumption.

Throughout the world, not just in Africa, it is this cash-crop sector that has received priority from development funding. When agricultural projects and innovations are analysed, almost all the beneficiaries are found to be men. In Nepal, for example, where women provide between two-thirds and all of the labour in many agricultural activities, and make many of the decisions about planting, use of fertilisers and so on, it was found that of all the agricultural advisors trained to work with villagers, only one was a woman, and she had been trained in home economics. Similarly, of all the development aid given to the Sahel, less than a fifth is given for food production — the subsistence crops grown mainly by women — and in 1982, only 0.05 per cent of the total UN allocations to the agriculture sector were to programmes for rural women.[15] Far more funds were allocated for large-scale, high-technology agricultural projects. Not surprisingly, only 15 per cent of those enrolled in African university agricultural courses are women.[16] New technologies to help with ploughing, irrigation and harvesting are invariably given to men growing cash crops. Using only indigenous agricultural techniques, and often pushed onto poor, marginal land, it is hardly surprising that women farmers have failed to increase productivity of crop yields to the levels found in other parts of the world.

According to Ann Whitehead, there is enough research available now to argue that there has been a 'widespread, systematic sexual discrimination against women in agricultural delivery systems'.[17] Not only are women's crops not targeted for improvements, but effective and innovative women farmers may be ignored in favour of less effective male farmers.[18] Alternatively, new technologies or new seed varieties may be offered to women, but in ways that have not fully taken their current farming practices into consideration. Two examples of the different effects of new technologies on the labour of women and men can be found in the introduction of improved cassava varieties in Zaire, and in the use of ox-traction — ploughing with oxen — as the case study below explains.

CASE STUDY: **Agricultural innovation in Zaire**

The women of Zaire grow most of the country's food. As men migrate out of rural areas into cities in search of work, women's role in agriculture has become even more crucial. At the same time, the main food crops grown by women (cassava, maize and groundnuts) face competition from tree-crops such as coffee, which are largely grown by men. The need to increase food production throughout Zaire has led to the development of a number of projects designed to improve productivity and efficiency, and hence food outputs. One innovation was the use of F100, an improved cassava variety, which provides substantial increases in the yield of the tubers without a loss of quality or leaves. But the introduction of F100 did not adequately take the pattern of women's work into account. F100 tends to become woody and inedible if left in the ground, unlike traditional varieties which can be left in the soil for a year or more after maturing. Harvesting and post-harvest preparation are largely done by women; and the need to harvest the new cassava varieties quickly, greatly increases their workload. Some areas of Zaire are prone to periodic food shortages, and cassava has traditionally played a role in famine prevention, because of its ability to remain in the ground — a store of extra nutrition and a vital resource for women to feed their families. Here, an apparently neutral innovation, a new variety of cassava, has advantages and disadvantages, but these affect the two genders differently.

The assumption that agricultural technology was the key to increased food production led Oxfam to fund pioneering work in ox-traction. Initially the intention was also to increase male involvement in agriculture and there was little attempt to encourage women farmers to benefit from the new technology. It soon became clear that the main use for ox-traction was in preparing land for sowing, traditionally men's work. Significantly larger areas of land can be brought under cultivation using ox-traction, but it is women who are responsible for all the other parts of the agricultural process, and they are unable to cope with the vastly increased amounts of work. While women may benefit from the use of the oxen to pull carts for collecting water and transporting produce, any time saved is taken up in farming larger fields. In one project there are now attempts to introduce ox-drawn weeders alongside the ploughs, and another project is investigating ways of using ox-power in women's domestic tasks, such as in grinding grain. Women are also being encouraged to join ox-traction groups so that they can use the technology on their own fields, to their own advantage.

S COLLINS/OXFAM

Some women farmers in Zaire are now being given an opportunity to use ox–power in their farming tasks.

Cash crops versus food

While there has been a gradual polarisation of agricultural production along gender lines the decline in food production is clearly not simply the result of a switch of resources to cash-cropping for export. For one thing, the growth in cash crops is not new; the growth of export crops such as cocoa from Ghana, groundnuts from Senegal, and cotton from Uganda was very rapid between 1900 and 1930, and in the first half of the century the area under export crops grew more rapidly than the area in foodcrops, but without chronic shortfalls in local food supplies. Indeed Whitehead argues that production data show that 'export crop production and food production tend to rise and fall together'.[19] It is certainly not the case that only men grow cash crops, or that women only grow food crops, or that cash crops have expanded so rapidly that there is inadequate land for growing more food. Rather, the problem seems to be the changing relations between men and women, tensions about the use of household labour, and increasing competition as to which crops should benefit from the scarce resources of both labour and agricultural inputs.

There have certainly been many instances of agricultural development programmes taking over communal lands where women enjoyed customary rights, and men being recognised as the new owners. This process has occurred all over Africa, and has been well documented in irrigated rice schemes in the Gambia, in the Kou Valley in Burkina Faso, and in Mauritania, Senegal and Zanzibar. The problem, is not just that men grow cash crops on this land, leaving women to grow food crops on the inferior land remaining, since most African families need both subsistence crops for their day-to-day requirements, and a cash income for their other requirements. It is that women find their labour appropriated by their husbands for work in their fields growing cash crops, yet they do not have control over the income generated by the sale of the cash crops grown on their husband's land and, because they have less time and sometimes less land available for their own agricultural work, they find it hard to produce a surplus to sell for cash for their own and their children's needs.

Such changes in agriculture have had a major impact on women's lives, though it is important to remember that '"rural African women" do not comprise a single category of rural actors', but have 'important economic and other differences between them'.[20] The development of commercial agriculture has therefore benefited some women who have found opportunities to increase their incomes, while at the other end of the scale, increasing numbers of women who maintain their own households without adequate land to meet consumption needs, find themselves joining the ranks of the casually-employed rural female wage-workers.[21] Other women are left to maintain households while their men migrate to work in industry in the cities. This has sometimes meant that, in their work as independent farmers, these women have found it difficult to get the resources they need because the land is not in their own name, but in the name of their absent husband. Consequently they have lost out in the competition for credit, for labour, and for improved agricultural inputs. Women whose partners produce cash crops have found an almost insatiable demand for their labour on their husband's lands, in their own fields, and in their households. As long as development planners ignore the independent nature of women's own farming work, they continue to assume that women's labour can be used as unpaid family labour on their husband's fields.

One of the consequences of this increase in the demands for women's labour is a growth in conflict, conjugal disharmony, and violence against women. The more women are coopted as family labourers, and their independence eroded, the more conflict arises. Women see themselves losing their autonomy and resent the dependence on the family unit that is imposed. The assumption that women's labour will be available as unpaid family labour has had incalculable consequences. A comment of the FAO sounds a warning which needs to be taken seriously: 'In the Third World agricultural productivity cannot be substantially increased, nor can rural poverty be alleviated, unless women's access to key productive resources and services is substantially improved. The consequences of patriarchy for agricultural productivity are very expensive. Developing countries cannot bear their heavy cost.'[22]

A crisis in the cities

The world's cities are growing at a phenomenal rate. In 1900, an estimated 1 in 10 of the world's population lived in cities. By the turn of the century, almost half the world will live in urban areas, from small towns to huge 'hypercities' with more than 15 million citizens. An enormous amount of national development is concentrated in cities; the stimulation of the economy through industrialisation is an urban phenomenon. Development has taken on what the economist Michael Lipton calls 'urban bias': resources, regardless of economic efficiency, are allocated to the cities.

According to the Bruntland Report, many of the world's cities have reached crisis point. Of the world's 100 largest metropolitan areas, 58 are in Southern countries, and the large cities of the South are growing more rapidly than the cities in the North ever have. Africa's urban population is growing at 5 per cent a year, which means a doubling of city sizes every 12 years. Growth is a result of push factors — from environmental deterioration and rural poverty, and pull factors — for more employment, infrastructure and opportunity, but also the result of high birth rates. In many developing countries 60 per cent of urban growth results from an excess of urban births over deaths and only 40 per cent or less is related to rural-urban migration.[23]

Few cities in the Third World have the resources to provide services for their rapidly growing populations; sanitation, water, housing, and educational and health infrastructures serve only a minority of city elites. Most of the housing used by the poor is makeshift, or decrepit. In some cities the bulk of the population live in slums and shanty towns, estimated to be growing at twice the rate of cities as a whole. Health problems abound; acute respiratory diseases, tuberculosis, diarrhoea, dysentery, hepatitis and typhoid are endemic. Poor Third World city-dwellers can expect to see one in four of their children die from preventable diseases, commonly from diarrhoea made worse by malnutrition, before the age of five. Growing cities need massive investment to address these problems. According to the World Commission on Environment and Development, between 1985 and 2000, developing countries will need to have increased by 65 per cent their 'capacity to produce and manage their urban infrastructure', including transportation and sanitation systems, utilities, schools and hospitals[24] — an almost impossible aim in a period of structural adjustment and trimmed down economies.

Poverty in cities is a gender issue, because of women's central role in the management and welfare of their families. If city life is difficult, it is women who bear the brunt of the difficulties. If water, fuel and food are needed, it is women who have to provide them, as in rural areas. To meet the need for fuel, women may have to destroy whatever vegetation remains in any patches of countryside near their settlements. According to one report, cities are becoming surrounded by 'eroded, deforested and desertified conditions that people fled from in the countryside'.[25] In some cities in India, water can only be obtained in the middle of the night. Sleepy women stand in queues at 3.00am with their water pots, waiting their turn at the communal standpipe.

Living in shanty towns or on pavements is a very stressful existence. Pavement dwelling women in Bombay, India, ask 'Do you think we enjoy living on the pavement? If they gave us proper houses we'd live as decently as they do.'[26] Tensions and marital problems increase under difficult circumstances and cities tend to have a higher number of households abandoned by men and headed by women. Poor urban households face major problems. Lack of state services means little or no welfare support; public transport may be slow, dilapidated or non-existent and fares rise repeatedly; health facilities may be minimal. In Bogota the capital of Colombia, there are only 90 public health centres for more than 5 million inhabitants. Describing conditions in her country, Sirocco Ramirez writes:

> As critical as the current situation is, however, Colombian society has managed to survive, thanks in large part to the efforts and long work hours of women. Women continue to wash clothes, prepare food and care for children while contending with blackouts, fuel

and water shortages, long queues, slow public transportation and houses without appliances and basic comforts. All of these activities are, in reality, another form of tax, paid in work, which women carry out to alleviate the effects of the current economic crisis. Yet these activities are neither measured nor compensated in any way. For example, it doesn't matter to society if women spend three minutes or three hours filling a wash tub; it only matters that women do the work.[27]

In Latin America many urban women have formed local organisations to help each other cope with the crisis in which they find themselves. The case study at the end of this section looks at Oxfam's partnership with one such organisation in the city of El Alto in Bolivia.

There is a paradox at the heart of city life. For all its difficulties, for all the hard work and struggle, most families who have migrated to the cities regard themselves as having made a positive choice. At least in the cities there is work, even if it is in the informal sector. The concentration of commerce, industry, administration and amenities in cities means that there are growing numbers of middle-class people, who need houses, services, food. Their houses are built by unskilled migrant labour; they employ servants; vegetables, flowers, fruit and a whole range of other goods are sold around residential areas by poor women and men. Many of the services that make life easy and convenient for middle-class people are provided by those in the informal sector.

CASE STUDY: Palu's story

Palu is building a house, in Bangalore, South India, one of the fastest growing cities in the world. She is one of a team of eight labourers building a smart bungalow for a doctor, in a quiet residential area to the north of the city. She comes from a village about 40km south of Bangalore, and is living in a shanty town about 15 minutes' walk away from the building site. Her own house is constructed out of the cement bags she collects from the sites, stitched on to a simple wooden framework. 'Very bad when it rains,' she smiled. She and her husband Rajagopal moved to Bangalore three years ago after the 1986–87 drought, when they couldn't find any agricultural work; she has been working on building sites ever since. She is 22 years old, and has cement dust in her hair; her slight form looks as if it finds the heavy loads of bricks that she carries on her head up the rickety bamboo ladder too much to handle. She prefers mixing the cement, though after a while that too is exhausting. What is a typical day like?

Woman worker in a brick-yard. In India, many women work in the construction industry as unskilled labourers.

I get up when it is still dark; it is the only time a woman has any privacy to answer the calls of nature. We walk up along the railway track. Then I make a fire with sticks saved from the day before, and make black tea, sometimes sweetened, but sometimes there is no sugar left. I give a cup to my husband, and to Moni, my eldest son. Shanti, my three year old daughter, shares my cup with me. I breastfeed the baby, and then share out the 'palliya soru', the rice cooked the evening before which is left in water overnight. We eat it with salt, and chillies. Then I make some rotis (chappatis) to take to the site with us. By 7.30 it is time to go to the building site again. We all go together; sometimes Moni goes to school with his friends, but other times he comes and helps on the site. Shanti plays with the baby while I work. Fortunately this bungalow is in a quiet street. Sometimes you work and the lorries rush by all day, and you always wonder if your children will end up under a wheel. We work from 8.00 until 1.00 and have a break. I feed the baby in the mid-morning too, when we stop for water. Then work again until the evening. The work is extremely hard; at the end of the day I get Rs15, and my husband Rs20. It is barely enough to keep us. Look at my sari; every day it rips some more. At the end of the day, my ears are ringing from the sound of the cement mixer, and I'm covered with dust. The children are filthy too. I go home in this state, and then take the pots for water, buy firewood and vegetables from the market and cook the rice and sambha for supper. Rajagopal goes to the arrack shop. Then I bath the children, and myself, and wash my sari, sweep the house, and eat, wash the pots, and sleep.

It is a hard life, definitely. But I wouldn't go back to live in the village. What is there for me? No work. What is there here for me? Work and more work. That is all a woman is for.

CASE STUDY: Taking control of food aid

La Paz, Bolivia draws women and men from the countryside like a beacon; they come hoping for a better life, and a chance to escape from the extreme poverty of the communities in which they were born. But Bolivia faces increasing economic difficulties; and even within cities poor people have to find their own solutions to the problems of unemployment, ill-health, and lack of basic services. The most serious problem that women face is also the most basic: not enough food for themselves and their families.

Over the years, Bolivia has become dependent on large amounts of imported food aid, particularly to feed its urban population, which has distorted the economy of the country, not least by changing patterns of consumption, which in turn has badly affected small farmers. While using food aid as one important element of their survival strategy, poor women also turn the raw materials of food aid into goods for sale — bread, and pasties which can be sold from street stalls — and are active in the informal economy. Food aid is distributed through women's groups, organised by the state and the church. But receiving food brings with it a range of obligations; members of the women's groups have to attend meetings, avoid membership of political parties or unions, fulfil quotas, and participate in a range of economic activities planned for them by food-aid organisations. At worst food aid is used as a weapon to ensure religious and political ends which neither permit the development of autonomous women's organisations, nor the personal development of the recipients.

Faced with this situation, in 1987 the women of El Alto, a district of La Paz, decided to establish an autonomous committee, the Comite de Mujeres Receptoras de Alimentos — the Food Receiving Committee — to defend their rights, and to challenge the use of food aid as a political or religious tool. By 1989, 4,000 women were meeting together, and the committee had gained the recognition of the local population. It began the task of calling for changes in food aid policies, demanding the right of women's organisations to influence decisions in aid policy, and to undertake the management of food aid distribution. By 1990, the committee was beginning to broaden its vision, and develop a programme of organisational training, with a view to forming a single women's organisation in El Alto, which would enable women to tackle together some of the problems they face.[28]

Growing population pressure

In the last few years, a growing number of publications have highlighted rapid population growth as a feature of the crisis in the South. Anxiety over population growth this century is not a new preoccupation of the North; industrialised countries have worried about rapidly expanding populations in the Southern hemisphere since the 1940s, despite the fact that people in the South can find this concern misplaced or offensive. By the 1950s demographers in the US believed that the introduction of 'family planning programmes for peasants' might slow down population growth, even in the absence of industrialisation and other developments that had been responsible for falling birth rates in the North. The enormous increase in funding of population programmes — usually in the form of family-planning clinics — in the South throughout the 1960s followed directly from this orthodoxy, and the many abuses and programme failures performed in the name of population control throughout the 1960s have been well documented.[29] In 1974 a World Population Conference was held in Bucharest at which the nature of the Third World 'population problems' became the context for a global political debate. The problems focused on were concrete ones — food shortages, underdevelopment, underemployment — and at the Bucharest conference a new orthodoxy emerged: instead of these problems of poverty being caused by rapid population growth, poverty itself was seen as the cause of rapid population growth. As a result, population policy was relocated within the context of general economic and social development, and the slogan 'development is the best contraceptive' became widely influential. By the early 1980s, concern about population as a global problem seemed to have diminished.

So why has population growth returned to the global agenda, particularly at a time when population growth rates are declining almost everywhere except Sub-Saharan Africa? This time the anxiety wears a different set of clothes: rapid population growth is seen as an environmental issue. As such, it is about both excessive consumption in the smaller populations of the North, and the burgeoning of young, impoverished populations in the South. Dr. Nafis Sadik, of UNFPA has put this view succinctly: 'Much of the environmental degradation witnessed today is due to two groups of people — the top billion richest and bottom billion poorest. The top consumers...consume resources and generate vast quantities of waste. The bottom billion...destroy their own resource base out of necessity and lack of options.' Unfortunately, protecting the environment can assume a legitimacy that blurs other issues in population growth. For example, some would argue that no direct cause and effect relationship has been proved between environmental degradation and population growth, and that, just as the North has tended to blame the South for Southern poverty, so now it is blaming the South for Southern use of environmental resources which are seen as belonging to the whole of humanity. Similarly, the relationship between the environment and numbers of people is not a simple one of consumption; factors such as poverty, land ownership, and trade play a key role. What concerns us here, however, is how and why population growth is a gender issue, and may represent a crisis for the world's poorest women.

The relationship between poverty, underdevelopment and rapid population growth is not fully understood, despite the apparent orthodoxy that grew out of the Bucharest conference. On one level rapid population growth may be related to underdevelopment because it affects the ability of governments to distribute resources and provide services. The need for schools, health facilities, and other aspects of infrastructure will rise dramatically throughout the South as populations grow. Despite falling birth rates, the high proportion of young people in the South means that the actual number of people will continue to rise for some time. Even to maintain the current rates of coverage for education, health services, and food output will require rapid increases of investment in infrastructure. As we have already seen, women tend to be the worst affected by cuts in services, and similarly, women will be disproportionately affected by the failure of services to keep pace with the number of people who need to use them. Another area of linkage is the economic and social pressures towards high fertility that exist in many Southern countries, particularly in Sub-Saharan Africa. In areas where few resources exist beyond the family members, children provide labour and incomes for family survival, and sons are particularly important as security for old

preference of sons

age. If infant and child mortality rates are high families need to have more children to ensure that at least some of them survive. Many women and men in the South want and need children; *machismo* culture, son preference, the need to satisfy ancestors, the quest for status in patriarchal households, the need for sons to support widowhood, the quest for a family labour force to work the land and contribute to family income are all mechanisms creating high fertility in women.

STEVE JONES/OXFAM

Health worker advising women on the use of the contraceptive pill, Bangladesh. Access to family-planning advice is an unmet need for many Southern women, and even if a service is available, this kind of personal counselling or follow-up is often lacking.

High fertility takes its toll of individual women, however. In some parts of Africa, women have the highest rates of fertility in the world, and a 1 in 17 lifetime chance of dying because they become pregnant. (In Northern Europe the figure is 1 in 9,850.) Between a quarter and a third of the 500,000 women who die each year of pregnancy-related causes do so following badly performed abortions. Many more women become seriously ill as a result of illegal abortion. There is an enormous and unmet need for contraception that is safe, appropriate and affordable, as part of a broader package of reproductive health care for women. Yet the gender role of millions of women in the South precludes them taking decisions over their fertility, and even when

fertility | reproduction .

they are able to, and wish to limit their fertility, the lack of good, safe facilities, adequate choice, counselling and follow-up make this difficult if not impossible. This failure to provide women and men throughout the world with the technical facilities for reproductive choice has as much of an impact on reproductive behaviour as coercive policies.

The availability of the social and technical means to plan births is a basic human need and right. Unfortunately, the provision of family-planning services throughout the South has been underpinned by a strong demographic rationale, and family-planning programmes have been charged with the task of lowering fertility rates in the absence of broader development initiatives. As a result, the available services have not served women well. In India, for example, the major emphasis on sterilisation, coupled with incentives, has prevented the development of a broader-based service to enable women to space their children using reversible means, and to take care of their reproductive health more generally. A range of services that take into account the different needs of women at different stages of their lives is essential. The growing understanding of the centrality of women to the development process has influenced organisations that provide reproductive health care services. There is now a strong movement within some organisations to start the process of guaranteeing 'quality of care' for all women, for example by ensuring their access to services offering wide choice, information, technical competence, good interpersonal relations between client and provider, follow-up, and an appropriate constellation of services, such as antenatal provision, or early abortion facilities.[30] The Women's Global network on Reproductive Rights is an organisation based in Amsterdam which is active on these issues.

The provision of good family-planning, or 'birth-planning', information and services is one aspect of meeting women's needs, but it needs to take place in a broader context. Tackling the interlinked problems of poverty and rapid population growth calls for an integrated response, including poverty alleviation, improvements in the health, education and autonomy of women, and challenging the inequitable access to resources both within and between countries.[31]

No water, no trees....

Women all over the Third World collect the water that their families and animals drink. For the Afar women in the Wollo region of Ethiopia collecting water is an arduous task; women may have to walk for four to six hours to reach a water source, using donkeys and goat skins to transport the water home. Because collecting water can take a whole day, women in families which are polygamous take it in turns to bring the water home.

With every passing decade, many parts of Africa are becoming thirstier. The same is true for India. In Uttar Pradesh, in Northern India, in the 1960s the number of villages with drinking water problems was 17,000; by 1972 the number had risen to 35,000.[32]

Common sense suggests that water shortages are due to lack of rain. The rains fail, there is a drought, women have to walk a long way to look for water, and crops fail. Then the rain comes and the problem is over. Unfortunately, the causes of drought and water shortage are not so simple; failure of rains only becomes a disaster in a context of a much broader network of environmental, agricultural, economic and political changes. Water shortages are more often a result of human activities than changing weather patterns; in some parts of the world they are made worse by modern, export-oriented agriculture and by industrial development; elsewhere, the commercial exploitation of forests, the over-exploitation of groundwater and inappropriate afforestation and irrigation projects have played a part.

Severe drought and famine, at one end of a spectrum of water difficulties, affect men and women differently. When central Somalia suffered from drought and famine in 1986–87 following two successive rain failures, Oxfam carried out a small study of pastoral women to find out what specific effects the drought had on them. They found that within the family it is almost always the woman who takes on the burden of keeping the children alive, often going hungry herself and that, as women and small children are less mobile than individual men, it is the men who go off to look for help, leaving the women and children to fend for themselves. The poorest groups in Africa are invariably women and children in female-maintained households, and drought and famine affect the poorest first, and hardest.

The study in Somalia found that the first response to drought is migration, but as the drought spread and animals and people weakened, many could no longer stand the long treks between water points. Once the animals had died, families often moved to towns, further disrupting their life-style. Some women who had lost their animals moved to water points and set up tiny tea-stalls, buying tea and sugar on credit and earning a few cents a day. Many women sold their jewellery and household utensils to buy food, and when that ran out, they ate wild foods. Drought led to an increase in marital conflict and the break-up of households, often because women and men dis-agreed on the best strategy for coping with the drought. The report concludes: 'For the women whose marriages broke up during the drought, the future looks grim. Divorce in Somalia is common, and the woman's family cannot always take on the burden of looking after her and her children. She may join the swelling ranks of single-parent households in the squatter areas of Mogadishu or a smaller town, eking out a living by small trading, bread making, mat weaving, and sending her children on to the streets to beg and survive as best they can...The most badly affected [drought victims] will be the women who are trying to support young children by themselves, who are caught between the struggle for survival and the prospect of once again being trapped in a marriage where they are often treated little better than servants.'[33]

JENNY MATTHEWS/OXFAM

Carrying water, Ethiopia. This is a physically exhausting and time-consuming part of daily life for the majority of Southern women.

Water is not only an important gender issue in times of crisis, how-ever. Returning to the example of Wollo in Ethiopia with which we started this section, women play a part here not only in collecting water, but as community managers, deciding where to collect water from in the various seasons, how much to collect, and how to use it. Oxfam became involved in a relief project to provide water in

November 1984 in the Wollo region, and in a longer-term water development programme from 1985. In this they worked with EWWCA, the Ethiopian water authority, in a delicate and complex political situation. April Brett, who studied the project, explains that this made it difficult to take 'a more typical Oxfam community-oriented approach'. As a result, women were missed out in the development of the project, despite their role as the community managers. Key issues of maintenance of the site and installation, design, the wider implications of use, storage of water, and health education were not adequately addressed. Instead, the traditional leaders were consulted — men, who had no specific knowledge of water sources. As a result, the practicalities of water collection were not properly understood.

Even the kind of vessel used by women in water collection was not considered. The traditional Afar water jar is round-bottomed, and cannot easily stand upright on a flat concrete surface. But to operate a pump, both hands are needed; in other words, one woman cannot operate the pump and hold the jar under the pipe simultaneously. Another problem was maintenance. Whenever pumps broke, wells became useless.[34]

These issues have been addressed subsequently, with new open-access wells being supplied with hand-lifting devices rather than pumps. At all the water sites there are now stands for the water jars so that women can collect water on their own.

The issue of gender, water and development has also been analysed in a broader context. Vandana Shiva's book *Staying Alive* contains a chapter which she calls 'Women and the vanishing waters', an account of the politics of water management and its effects on women. She argues that women's role in water management has been overlooked. In Maharashtra, India, the so called 'sugar barons' who grow vast tracts of sugar cane have relied on bore-wells to irrigate their crops, and in some places have significantly lowered the water table, leaving poor farmers and water-gathering women literally high and dry.

The cutting down of forests is another example of short-term development priorities taking precedence over long-term implications for water supply. Deforestation affects water supply because forests act as giant sponges, absorbing and releasing water in a cyclical pattern over a period of time. Without tree cover the land looses its capacity to absorb torrential monsoon and tropical rains. Research has suggested that 75 per cent of rainfall in rainforest regions is contributed by the rainforest itself.[35]

According to Vandana Shiva, most water projects work against the logic of the water cycle, and violate the integrity of water flows which allow rivers, streams and wells to regenerate themselves. There is considerable evidence that if planners of water projects fail to think and act ecologically, to 'think like a river' and to work with the natural flow of the water, after a while they end up by making the problem of water shortage worse. Once the integrity of a water system has gone, it is very difficult to recreate it. Perhaps one of the most fundamental mistakes that development planners and water engineers make is to overlook women's gender role in and understanding of water management.

As the waters have vanished, so have the trees. Figures for the rate of deforestation this century in different parts of the world make uncomfortable reading. In 1981 the FAO/UNEP Tropical Forest Resources Assessment study concluded that Africa was losing forests at the rate of 1.3 million hectares per year, an area about half the size of Rwanda. The clearing of Latin American forests have attracted considerable attention, and so too has the felling of the forests of Sarawak, Malaysia, home of the Penan community. For all the stories of forest clearance that make news, there are many more communities suffering the long-term consequences of the change to their environment that deforestation means.

Trees are cut down for a variety of reasons; for the value of the trees themselves, whether for paper-making, rayon, furniture, or building material, or for the speculative value of the land on which they stand which can be used for agriculture, for ranching, for building or roads. But the main reason trees are felled is for fuel, both industrial and domestic, either to be turned into charcoal, or simply burnt in sticks on domestic fireplaces. In many cases, there is a conflict between immediate and longer-term factors in clearing forests. Acute shortage of land for agriculture to feed hungry people or the prospect of earning foreign exchange from a cash crop may seem a more pressing priority than more general issues of global well-being. The Indonesian Vice-President summed up the conflict when he asked: 'How much land for the hungry of today? And how much for genetic resources to be preserved for tomorrow? In the past, we have neither received a fair share of the benefits, nor have we received a fair share of assistance — other than inexpensive advice and even more inexpensive criticism — in the efforts to save the common global natural heritage. Unless such responsibilities are equally shared, all our good intentions will only lead to global environmental destruction.'[36]

But the question of forest clearance is not only a political and environmental question between nations, between North and South. It is also a question within nations, between different groups and, in some instances, between genders. In India for example, forests are cleared to feed an industrial system which at present benefits only about one in five Indians. Half of India's industrial output is reckoned to be based on natural resources, such as wood, or minerals or cash crops, many of which come from areas formerly covered with forest. The people who live in the forests, often tribal people, depend on the forest products for their traditional way of life, and for them the forest is the context, the condition of survival. As they lose their habitat, so they lose their means of production, and everything else besides.

The India scholar Anil Gupta carried out an interesting exercise when he asked village people — women and men — to draw their village, or the parts most important to them. The women's drawings included trees, plants and, almost without fail, temples. The equivalent drawings of men usually included transport links between villages, whereas the drawings of the women showed virtually none, reflecting the fact that the movement of women beyond the village boundaries, except to collect wood and water is very limited. Women's perceptions of the importance of trees differs from that of men. According to Jennifer McCracken, 'If asked to rank a number of different tree species in order of preference they often use criteria such as the value of the tree as a source of fodder or fuel, the thorniness of the branches (i.e. ease of handling), the smokiness of the wood (when used for cooking) or even the aesthetics of the tree. Men, on the other hand, use very different criteria, reflecting their different perspectives. They may rank the species on the basis of the strength of the wood for construction purposes, or the spread of the canopy (i.e. the area of cropping and which it would cast in shade).'[37] In other words, the relationship between women, men and trees shows clear gender differences. And just as gender is an issue in terms of the use of trees, and the kind of trees that village people choose to plant, it is also an issue in the case of deforestation.

People who live in forests take food, fodder, fuel, fertiliser, fibres, medicines and the raw material for craft products and construction from them. The Soliga tribal people in Karnataka, India, collect 27 different varieties of leafy vegetable from the forest at different times of the year, and a wide variety of tubers, leaves, fruits and roots, which are used both as food and medicine. Forest-dwelling people are usually protected against famine, even when it affects neighbouring areas, since they can collect at least half of the calories they need from the forest.[38] Food gathering, and fodder and fuelwood collection tends to be a gender-specific task, done by women. As forest land recedes, women are still charged with these tasks, even if it means walking twice as far, and searching twice as hard for the products. But this is not the whole story. Forests, as we saw in the section on food, play a vital part in the food chain, which is why women in the Himalayas sing 'Give me an oak forest and I will give you pots full of milk and baskets full of grain'. It is why the women of the Chipko movement sing 'What do the forests bear? Soil, water and pure air'.

BERNARD TAYLOR/OXFAM

Carrying fuelwood, Senegal. Women often have to walk long distances to gather the fuelwood needed for cooking.

The forest ecosystem acts to stabilise soil and water; forests act as reservoirs and lungs, guaranteeing a stable rain supply, producing oxygen, absorbing rain water, and releasing it slowly through underground water flows. The deforestation of the Himalayas, the floods, landslides and consequent soil erosion, led to a popular protest, organised and sustained largely by women, and known as the Chipko movement. Chipko literally means 'to embrace', which is exactly what the women did to the trees that were due to be felled. The embracing of trees spread throughout villages in the Garhwal Himalaya in the late 1970s, and south, down to Karnataka. In some of the conflicts that followed, the different gender issues of women and men were painfully highlighted, when women embraced the trees that were to be cut down by their own husbands, employed by the forest contractors. The demands of the women, for a supply of fuel, fodder and water, conflicted absolutely with the demands of men for a cash income. In one struggle in the Balganga Valley in Garhwal, the women held out against the forest department, and their own partners for four months in order to save a patch of trees in an otherwise degraded forest. Subsequently the women mounted a protection on the forest, about 10 or 12 women watching over it each day, preventing goats from grazing, or humans from lopping and cutting trees for wood. 'On these days we leave our own work and protect the forest because our oak trees are like our children.' As a result the forest is beginning to regenerate.[39]

In this chapter we have looked at food, water, and forests separately. Of course, agriculture, water, and forests are highly interdependent systems, the environment in which most Third World women produce and sustain their lives. As long as the land, water, and forests remain the means of production for millions of the world's women, and as long as this fact fails to be central to the planning of resource management by governments and international agencies, the future looks bleak. For millions of women in the world, there is indeed a crisis — a time of decision. Unless they are involved in making those decisions, it is hard to see how their environments, their livelihoods, will be allowed to survive.

..but plenty of guns...

The trees and waters of the world may be vanishing, but there is no shortage of global resources for bombs, guns, missiles and all the other apparatus of war. During the 1980s world military expenditure grew to unprecedented peacetime levels. In 1987 the world invested $1.8 million dollars a minute on arming itself. The industrialised North is responsible for the vast majority of the money spent on arms, but each year the proportion spent by the Third World rises. In 1986 developing countries spent $159 billion on their armed forces, five times the amount that they received in aid. A glance at tables of central government expenditure on health, education, social services and defence for many developing countries shows where government priorities really lie: India spent 19.3 per cent of its government budget on defence in 1988, 2.9 per cent on education, 1.8 per cent on health and 5.8 per cent on social security, welfare and housing. Burkina Faso spent 17.9 per cent of its budget on defence, but only 3.3 per cent on housing, social security and welfare. Moreover, under programmes of structural adjustment, many countries have cut their social services more stringently than their defence budgets, reflecting the fact that armed forces are used to surpress discontent arising from poverty in many parts of the world.

Whilst there can be no guarantee that arms spending would necessarily be switched to more constructive objects, these figures represent, at the least, enormous opportunities that have been lost and are being lost every day for more peaceful and equitable development. It does not take much imagination to think what might have been produced with the same capital, labour skills and raw materials. It is estimated that half of the world's scientists are employed in weapons research, half a million highly educated people who might otherwise be working on some of the major global problems — pollution, disease, environmental crisis — that assail us. While there is no simple relationship between reducing defence-spending and increasing aid, a UN Group of Experts came to the conclusion that there is a competitive relationship between the arms race and development, not only in terms of resources, but also in the dimension of attitudes and perceptions.

The figures also represent an immense amount of human suffering, for tanks, rockets and guns are not only abstract figures on paper; the world over, armed conflict, besides causing thousands of deaths and mutilations, creates huge refugee populations and violates human rights. The vast majority of the world's refugees are women and children, whose husbands, fathers, and brothers have either been killed or are fighting. In 1985, 90 per cent of the Ethiopian refugees in Somalia were women and children under 15; 80 per cent of the Kampuchean households along the Thai-Kampuchean borders were headed by women and over 80 per cent of Salvadorean refugees in Nicaragua were women, children and old people. Women refugees face a multitude of problems made more acute by their gender. They face the insecurity of sexual vulnerability, of harassment, discrimination and rape; they come from cultural backgrounds which may well have defined them as subordinate yet they have to take on the full responsibility of trying to build new lives for their families; many face health problems, without the support of traditional kin networks; almost all face acute anxiety, bereavement and loss; most have to learn to change their traditional behaviour and take on the new gender roles that are expected of them if they are to survive. It is an extraordinary fact that the gender-specific nature of so many refugee populations should have failed to register for so long, and that the specific needs of women refugees, both as individuals and as women, should only just have begun to affect planning for refugee populations. (Chapter 8 contains a section on the particular problems of women refugees.)

Armed conflict has other, less obvious effects on the gender roles of women and men, but which are none the less deeply disruptive to the long-term well-being and development of communities. Evidence from the Philippines suggests that the displacement of women and men — 'internal migration' — can cause just as much disruption as migration across international borders. Men, particularly in areas seen as 'rebel' districts, may be forced to flee, or join one of the opposing armies, leaving women to adopt the responsibilities traditionally assigned to men, at the same time as fulfilling their own roles. Some areas of the Philippines have been declared 'free fire zones', a term meaning the removal of the civilian population: anyone staying on is automatically assumed to be a rebel. For civilian men who are dis-placed to urban areas, traditional male skills such as farming may become redundant, and family survival rests on the women's shoul-ders. Even among families who do not resort to leaving their homes, armed conflict in the countryside reduces the mobility of men, leaving the burden of household and community survival to the women. Armed conflict significantly disrupts local and national economies, so that women have to cope with diminishing incomes and dwindling supplies, which in turn reduces their ability to feed their families. Under such circumstances, social life and recreation tend to become low priorities, and marital problems increase, both of which under-mine the ability of women to cope with all the other stresses.

A report on the impact of conflict on gender in the Philippines found that a high proportion of the many single young women migrating to cities, or abroad, as domestic helpers or workers in the 'entertainment' industry, came from the regions most affected by armed conflict. These women can end up in situations in which they are extremely vulnerable, as the plight of many Filipino contract workers in the Iran-Kuwait conflict demonstrated. Kuwait was home for some 60,000 Filipino workers, 80 per cent of whom were women working as domestic helpers. The majority of the Filipino men were working on construction sites or industrial operations and living in worker's compounds when war broke out. As a result they had better information and more access to help; the first evacuation flights for overseas workers from Kuwait brought home mainly male evacuees. Women, living in the homes of their employers, had little access to information, and no social support. Leaving Kuwait became a night-mare for hundreds of Filipino women. Some were raped by Iraqi troops; others had to sell sexual services to secure safe passage out of Kuwait. Even for women who managed to locate and use official channels for escape there were enormous difficulties. Food and water in evacuation camps in Baghdad were scarce and sickness rife. Many women had to use much of their hard-earned savings and sell their possessions simply to buy their basic needs.

In areas of the world where women are faced with direct armed aggression, the constant anxiety they face has a major effect on both physical and psychological well-being. Rape of 'enemy' women is regarded as one of the 'spoils of war', and women may be captured and used as prostitutes by the army. War may lead to a dramatic cur-tailment in the availability of medical facilities available to civilian populations, just when women in particular may most need such resources to help them cope. There is evidence that miscarriages and other health problems occur more frequently when women suddenly find their homes have become part of a war zone. Conflict destroys crops and infrastructure; restricted mobility may prevent the collec-tion of firewood, water and food; access to fields and income-generat-ing activities may be severely curtailed. This was the experience of women in conflict zones in Angola, the Sudan and Eritrea where, as a result, community and household structures broke down.

Gender and conflict is a matter of considerable importance to Oxfam, as much of Oxfam's work around the world is affected by war. Until very recently, the gender dimension of conflict was little researched and even less understood. As more evidence is collected, it seems certain that the very different effects of armed conflict on the two genders will become clearer, making relief and rehabilitation efforts better targeted. In the Philippines for example, recognition of links between armed conflict and women's sexual and reproductive health has led to a programme focus on activities which support women's health and within which women can address issues of sexu-al violence. During the early months of the Gulf conflict, the local Oxfam programme supported the activities of an NGO providing ser-vices, including counselling and medical referrals to returning migrant workers, virtually all of whom were women.[40]

Why gender is a development issue

Whichever facet of global politics and crisis we consider — the eco-nomic crisis, the pains of structural adjustment, the crisis in food production, in the cities, the environment, or in the continuing conflicts in Southern countries — we find that women and men are affected differently. The pattern of development pursued in recent years, with priority given to economic growth, export orientation, high levels of defence-spending, has been in a very literal sense of the word, a 'man-made' agenda. If it had been women — poor women — who had set the priorities of national development, perhaps fewer of them would be suffering now. This is not to claim any inherent feminine wisdom, it is simply to point out what has not been properly acknowledged — the importance of women's work and well-being. Women's work, women's priorities, women's lives have not counted on the agendas of the Third World's national planners. As a result, the models of development that have been followed have failed to perceive, let alone use, what was missing: the contribution of at least half the world's citizens.

7

REASSESSING THE ROLE OF WOMEN

Development and women: a brief history of different approaches

It is over 20 years since the first text to be labelled as part of the 'women and/in development' literature was published, Esther Boserup's book, *Women's Role in Economic Development* (1970). The book begins with the words: 'In the vast and ever growing literature on economic development, reflections on the particular problems of women are few and far between.'[1] At the time, she was right, but in the three decades that have followed, the literature on the 'particular problems of women' has burgeoned, and women in development (WID) has become a major aspect of the development 'industry', with women's development bureaus, specialist consultants and planning divisions proliferating the world over.

The aim of this chapter is to look at some of the ideas that have come out of all this activity, and to indicate the different directions in which thinking about women in the development process seems to be going. One of the problems with using terms like 'women in development' is the assumption that everyone knows what is meant, and that there is one particular theory about the subordination of women that can be applied across the board. This is by no means true. In the first place, the problem of gender in development is, as the economist Amartya Sen put it, 'far to complex and basic to be "resolved" by any kind of simple model'.[2] In the second, gender and development is still a very new concept, and is not fully incorporated by all academics or practitioners, especially those dealing with macro analysis. Many of the models described in this chapter, such as 'welfare' or 'equity', are ways of describing particular approaches, rather than clear-cut methodologies.

Beginning to work with women: modernisation, welfare and equity

Esther Boserup looked back over the development process of the 1950s and 1960s with gender-sensitive eyes. Instead of assuming that women were confined only to their reproductive roles as wives and mothers, Boserup looked at their productivity, and emphasised the vital role of women in agricultural economies. Boserup's work has been criticised for its adherence to the dominant economic approach of the time, modernisation; subsequent writers have argued that her book also fails to pay attention to women's household labour as a basis for subordination, and to the affects of capital accumulation in colonial settings, two themes that have become very important to subsequent WID theorists.[3]

Modernisation, as we saw in Chapter 2, was a model of how to transform 'backward' economies by means of industrialisation, urbanisation, the transfer of technology, financial aid, and the integration of Third World economies into the capitalist market system. Economic growth would slowly 'trickle down' and eradicate poverty. Under this approach to development, women were either overlooked, or seen as part of the 'household' or 'community', or they were objects of welfare. Development assistance took the form of financial aid for economic growth (largely targeting men) and relief aid for the socially vulnerable groups who were failing to gain any of the benefits from the long-awaited economic growth (targeting poor women). In many cases the projects developed were necessary to ameliorate the impact of the dominant development model. The fact that the welfare approach targeted women was a result of a particular perception of women, already documented in this book: that motherhood and child rearing are the most important roles of women. It also made another assumption: that women are only passive recipients of development.[4] 'Welfare' includes many of the best-known kinds of development — mother-child health programmes, feeding schemes, family planning services, food aid, and so on. Welfare programmes remain very popular as a way of reaching women, though they make little contribution, if any, to creating independence and self-reliance. Rather, they tend to encourage dependency; but because they are politically 'safe', and do not question the *status quo* in terms of values, economic status (particularly unequal access to and control over resources), or an established sexual division of labour, they are preferred by governments and agencies who are anxious about upholding cultural and social values.

By the 1970s it was becoming clear that the modernisation strategy was failing to eliminate poverty from the South. It was also clear from analyses such as Boserup's that women, far from benefiting from development programmes, were actually being harmed by them, a situation that welfare programmes could do little to alter. A change in thinking about both development and women in development was well overdue. The shift in direction among development planners and donors was towards the direct provision of health, nutritional and educational services. The World Development Report 1980, marshalling all the evidence available at that time, argued that improvements in health, literacy and nutrition were important not only in their own right, but because they promoted growth in incomes, nationally and for the poor themselves.[5]

During the 1970s this analysis was applied not only to poor people in general, but to women in particular. The argument was put forward that if women's traditional work was not recognised as part of the national economy, efforts were needed to give them work that could be counted: they needed to be 'integrated into development', or at least integrated into the market economy, producing goods or services which would ensure an income for them and would contribute to the development process as measurable by GNP. Education, vocational and technical training were seen as essential prerequisites for this. Women were to be given the same chance as men, in an essentially liberal view of the system which simply saw women as having been missed out — it was all a question of equal opportunities. Few people stopped to ask whether the system into which women were to be integrated was the right one. So it was that in 1975 the UN launched its International Women's Year, under the themes of 'equality, development and peace', and a decade to concentrate on women.

The International Women's Decade provided a major spur to research and discussion about women in the development process. The idea of equality became an important criterion for thinking about what women needed from development. The policy approach to women and development that grew out of this concern for equality — the equity approach — has been characterised by Caroline Moser as recognising that:

> Women are active participants in the development process,
> who through both their productive and reproductive roles
> provide a critical, if unacknowledged, contribution to eco-
> nomic growth. The approach starts with the basic assumption
> that economic strategies have frequently had a negative
> impact on women, and acknowledges that they must be
> 'brought into' the development process through access to
> employment and the marketplace... However, the equity
> approach is also concerned with fundamental issues of equali-
> ty which transcend the development field... its primary con-
> cern is with inequality between men and women, in both pub-
> lic and private sphere of life... It identifies the origins of
> women's subordination as lying not only in the context of the
> family, but also in relationships between men and women in
> the marketplace.[6]

There are three important elements here. Firstly, the recognition of
the economic value of women's paid and unpaid work (worth a third
of the annual global economic product, or 4,000 billion dollars in
1985).[7] Secondly, there is the recognition of the way in which much
development has affected women adversely. Thirdly, there is the
argument that the pursuit of equality, in the marketplace and in the
home, will remedy these problems. Yet it is here that the equity
approach has come up for criticism, both as a rather top-down
approach and as a reflection of a First World feminist preoccupation
with equality. A recent document produced by the UN on how far the
Forward-Looking Strategies of the decade had been implemented
illustrates the first of these criticisms, because it is mainly concerned
with government implementation of equality. Its draft recommendations are as much to governments as NGOs, and include promoting
an increased awareness of women's rights; equal pay for work of
equal value, including measurement of comparable worth and
women's unpaid work; equality in economic decision making; measures to counteract stereotyping of women in the mass media, and
improvement in the situation of female-headed households. Most of
these recommendations are not about empowering women to bring
about change themselves, but require government interventions, such
as changing school textbooks to eliminate sexist stereotypes.

The equity approach to women in development has fallen from
favour among many aid agencies, and has been viewed with suspicion by many Third World governments. In the case of aid agencies,

the implicit redistribution of power implied is seen as unacceptable intervention in a country's traditions. Some Third World governments, even though they signed the Nairobi Forward-Looking Strategies for Advancement of Women, felt that the call for equality was a legitimisation of Western-exported feminism. Nonetheless, the Strategies provide an important framework for those working within government to improve the status of women through official legislation.

Three other approaches to the role of women in development have been labelled by Moser as the 'anti-poverty approach', the 'efficiency approach', and the 'empowerment approach' to women in development. Other writers have labelled the evolution of approaches as moving from WID (women in development) to WAD (women and development) to GAD (Gender and development). We will look briefly at each in turn. These approaches were not 'tried out' consecutively and it is still possible to find examples of projects typifying all these approaches, and many other projects and programmes that seem to combine elements of several.

The anti-poverty approach

By the end of the 1960s it had become clear that the poorest of the poor remained poor, and that many of them were women. It was also becoming clear that education and vocational training was at best only going to benefit a tiny proportion of women. The anti-poverty approach to women in development took as its starting point poverty rather than subordination as the source of inequality between women and men, and set out to improve the incomes of poor women. In this it reflected both World Bank and ILO priorities and the 'basic needs strategy', with its primary aim of meeting the basic needs of food, clothing, shelter and fuel. Low-income women were identified as a particular target group, not least because of their central role in providing these basic needs to their families.

The anti-poverty approach focused on income generation for women through better access to productive resources, such as land and credit. Since the 1970s, income-generating projects for poor women have proliferated, and become one of the most common forms of development activity, particularly of the kind supported by NGOs. Many of these projects aim to increase the productivity of work that women are already doing — for example, small-scale marketing or food production. There have been many criticisms of income-generating projects. They often take little account of the fact that women are already over-burdened with work; that saving, where they do not control the family budgets, may be very difficult for women; that freedom of movement for many women is restricted; that the capacity of the informal sector to generate employment and growth is limited. On the whole, women's income-generating projects are seldom treated as seriously as those for men. But income-generating projects may also offer a possibility of empowering women. One example drawn from an Oxfam project in Bangladesh featured many of the problems listed above. Yet out of unpromising circumstances was created a small-scale project that has both generated an income, and led to other social changes.

CASE STUDY: **Income generating in Bangladesh**

The women's group had been meeting for just over a year, and had built a meeting place out of bamboo and tin. Since saving was difficult, many of the women saved a handful of rice each week which they then turned into cash, with the aim of contributing Rs2 per week. The group managed to save Rs2,500 in the course of a year. None of the women had worked outside their homes before, and took no part in the public economic life of the village, but eventually the group took over the lease of a piece of land. A man in the village, Tofajol, had taken a loan of Rs10,000 by mortgaging his land, and was given three years to pay it back. When he failed to repay the money, the money lender threatened to seize his land. This is where the women's group stepped in, paying off the loan, and cultivating the land until Tofajol was able to pay the money back to them. The women's group grew rice on the land, earning additional income for themselves. Yet the income was almost secondary to the other changes that have occurred; together with other village groups, they have managed to have the road to their village repaired; and by applying to the government public health department they have managed to get latrines.

More importantly for the long term, the women are focusing on the problem of dowry. So far they have managed to reduce the amount of dowry demanded, but they are trying to stamp out the practice altogether. This project demonstrates that an income-generating project can have important long-term effects, particularly when generated and managed by the women concerned.

Women in Development

The phrase 'Women in Development', and its accepted abbreviation, WID, more or less sums up the earliest phase of thinking about women's role in development and the approaches we have covered so far. It was coined in the early 1970s by the Women's Committee of the Washington DC Chapter of the Society for International Development as part of a deliberate strategy to bring the new thinking by Boserup and others to the attention of American policy makers. Since then, WID has been used as shorthand for approaches to the issue of women and development largely based on the modernisation paradigm.[8] The WID approach focused on initiatives such as the development of better, appropriate technologies that would lighten women's workloads. WID has tended to over-emphasise the productive side of women's work and labour — particularly income generation — ignoring their reproductive side, and in this it shows its origins in the liberal preoccupations of the North in the 1970s and 1980s.

The efficiency approach

The efficiency approach to women in development is well illustrated by two recent documents, one from the World Bank and one from the British ODA. In a 1987 publication entitled 'The World Bank New Approach to Women in Development' the Chief of the Women in Development unit, Barbara Herz writes the following:

> We want to show what can actually be done to include women in development programmes and how that contributes to economic performance, easing of poverty and other development objectives... The Bank has just adopted a new, more operational approach to women in development... it emphasises gains in economic productivity attainable through more effective involvement of women and focuses on practical ways to involve women in normal operations in agriculture, education and PHN [Primary Health and Nutrition].[9]

The ODA policy statement is dated 1989 and says:

> To achieve a better deal for women is, at one and the same time, a major step forward towards relieving poverty, a broadening of social opportunities and a stimulus to economic development. Women make up the greater part of the poorest of the poor. Helping them can make a major contribution to the relief of poverty. Women hold the key to a more productive and dynamic society. If they themselves are healthy and knowledgeable, if they have greater access to knowledge, skills and credit, they will be more

economically productive. Even more, women are the dominant influence on the next generation through their attitudes, their education and health. Equity and economic growth go together. If the challenge of this enterprise is formidable, so will be the rewards of any success.[10]

These two statements have one important thing in common: the belief that development will only be efficient if women are involved. The recognition that '50 per cent of the human resources for development were being wasted or underutilised'[11] represents a shift in emphasis from women themselves as the focus of concern, to their contribution towards getting development to work. The anxiety among development planners that enormous quantities of money and other resources were failing to make any significant impact has, according to Moser, led to the efficiency approach being rapidly appropriated as the model for women and development.

Historically, the efficiency approach grew out of the decline in the world economy from the mid-1970s onwards, the phase of structural adjustment policies and a global emphasis on increased efficiency and productivity. As Chapter 6 argued, much structural adjustment has entailed a shifting of costs from the paid to the unpaid economy, through the use of women's unpaid time. Moser's account of the efficiency approach explains that it has 'implications for women not only as reproducers, but also increasingly as community managers. In the housing sector...one such example is provided by site and service and upgrading projects with self-help components, which now regularly include women in the implementation phase. This is a consequence of a need for greater efficiency: not only are women as mothers more reliable than men in repaying building loans, as workers they are equally capable of self-building alongside men; while as community managers they have shown far greater commitment than men in ensuring that services are maintained.'[12]

The efficiency approach operates at two different levels. Ensuring efficiency in development projects demands the involvement of women because they are often more efficient and committed than men. A development project, whether a subsistence food-growing project in Africa or a 'food for work' scheme in India is more likely to be successful if women are fully involved, even though the efficiency approach is based on an idea of the elasticity of women's time (and therefore the cost to women in terms of the time demanded of them may be intolerable). The second aspect is at the macro level of development policy pursued by governments, supported by organisations such as the World Bank and IMF, who also demand efficiency and productivity in programmes of structural adjustment. It is at this level that efficiency is brought about by shifting the costs from the paid economy — social welfare payments, food subsidies, free education and health services — on to the unpaid economy, which tends to be made up of women's unpaid labour. At times, these two levels come together. Moser cites the example of a programme in Lima, Peru, the *Vaso de Leche* (glass of milk) direct-feeding programme, which provides a free glass of milk to young children in low-income areas of the city, and is managed by women in their unpaid time. The significance of the programme is that it is one that has received the approval of UNICEF, fitting into UNICEF's definition of 'adjustment with a human face'. It is an example of project efficiency (the project works: the children get their glass of milk), and also an example of efficiency in terms of the costs, because it relies on women's unpaid time. In fact, the project only achieved its efficiency by its reliance on the 'freely available' time of women. Much the same thing could be said about activities such as communal kitchens and other self-help services that have developed, particularly in Latin America in response to the crisis of debt and adjustment.

Women and development

Women and development (WAD) is a neo-Marxist feminist approach, which emerged in the latter half of the 1970s out of a concern with the limitations of modernisation theory. Rather than focusing on strategies for 'integrating women in development', it points out that women have always been important economically, and the work they do in their households and communities is fundamental to the maintenance of their societies. WAD recognises that poor men are also victims of a development process that ignores them, but it tends to group women together without sufficiently analysing class, race and ethnic divisions between them. The WAD approach assumes that women's position will improve as and when international structures become more equitable, and in this it tends to underplay the nature of women's specific gender oppression; women's position is seen as part of the structure of international and class inequalities, rather than being a result of an ideology and structure of patriarchy. WAD approaches have tended to focus on income-generation activities and have underplayed the labour women invest in family and household maintenance.

The empowerment approach or gender and development (GAD)

The only approach to women-in-development that looks at all aspects
of women's lives and all the work that women do — productive and
reproductive, private and public — and rejects any attempt to undervalue family and household maintenance work, has come to be
known as 'empowerment', or more generally, the 'Gender and
Development' (GAD) approach to women-in-development.

Although popular among development practitioners working
within a feminist framework, the empowerment approach is viewed
with suspicion by many aid agencies and Third World governments.
It questions the commonly accepted theories of what good development entails, arguing that there is more to development than economic growth and the efficient use of money, and challenges the idea that
women want to be 'integrated' into the mainstream of Western-
designed development, in which they have little chance of determining the kind of society they want. Empowerment differs from other
approaches in its analysis of the origins, dynamics and structures of
women's oppression, and in how it proposes to change the position of
Third World women. The process of change, and its effects on the
consciousness of the people bringing about their own development, is
often as important as the changes themselves.

Empowerment is associated with a bottom-up rather than a top-
down approach, and much of the thinking about empowerment has
arisen out of the feminist writings and emergent women's movements
of the South. It is essentially a Southern women's approach to development, rather than a Northern, white man's approach. It traces the
roots of subordination to race, class, colonial history, and the position
of Southern countries within the international economic order. It sees
the goals of development for women in terms of self-reliance and
internal strength, and places much less emphasis on legislating for
equality between women and men then on empowering women
themselves to work to change and transform the structures that have
been so inimical to them — such as labour codes, men's control over
women's bodies and reproductive rights, civil codes, and property
rights.

While the equity approach also sees the need to reform these structures, it differs from empowerment in its belief that change imposed
from the top is most effective. The empowerment approach, while
recognising the need for supportive legislation, argues that the
growth of women's organisations, leading to political mobilisation,

consciousness-raising and popular education, is the necessary condition for lasting social change. Women's organisations offer the possibility of personal empowerment and change, and also provide a context for this personal transformation to lead into direct political action. The most successful women's groups have been those that have mobilised around specific needs, in health or employment for example, and have then gone on to work on longer-term issues.

A woman rag-picker rummaging through a dustbin in Hyderabad

The empowerment approach is much easier to understand by looking at a specific example. The following case study looks at the paper pickers of Ahmedabad, Gujarat, India who received a small grant from Oxfam. The details come from a study by Elizabeth Bentley on behalf of the Self Employed Women's Association (SEWA) of Ahmedabad.

CASE STUDY: The paper pickers of Ahmedabad: a case of empowerment

There are about 20,000 paper pickers in Ahmedabad, mostly women and children. Paper picking is the collecting of used paper — newspapers, office waste, packaging or household rubbish. It is the first rung in a vital recycling industry in India, a country where nothing is wasted. Each picker sells her collection to middle-men, who sell it to contractors who then recycle it. Women are hugely exploited by the middle-men, getting only about 10 per cent of the value of the waste they collect. Despite the meagre earnings of most paper pickers, the money they make keeps their families together.

How did there come to be so many paper pickers in Ahmedabad? Many of them have been in some way dependent on Ahmedabad's textile industry. As the textile industry expanded earlier this century, it destroyed the market for village handloom weaving. By the 1930s many weaving families from surrounding villages had migrated to Ahmedabad to find work in the mills. Their slum houses were too small to accommodate the traditional looms, and the weaving skills of women began to die out. As the industry grew, more women found employment, but often in low-skilled jobs, like cleaning. Then, as India and Ahmedabad began to loose its place in the world textile trade, the industry came to a standstill, and women were laid off first.

Unemployed women turned to working in private workshops for contractors who exploited them. With the major recession of the 1970s, most of Ahmedabad's mills closed and thousands of women, many the sole breadwinners of their families, were forced into the only work available — paper picking. Many women are ashamed of the work they have to do: 'Picking paper is a real come down for me. When I was in the mill, we used to look down on paper pickers. We would say we are the mill workers, we earn a good salary. These paper pickers they wander around everywhere without shame. They are dirty. Today, I am degraded too. When I first had to start picking paper, I would try to make sure no one could see my face. I was so ashamed. How low I have fallen.'

Empowerment seems a forlorn hope for people whose plight was so desperate, and whose position on the edge of the economy so precarious. But the paper pickers became involved with the Self Employed Women's Association of Ahmedabad. This started in 1972 as a trade union, and by 1991 had 25,000 members, had set up its own Bank, ran numerous training programmes, and supported its members through a joint strategy of struggle and development.

Struggle and development sums up well the work of SEWA with the paper pickers. It began by supporting the women in their struggle for a higher wage, through persuading the mills to turn over their low-grade waste paper to paper-picker members of SEWA. In an attempt to guarantee a regular supply of waste paper, SEWA and the paper pickers negotiated with the State Government to give SEWA members preference for waste paper from government offices. The government demanded a lump sum of Rs 10,000 from the women as security in case they failed to collect the paper, which SEWA duly paid. But the women still faced a great deal of corruption and obstruction, as people with vested interests in controlling the paper trade tried to block their way.

To deal with these kinds of pressures, the paper pickers organised themselves into a series of co-operatives. Drawing strength from their collective position, they have adopted a wide range of imaginative solutions to get what they wanted: instead of relying on good will to provide them with access to paper, they researched the tender system and learnt to compete with contractors on their own terms; when invited to participate in a television documentary on corruption in local government, one of the organisers told the story of their struggle with the government offices in detail, carefully mentioning the names and positions of all the men involved, and within a week the women began to receive the full amount of waste paper that was their due. They also blockaded trucks trying to take away paper rightfully theirs, and they petitioned the Chief Minister of Gujarat directly.

By exercising their united strength and refusing to give up, the paper pickers have established themselves as a force to be reckoned with in the eyes of the government, the contractors and most importantly, in their own eyes. This is empowerment, and it is the start of a process that the paper pickers intend to see to its logical conclusion, which is exercising control over all the stages of the recycling process. They have now acquired their own warehouse where paper pickers can get a better price for their paper, and they are working to achieve complete independence from middle-men, hoping eventually to own their own paper reprocessing plant.

At the same time, SEWA has been working with the paper pickers to find alternative ways of generating an income. Most paper pickers hope that their daughters should not also have to become pickers, and some girls have now been trained in electrical wiring. Four new co-operatives of ex-paper pickers have been formed: weaving, cleaning, electrical wiring, and file production.

Elizabeth Bentley's report sums up this process of empowerment:

Their involvement with SEWA has allowed the women to experience themselves as the equal of anyone with whom they come into contact. They are far less afraid of the more fortunate in society and they are not ashamed of themselves for the work they do — no longer feeling as though it is their own shortcomings which have condemned them to such a life. They are aware that their position in society is a result of many forces they are able to understand and work against. Apart from the organising and business skills SEWA has helped the women to develop, their involvement has helped broaden their general awareness...Many of the advances made by the paper pickers through their association with SEWA are not measurable in...objective terms. The leadership skills, confidence and the courage to define their own lives and values in the face of oppressive traditional beliefs are invaluable benefits of the women's experience with SEWA which only becomes visible by looking at the lives of individual women.[13]

Women's gender needs and interests

One of the key assumptions underlying gender and development analysis is that women and men, because they have different gender roles and power, also have different gender interests. If those who plan projects and programmes were better able to understand women's gender interests, so the argument goes, they would be in a much better position to ensure that their gender needs were met. It is more useful to talk about 'gender interests' than about 'women's interests' because this recognises the fact than an individual woman's interests may be determined as much by her social position or ethnic identity as by the fact that she is a woman; the interests that women share by virtue of the fact that they are women are therefore 'gender interests'.

One of the most useful ways of looking at women's gender interests is to make a distinction between improving the immediate, difficult conditions that most poor women in the South face daily — addressing their practical gender needs — and tackling the underlying structural issues that cause these conditions. DAWN argues that 'studies show that rather than improving, the socioeconomic status of the great majority of Third World women has worsened considerably throughout the Decade...'[14] Other reports and statistics show improvements in literacy levels, child mortality and in growth of per capita incomes for at least some Southern countries. The contradiction may be explained by the fact that most of the benefits of development have neither been shared evenly between women and men nor between women of different classes. Women's relative access to economic resources and employment has worsened, even though the 'pie' of resources may have increased. Improvements in health, housing and education have never reached those who are the real focus of women-in-development literature, the poorest of poor women.

Peggy Antrobus, co-ordinator of DAWN, believes that poor women have not benefited from development because the underlying forces and ideologies that prevent change have been ignored; for Antrobus the emphasis on women's practical needs went wrong, not because these needs were unimportant, but because in meeting them there was a failure to recognise that 'these practical gains are easily reversed if women lack the power to protect them when resources are scarce... [which] is what happened in the context of structural adjustment policies pursued by most of our governments in their efforts to deal with the problem of debt...'[15]

By proposing a distinction between 'practical' gender needs and longer-term, or 'strategic' change, gender and development analysis has suggested ways of tackling not just immediate problems, but their underlying causes. The terms 'practical' and 'strategic' gender interests were coined by Maxine Molyneux in 1985.[16] She differentiated between the needs generated by women in performing particular social roles and their interests as a social group with unequal access to resources (economic, social and political). This distinction has gained wide acceptance in gender and development literature, and has been developed and refined by other writers. Caroline Moser, for example, suggests that meeting women's practical gender needs can work to preserve and even reinforce the sexual division of labour, since enabling women to perform their traditional gender roles more effectively fails to challenge the assumptions of what it is a woman's task to do — tantamount to propping up the system.

The definition of strategic gender interests and needs, as far as long-term change is concerned, is the nub of the gender and development issue. It is also the centre of a cluster of ideas and anxieties about the role of donor organisations, and the right of donors, whether bilateral or NGO, to pursue policies that might lead to structural change in the politics of gender within societies; though it is ironic that few such qualms are raised about structural adjustment, which has equally profound effects on Southern societies.

Strategic gender interests are those derived from an analysis of women's subordination. They point to an alternative, more just, and more satisfactory organisation of society in respect of the relationships between women and men, and the upbringing of children. In this sense, the identification of women's strategic gender interests is part of a feminist strategy directed at changing the existing power relations between women and men which structure all areas of life — the family, education, welfare, the worlds of work and politics, culture and leisure. The areas of change might include some of the following (taken from Moser): 'abolition of the sexual division of labour, the alleviation of the burden of domestic labour and child care, the removal of institutionalised forms of discrimination, the establishment of political equality, freedom of choice over childbearing, and the adoption of adequate measures against male violence and control over women.'[17]

It is clear that only two of the various approaches to women-in-development that we have looked at could operate in favour of women's long-term strategic interests — the equity and the empowerment approaches; and of these, empowerment may be the most effective at bringing about the kinds of transformation envisaged.

This analysis raises some important questions about the nature of the development process itself; above all, the question of what, for women, development actually is. Answering this question reveals a dilemma, and echoes a theme that has occurred again and again in feminist debate since the nineteenth century. This is the question of whether women are to achieve liberation — or in the terms of this discussion, development — on the basis of their similarity to men, or their difference from men. The equity approach, as we have seen, argues that the way forward is to enable women to participate on the same basis as men, by upgrading women's skills so that they can lift themselves out of the informal sector, and become a part of the wage-earning economy. In this view, women are not already central to development, but peripheral. By 'de-gendering' them they can become 'as men' in the development process.

The contrasting view, asserting women's centrality to development, calls for a proper recognition and valuation of women's traditional work (by including it in figures for GNP, for example). At its most radical, it argues for the recovery of the 'feminine principle' in development. In their traditional gender roles, women have pursued forms of development which are environmentally sensitive, ecologically sound, sustainable, life-enhancing, and just. This view of women's development calls for a revival of the means of preserving and protecting that work, rather than challenging it.

The conflict between these two models seems irreconcilable. On the one hand, we have a picture of women's development in which, for example, well-paid, trained women contractors in pursuit of government policy decided by women as well as men, work on a commercial wood-pulp project to increase the per capita consumption of paper — sometimes seen as an indication of development. On the other, we have village women embracing 'their' trees to demonstrate to male forest contractors the importance of trees to the community. Those who uphold the centrality of women's role in 'good' development would probably argue that for women to cut down trees or build dams would be an example of women's co-option into 'maldevelopment', based on principles of economic expansionism, ecological exploitation and neo-colonialism. The counter argument is that women have for too long been denied the material rewards of development, and to insist on their ideological purity effectively works as another way of ghettoising them — another manifestation of paternalism.

It is not only Southern writers who pursue the idea of a revaluation of women's traditional gender role as a basis for a better kind of development. Kate Young, for example, argues that women's activities around producing and raising children are 'nowhere recognised as being of the same order of importance as those directed to the production of things... So one starting point for a feminist critique of development must be that the production or maintenance of things in no way should take precedence over the production and maintenance of people. And that planning for economic growth must give equal weight to the production and maintenance of human beings and of social relationships as to the production and distribution of goods and services.' [18]

Young goes further and argues that development practitioners should build development models around such 'feminine' characteristics as altruism, co-operation and sociability, enhancing them rather than minimising them. There remains the question as to how far development practitioners can affect human behaviour, particularly that rooted in gender roles, which goes beyond the question of individual volition to the structures of society itself.

International gender politics

To advocate this kind of strategic change raises another important issue which has already been touched on in this chapter: the 'right' of outsiders to intervene in the internal gender politics of another society. It is sometimes argued that changes in gender roles and relations are a current western feminist obsession, and should not be imposed on the traditional cultures of Third World countries. An elegant paper by Sara Hlupekile Longwe, a consultant in women's development based in Lusaka, makes the point that all forms of development funding are forms of intervention, since all follow the same pattern of taking a deliberate action to change a situation which would otherwise remain unchanged. Whether the intervention is on behalf of the poor, or on behalf of women, it is intervention in the political structure of the recipient community.

Longwe also makes the point that all member states of the United Nations have assented to the Nairobi Forward-Looking Strategies. They have thus committed themselves to: '...take the relevant steps to ensure that men and women enjoy equal rights, opportunities and responsibilities', and have assented to the fact that 'for true equality to become a reality for women, the sharing of power on equal terms with men must be a major strategy'. For Longwe, the question of women's equality is not simply a development issue, but a human rights issue. The 1979 UN Convention on the Elimination of All Forms of Discrimination Against Women (which by 1987, 94 out of 171 countries had ratified) makes this clear.[19]

BRIAN BEARDWOOD/OXFAM

Oxfam woman project worker in Chad, talking to members of a women's pastoralist group. Sensitive ways of working with women, which respect their culture and the demands on their time, can encourage them to express their needs and challenge and change their situation.

Another argument frequently put forward against gender-based intervention is that women in the Third World are quite content with their position in society and do not want equality with men. This view fails to take into account the fact that the worldwide women's movement has been growing steadily, and that now much of the vitality of the movement, and much of its cutting edge, comes from women in the South. Many countries of the South have traditions of women's protest with roots in their national liberation movements. In the last 15 years particularly, much gender and development thinking has come from the South, as the women's movement has increased in size and as more women's organisations and NGOs with a feminist focus have come into being. There has also been a huge surge in research and thinking by and for Southern women, with a result that the agenda for development is increasingly being set by women's groups in Third World countries, though their ideas and voices are often drowned out by the official machinery of development.

The argument that women in the Third World are already content ignores the fact that millions of women have never had an opportunity to question their lot, and to ask why they have to work so hard for so little reward, be beaten, have so many children and watch some of them die, be so poor, and submit to the will of their fathers and husbands. Resignation in the face of a lack of alternatives is often the best way to survive. Oxfam's experience of working with women the world over shows that, given the opportunity and the support, and sensitive ways of working which respect culture and women's pace, women readily question the reasons that their lives are as they are and, far from being content, seek out ways of challenging and changing their situation.

Models of transformation: engendering change

Thinking about women in development means envisaging a situation in which the ills of the present are transformed. The process of planning for women's strategic gender needs is all about engendering models of change. An empowerment approach means that models of change have to be generated by women themselves. (No external foreign funding agent could have dictated the kind of changes that the paper pickers of Ahmedabad needed to make to start their process of empowerment, for example.) We will now look at just some of the models of change and transformation that have been developed in the last decade.

DAWN

A frequently quoted document in recent women-in-development literature is the book put out by DAWN, *Development, Crises and*

Alternative Visions. Their alternative vision provides a picture of transformation that has been echoed widely by the women's movement worldwide:

> We want a world where inequality based on class, gender, and race is absent from every country, and from the relationships among countries. We want a world where basic needs become basic rights and where poverty and all forms of violence are eliminated. Each person will have the opportunity to develop her or his full potential and creativity, and women's values of nurturance and solidarity will characterise human relationships. In such a world women's reproductive role will be redefined: child care will be shared by men, women, and society as a whole. We want a world where the massive resources now used in the production of the means of destruction will be diverted to areas where they will help to relieve oppression both inside and outside the home. This technological revolution will eliminate disease and hunger, and give women means for the safe control of their fertility. We want a world where all institutions are open to participatory democratic processes, where women share in determining priorities and making decisions... The transformations of the structures of subordination that have been so inimical to women is the other part of our vision of a new era. Changes in law, civil codes, systems of property rights, control over our bodies, labour codes, and the social and legal institutions that underwrite male control and privilege are essential if women are to attain justice in society. The consequences of the prevalent injustices and inequities in terms of women's health, work burden, access to employment and income, and even mortality rates are well documented. Only by sharpening the links between equality, development, and peace can we show that the 'basic rights' of the poor and the transformation of the institutions that subordinate women are inextricably linked. They can be achieved together through the self-empowerment of women.'[20]

What is novel about this message is the people who are saying it and those whose interests they represent — women of the Third World, who are committed to changing structures nationally and internationally. DAWN's strategy for change involves restoring to women control over the economic decisions that shape their lives, and using grassroots women's organisations as forums for working out policy that incorporates the experiences and concerns of poor women.

In the economic sphere, they argue that the needs of the poor must become central to the planning process, and advocate policies that return countries to self-sufficiency in food and energy, health care, water provision and education. This would involve a shift away from export-led production in agriculture and industry. Cuts in military spending and control of multinationals are seen by DAWN as not only necessary in themselves, but also a step towards removing the inequalities within countries. Land reforms which give women equal status with men are another vital part of the strategy.

Realising the vision depends on political mobilisation, legal changes, consciousness raising and popular education, and DAWN looks to an international movement of 'women and the oppressed'. DAWN is well aware of the problems that will be faced in pursuit of development that puts the needs of poor women first; they realise that they are proposing not a programme for women alone, but a much broader one. For DAWN, self-empowerment is the only way for women to bring about the kind of society they envision.

The wisdom approach

One woman who has tried to make an alternative vision more concrete is Peggy Antrobus. In her paper, 'Women in Development' she outlines five elements for an alternative, gender-sensitive analysis, which she calls the wisdom approach. She begins by making the distinction we have already looked at, between change at a strategic level and approaches that maintain the *status quo*. Her second point is that experience at the micro level (community, project, or household) should be used to inform macro-level policies, and vice versa. Thirdly, the approach must be holistic in order to integrate social, cultural and political dimensions into economic analysis. The fourth point is that the political nature of the processes of development must be acknowledged, and also that the causes of development and 'underdevelopment' lie in 'imbalances of power within and between nations rather than the presence or absence of resources'. Finally, Antrobus calls for 'an analysis which is feminist in orientation. We need to reject the separation of private and public domains; of the household from the economy; of personal and political realities; of the realms of feeling and intuition from that of rationality; above all we need to reject an analysis which lies within the monetised sector of the economy.'

The effect of this kind of analysis should be the development of 'feminism as a transformational politics, with the capacity to transform not only individual lives, but all the structures of oppression and domination which shape women's lives, including racism, class and nationality'. For Antrobus, this kind of analysis leads to a transformation in the concept of feminism, since it is seen as a tool not only for the transformation of women's lives, but 'for our world'.[21]

A perspective from India

In her book *Staying Alive*, Vandana Shiva sums up her alternative vision like this:

> Recovering the feminine principle as respect for life in nature and society appears to be the only way forward, for men as well as women, in the North as well as the South...[the] dominant mode of organising the world today is being challenged by the very voices it had silenced. These voices, muted through subjugation, are now quietly but firmly suggesting that the Western male has produced only one culture, and that there are other ways of structuring the world. Women's struggles for survival through the protection of nature are... challenging the central belief of the dominant worldview that nature and women are worthless and waste, that they are obstacles to progress and must be sacrificed.
>
> The two central shifts in thinking that are being induced by women's ecological struggles relate to economic and intellectual worth. The shift relates to our understanding of what constitutes knowledge, and who the knowers and producers of intellectual value are. The second involves concepts of wealth and economic value and who the producers of wealth and economic value are. Women producing survival are showing us that nature is the very basis and matrix of economic life through its function in life-support and livelihood... They are challenging concepts of waste, rubbish and dispensability as the modern West has defined them. They are showing that production of sustenance is basic to survival itself and cannot be deleted from economic calculations: if production of life cannot be reckoned with in money terms, then it is economic models, and not women's work in producing sustenance and life, that must be sacrificed...By elbowing out 'life' from being the central concern in organising human society, the dominant paradigm of knowledge has become a threat to life itself. Third World women are bringing the concern with living and survival back to the centre-stage of human history.

Shiva shares the view put forward in the DAWN manifesto: that it has to be those missed out of the debate so far — the poorest women of the world — whose perspective informs the debate now. We should listen to the poor women of the world because, as we have already seen, they do the majority of the work in the world, hold households together, and are the key to sustainable development in the South. Shiva's perspective on ecology, survival and the environment offers an urgent and cogent analysis of development. She, too, touches on the dichotomy of 'things versus people', or the production of life versus the production of commodities, and refuses to accept that human value is measurable only by what we accumulate and possess.

A Central American manifesto

The Fifth Latin American and Caribbean Feminist Encounter was held in 1990, around the theme of feminism as a movement of 'transformation, evaluation and perspective'. One of the delegates at the Encounter was the poet Elizabeth Alvarez (an Oxfam project partner), whose account 'The feminism of 90s in Central America' was published in the journal *Otra Guatemala* in February 1991. The extract below is Alverez's account of the manifesto of the women of Central America which grew out of the Encounter.

> [They] manifested their hope for peace, noting that this cannot be reduced to the silencing of weapons but must be a peace which democratises all spheres of life (private and public). They spoke of peace as the struggle for a new quality of life, where women are not subordinated to others and no one appropriates their actions. They spoke of peace which allows women to decide if they want to be mothers or not and how many children to have, peace where women do not die after illicit abortions, where children are a family and social responsibility, of peace where violence and rape are not a daily trap, of peace which eliminates the sexual hierarchy and allows women equal conditions for training and development, of peace which denies illiteracy among women and among all, of peace which will destroy the triple oppression of women... They spoke of peace which guarantees air to breathe to all, peace which is inclusive and not sectarian, peace which allows the elimination of all types of authoritarianism and which eliminates patriarchy and its free play in all spheres of society...This is the feminism [which] is growing in both Latin America and a world context...there is a feminist memory which bears witness to a reality leading to the construction of a new social subject in the conti-

nent and which, beyond its specific struggle against patriarchy, is essentially bound to the struggle against exploitation and all forms of oppression and discrimination.

Conclusion: empowerment and change

In considering how attitudes to women in the development process have changed and are changing, it is clear that the different approaches over the years reflect fundamentally different views both of appropriate develpment paradigms and of women's social and economic roles. A failure to consider women as individuals with particular needs, rights, and abilities, will only result in an increase in women's workloads and levels of stress, rather than an improvement in their status and range of choices. It is important to recognise that, unless the root causes of women's subordination are addressed, and their own stated needs prioritised, development projects and programmes involving women will not lead to significant and lasting improvements in their lives.

8

SOME PRACTICAL ISSUES IN DEVELOPMENT

As a first stage, a few small projects sprang up which helped to lighten the workload of women to some small degree. However, the huge theoretical speeches have not led to great changes in women's lives. The second stage was to set up income-generation projects, with talk of empowering women. But these have not in fact generated much income. The third stage was to organise women into collective co-operatives...But there was no assessment of how such collectives might operate in these [African] societies, and they have not worked for the women, who want to have their own individual plots, not to share land collectively with everyone else. All three stages have thus failed. What is said in London, Paris, or Mexico does not bear fruit in Africa: 90–95 per cent of the women in Africa remain 'invisible'.

Lalla Ben Barka, ACORD, in a talk to Oxfam, 1990

...The 1991 [Indian] census furnishes proof, if indeed proof were needed, that women have been short–changed in the development process... The plight of women working in the unorganised sectors is pathetic... The 1991 census is both an eye–opener and a mandate for concrete action...

S. Gangadharan in *The Economic Times*, Thursday, 18 April, 1991

Of course we can change things, but when? I wanted to study, but I couldn't. I wanted to finish my courses and be a professional. But I couldn't study because there wasn't enough money. We'll have to find a way forward.

Rosa, quoted in *Just Ordinary Feminists*

Linking women's experience to development projects

We travelled for about three hours this morning to reach the project where, according to the project application form, the women were well-organised into small meeting groups — sangams — and "mobilising for social change". We spent the first hour of our visit sitting with the project holder — male, very articulate — who described all the activities that he and his team (also present but very silent unless spoken to) have been doing since funding from Oxfam started. After lunch, cooked by women team members, some of whom missed the morning session as a consequence, we went to visit some villages. They were obviously well-prepared for our arrival. The women were in their beautiful embroidered tribal dress and as soon as we drove up began to dance — a complicated circle dance with much banging of sticks. They danced for the best part of an hour. When at last we sat down to talk they had much to say. How could they make their lives easier? Did we understand that their poverty was increasing, rather than decreasing? Why was there less rain now than ever before? Yes, they met in their sangam every week; they had revived their traditional dancing; they shared their problems, but this didn't solve them. One elderly woman with astonishingly white hair and a deeply lined face gesticulated her frustration with the slowness of change and the arduousness of their lives. Somehow the project is passing the real needs of these women by. But what can one project do? These women need to make a living for themselves and their families. They need an income to solve the problems of acute and chronic poverty. Yet in this isolated tribal village, in a denuded forest area, what possible means of earning an income can there be?

Author's diary entry, 11 January 1988, South India.

How can development be made to work for those for whom it is intended? The diary entry above must be typical of many project reports of many hundreds of field visits where the real needs of people are not being met. In the project above, those running the projects had decided, rather paternalistically, that encouraging women to revive their traditional tribal dances was the best starting point for social change, yet the project's work with men tended to focus on income generation. The women, however, also wanted an income, a way of dealing with their poverty, rather than being offered a way of maintaining their traditional gender role as cultural guardians of tribal customs. Of course it is possible that reviving a sense of cultural distinctiveness would give the women a social cohesiveness with which to begin to tackle their other problems, and the revival of danc- ing might prove a good first step towards this. But at the time, the women certainly felt that there was a long way to go.

In this chapter, the focus will be on practical project experience and the way in which gender-sensitive planning has been developed in different sectors. Limitations of space mean that this chapter cannot do justice to the variety of gender-sensitive projects and programmes developed in the last decade; consequently the focus in the last part of the chapter is on just three areas of project and programme experience — the gender needs of women refugees; gender and housing; and gender and health. Underlying any form of project designed to address women's gender needs lies the question of their participation, particularly the barriers to participation. The first part of the chapter looks at issues surrounding women's participation, including the ways in which some projects have addressed questions of self-esteem and confidence building among women. The chapter also looks briefly at the crucial issue of why women organise, and the role of social organisation as a means of social change.

Women and participation

Women face a multitude of barriers to participation. This is one of the clearest lessons that has come out of the last decade of women's organisation. A study in Costa Rica demonstrated the existence of these barriers. Women who belonged to one of three types of organi- sation; productive (directed at income generation); community (directed at obtaining services for the community); and political (ori- ented to a political party) were interviewed and asked to answer a questionnaire. One of the first observations made by the study was that the deteriorating quality of life caused by the overall crisis in Costa Rica was particularly felt by Costa Rica's poorest women, and affected their involvement in organisations. The first constraint to par- ticipation documented by the Costa Rican study was women's domes- tic work, particularly in the context of economic crisis. When poor women also have to earn an income to support families they may expand their working day to as much as 17 hours, or more, leaving no time for anything other than sleep. Another major constraint was the cult of *machismo*: 'sexist cultural patterns' which 'limit the effective participation of women'; '*machismo* is a form of discrimination against women across the whole structure of society... It affects the sexual, procreative, labour and emotional life of women and determines the relationship they have with their partners... [and] between a man and his family.'¹ An additional barrier was the women's own negative perception of themselves, itself a reflection of the social and economic context. The study found that the anxiety of women to fulfil their roles as mothers and carers, and their concern for the well-being of their children, permeated every aspect of their lives. They were too tired and too overworked, and it was this, and the guilt at neglecting their family, that prevented them spending time in political and community organisations. The women also expressed their frustration at not being able to fulfil their potential, at having married 'too young', at having had too many children, at having missed out on opportunities for education.

The most important conclusion the study reached was that it is only possible to understand the nature of women's participation in organisations when the barriers to that participation are recognised. Once these barriers are recognised, appropriate work can be started to overcome them and, for many women's organisations, addressing these issues is one of the most important areas of their work.

The following case study illustrates how one women's organisation in Honduras, Central America, addressed the problem of women's negative self–perception. It grew out of the realisation of one women's perception that before women became involved in activities to improve their material circumstances, they needed to begin to develop self–esteem.

CASE STUDY: 'Getting to know myself': a women's educational programme in Honduras, Central America

If I don't know who I am,
If I don't know what my virtues are.
Or my strengths and abilities,
Then nor do I know
My weaknesses and shortcomings,
I can't value myself for what I am,
I have no self-respect, I don't even like myself.

I need to get to know myself
So that I can grow and develop as a person.
If I know myself better,

I can help other people.
And I'll be able
To help myself.

This is the voice of women from Honduras, expressed in a training manual written by and for women, whose voices are rarely heard and whose needs are seldom articulated. Poor women in Honduras live demanding and difficult lives; unable to migrate to look for work on the banana and sugar plantations, many women work tiny plots of marginal land in the mountainous regions of the western provinces, cultivating a subsistence crop of maize. beans, and the occasional coffee shrub. Woman-maintained households are common, yet land reform laws rarely favour women. From birth onwards girls imbibe the values of *machismo* culture and grow up believing that they were born to serve others — their children, their husbands and other menfolk. The socialisation of rural women makes it extremely difficult for them to put their own needs first, or to even recognise that they have legitimate needs.

In 1985, an organisation called the Women's Educational Programme (PAEM) began its work under the auspices of the Catholic Church. Its coordinator, Maria Esther Ruiz, came to believe that one of the main constraints on women grew out of the culture in which they were socialised, a constraint that lay first and foremost within their own minds: 'From when we're tiny they told us so often that we're stupid, that we ended up believing it...Fear stops us thinking properly, so we make mistakes. It's fear that makes us get things wrong. It's not because we're stupid.' The consistent failure of 'projects for women' — whether welfare projects, income–generation or food–for–work projects — reinforces the same message: 'women are too stupid to want to improve themselves.'

The idea of producing a manual grew slowly over several years, and Maria Esther Ruiz was supported in particular by Luisa Maria Rivera Izabal, currently working for Oxfam in Mexico and Central America. The two women developed a methodology for working with small groups of semi-literate women. The group coordinator reads passages aloud and passes round photographs to encourage free discussion. The women begin to consider power relations which work against them but which they have always considered to be natural. A range of techniques, such as role play and group work, encourage the women and their children to become fully involved.

Most of the problems we have
Are the same as the ones which other women in the community
have got.
We need to break out of our individualism,
We need to join with other women
Who have the same problems
And the same concerns.

Getting to know myself is essentially about enabling women to find a language with which to talk about shared experiences encoded in their gender role, their sexuality and the oppression they suffer because of it. It is a step in giving women back their right to themselves.[2]

Women organising

Women the world over are organising; and funding agencies of all types are looking for effective women's organisations to support. Since the start of the UN Decade, organisations of women working for change, for incomes, for support and solidarity have mushroomed, and much of their work is proving highly effective. Womankind Worldwide, for example, states its support for women's groups because 'it has been found that initiatives developed by women themselves are potentially stronger, more adaptable and more sustainable than projects undertaken on their behalf...the support of women's organisations is the key to development for women and can make an enormous contribution to society as a whole.'[3] Oxfam supports women's organisations working on local issues the world over, and also broader coalitions of women's groups working for change in a wider context.

What are women's organisations and how do they function? DAWN identifies at least six different types of organisation ranging from the very traditional to those with a specifically feminist analysis and agenda. First there are the traditional women's organisations, often of long standing (the Women's Institute in Britain would be a good example of this type). Such organisations tend to cohere around traditional gender roles, though they have made significant achievements in the areas of women's education, health and related services. They are also supported largely by middle–class women, and may have a patronising, 'welfare' approach to poorer working women. Their strength lies in their access to resources and policy–makers, though they may not always exploit these links. Secondly, there are those groups affiliated to a political party, such as the women's wing of the ANC in South Africa. Such organisations may have problems asserting an agenda of their own, out of fear of being seen as divisive. Thirdly, there are the worker-based organisations, including both trade unions of workers in the formal sector, and the growing number of organisations of poor self-employed women, such as SEWA in India. They usually start by addressing issues such as conditions of employment and availability of credit, but may move on to a more explicitly feminist agenda, such as childcare, sexual harassment at work and so on. DAWN argues that such organisations tend to be very successful at empowering poor women in their own personal life situations.

A fourth type of organisation has flourished in the years since the UN Decade was launched, arising from project funding; credit co-operatives, income-generating projects, and other initiatives for poor women. Many such organisations suffer from structural weaknesses and a top-down approach. A stronger kind of organisation is the fifth type identified by DAWN: those grassroots organisations which, while again related to a specific project, tend to look at issues such as health, literacy, violence, legal issues, and broader political questions, often from a feminist perspective. DAWN sees the weakness of such groups lying in an inadequate resource base, and in the fact that they tend to have a middle-class, urban membership and perspective. On the other hand, those which succeed in building genuine links with poor working women have considerable potential. Finally, the sixth type of organisation is the research and resource organisations, which have sprung up in recent years; such groups have considerable opportunities to influence public policy debates and to feed into the work of international funding agencies and governments. At best they are committed to breaking down the traditional gulf between the researcher and researched. At worst they fail to challenge standard research methods, where only the researcher benefits from the work. Alongside these six types are a whole range of other organisations not so easily classified.[4] Groups that come together on single issues, such as peace camps, or umbrella organisations that link up women working in different sectors, would come in here, as would women's cultural and religious organisations, for example, the 'secret' societies, still strong in some African countries, such as Sierra Leone.[5] Many of the women's organisations supported by Oxfam fall slightly outside DAWN's six categories. For example, Oxfam supports many groups that organise for subsistence. A specific example would be the housewives committees formed, particularly in many Latin American countries, in order to ensure family survival in times of severe economic crisis. This form of organising, essentially on the basis of women's reproductive role, may lead in time to women playing a role in policy development and campaigns for state services (as the Brazilian example on page 184 illustrates). Such committees are an important space for women, in which they can begin to develop their skills as leaders, and prepare for greater control in the public domain.[6] Another important form of women's organisation are those that exist to resist oppression and the abuses of human rights. In Latin America such organisations have often been the starting point of poor women organising. Taken together, these organisations have built up enormous expertise in organisation for change, and produce a considerable quantity of journals, books and pamphlets as material, tangible evidence of their activity.

Further evidence of their effectiveness becomes clearer when we look at the particular strengths of women's groups. Caroline Moser argues that 'historically it has been shown that the capacity to confront the nature of gender inequality...can only be fulfilled by the bottom-up struggle of women's organisations.' This is because such grassroots organisations, whether of village women in Bangladesh, or urban women in downtown Rio de Janeiro or Nairobi, offer women who would otherwise have no opportunity for organisation, a space of their own. This space, both physical and conceptual, is the prerequisite for identifying needs and then mobilising to meet them. Women's groups offer a legitimate forum beyond the private, domestic world; membership of an organisation offers an initial substitute for lack of bureaucratic know-how, and inexperience with public discourse. A successful women's organisation encourages in its members a capacity to interact with a wide range of public systems and structures, and in time, is able to transform them into participants in development — active partners in the development of goods, services and resources, rather than passive recipients or 'targets'.

The long-term growth of expertise and confidence within women's organisations, and their increasing effectiveness in the public domain, are key to the process of structural change. Gender inequalities, institutionalised at all levels of society, can only be challenged by this kind of collective action, which reaches from the bottom to the top of society. Chapter 9 looks at the process of linking up and 'scaling up' for broader action in more detail. It is clear that women's organisations in the South have a voice that can no longer be ignored, and an understanding of development that challenges all development paradigms, at the macro and micro levels. Women's organisations are posing questions related to the exercise of power, whether in participatory democracy at grassroots level, in the funding policies of donors, or in the priorities of official development funding. In the process they are proposing horizontal forms of organisation, such as networks, which break with hierarchical and authoritarian structures.

The following case study tells the story of different groups of women organising in North East Brazil, who came together to record their experiences in a book.

⚡ CASE STUDY: 'Why We Should Work with Women'

Why We Should Work with Women is the title of a book, written and published by a group of women in north–east Brazil, with support from Oxfam, who had never contemplated expressing themselves in the public arena until they discovered the collective strength of an organisation of women. In essence the book is a history of their own work in Brazil over the past decade, but a history rooted in an analysis of the gender relationships by which women are defined:

> We are discriminated against by the simple fact of being women, because we have a different body, because we seem to belong to a world that doesn't seem to be as 'concrete' as the male world. Emotions, sexuality and fantasy imprison us in a set of prejudices that are difficult to break down or question. It doesn't matter if we are black, white, poor or rich, young or old, our identity always seems to be defined by a way of seeing the world that is essentially male.

The book, which grew out of the experiences of many different women 'like a huge patchwork quilt' describes and analyses the process of women becoming the catalysts of social change. Through the project, those involved became aware that they had not only a future, but a past: 'We have discovered our history, the history of the rural women workers, of the housewife, the prostitute, the industrial worker, the domestic worker.' The spur to producing the book, however, was the desire to feed the new perspectives gained in a multiplicity of small initiatives — itself the basis of a social movement — into the larger process of 'structural and qualitative change' in Brazilian society.

Some of the work described in the book has already been used as case material in Chapter 3 (page 39) and Chapter 5 (page 103). Both the domestic workers and MMTBP are good examples of women organising for social change. *Why We Should Work with Women* takes the story further, however, and describes the exciting growth of MMTBP as it began to network with other women's groups:

> MMTBP began networking with other groups of workers in the region, and in other states in the country and internationally. In 1985, representatives of the MMTBP took part in the Third Latin American and Caribbean Feminist Meeting in Bertioga S. Paulo...In 1986, the first State meeting of women workers was held in Guarabira bringing together 150 delegates from the whole state, urban and rural, of organised women's groups...Mobilisation and networking...is very important for the consolidation and regeneration of the movement. On these occasions women have to face the public world, exchange experiences and breakdown their isolation.

> If we look at the history over these last ten years we can see that there have been real gains. The most obvious is that the women have come to understand that they have their own identity, and that they are representatives of a new social force. This awareness encourages their greater social participation as they seek to inform themselves more. The advances cannot be denied, but it is still necessary to widen the work to reach a larger number of women...Finally it is crucial to link the town and country, as well as secure financial autonomy...The great challenge is thus to integrate a feminist perspective within the analysis and strategies of class struggle...[7]

Practical project experience

The effectiveness of women's groups in organising for change has been illustrated many times in this book. The following section looks at some of the gender issues and analysis that has emerged from development initiatives in three different sectors; work among refugees, in housing, and in health, giving examples of the specific work of NGOs to address these issues at each point.

The gender needs of women refugees

Emergency relief work with refugees has traditionally been very top-down, and has suffered from the idea of 'bringing relief to the poor'. Even in cases where refugees are offered the opportunity of participating in the planning of their own 'relief', women refugees are invariably excluded. The majority of refugee populations the world over are girls and women — up to 70 per cent of UNHCR target populations — and, while refugees are in no senses a homogenous group (compare the different life experiences of nomadic women in a Somali refugee camp with young Tamil girls and women fleeing from Sri Lanka and Guatemalan refugee women in Mexico City), there are certain aspects of their experience as refugees and as women that they share in common. According to the UNHCR Commissioner:

> Refugee women and girls represent the majority of refugee populations in many countries hosting sizeable refugee caseloads today. They, like most refugees, are confronted with the inherent dangers characterising their flight to safety, together with insecurity and often interminable waiting periods in camps pending identification of desirable solutions on their behalf. Yet it is evident that refugee women are doubly disadvantaged for, confronted with the trauma of uprooting, deprived of normal family and community ties, property and personal belongs, they have been forced to assume abrupt changes in role and status. Faced with loss, due to death or frequent absences, of husbands and young male family members, women–headed households are a common phenomenon in many refugee populations today.[8]

CHRIS JOHNSON/OXFAM

Refugees in Mozambique. The majority of refugee populations the world over are girls and women.

Being a woman and a refugee raises specific gender needs: women are more vulnerable to violence, sexual and otherwise, and to coercion, sexual harassment, intimidation, and abuse. Women are the ones who care for the sick, the elderly, the children, and the daily needs of the household, taking on the added burden created by the refugee situation. While women are often heads of households, few programmes for refugees target women as household heads; training and employment opportunities are designed for men. Allocations of food, land, tools, jobs, and legal identity papers go first to men; food rations are often distributed through men, leaving women intensely vulnerable, as male refugees may abuse the power that this gives them. The fact that women are not issued with their own separate legal identity papers adds to their dependency and vulnerability. Women refugees suffer from many health problems, yet still have to do a good deal of heavy work. In the camps in Somalia, researchers report that women refugees have been pushed to the very brink of survival through the combination of a poor diet, the cultural habit of eating only when everyone else has finished, continual childbearing, and the trauma and stress of refugee life.

It is this trauma and stress which is most often neglected in the provision of basic needs for refugees, and it is most often the women who suffer the brunt of the psychological upheaval as they try and settle their families into a completely new way of life. If relief, and subsequent development work with women refugees, is to be effective, the involvement of refugee women in planning and decision-making at the grassroots level is essential. Yet involving women is not easy. Tina Wallace outlines some of the obstacles to women's participation, such as the resistance of men, women's reticence, and acute lack of time available to them for meeting and talking; women's lack of experience in being consulted, and religious and cultural barriers.[9]

The following case study is the story of one Oxfam-funded project that worked specifically to overcome the stress and trauma of refugee life, and which recognised the cultural constraints imposed by the women's gender, actively finding ways of overcoming them and building on the strengths of refugee women.

CASE STUDY: 'Sharing our lives': A project with Guatemalan refugee women

As repression and counter-insurgency took over in Guatemala in 1980, many thousands of men, women and children were faced with the choice of fleeing from Guatemala or dying under the repressive rule of the Guatemalan military government. Many fled the invasion of the Guatemalan army who burnt villages and destroyed crops, and some 200,000 refugees escaped into Mexico, mostly illegally. In 1982 a committee — The Comite de Ayuda a Refugiados Guatemaltecos — was set up to counsel and offer support to the refugee families.

In September 1984 the committee decided to include in its work an explicit focus on the particular gender needs of women, recognising that the tensions and forces shaping women's lives were still unexplored. As a result, a group of 12 women, Indian and *ladinas*, peasant women, workers and housewives, came together in October 1984 to help each other face the problems of being a refugee in Mexico City. In an article 'When broken-heartedness becomes a political issue', Claire Ball outlined some of the loss and dislocation that was specific to the women:

> The need to conceal their origins... forces them to abandon their traditional dress, which in their native Guatemalan community identifies them as a member of a particular village or community. Having to grapple for the first time with unfamiliar zips and fasteners, cumbersome Western clothes; having to awkwardly twist their bodies to carry their babies across their breast instead of on their back, bundles under their arms rather then on their head, are only the physical manifestations of their tremendous trauma, the total loss of cultural and personal identity, which are experienced by Guatemalan women refugees in Mexico City.[10]

Broken-heartedness — *tristeza de corazon* — was recognised by all the women as a symptom of the loss that they shared as a gender, although divided in many other ways along ethnic, linguistic and class lines. They decided to explore their lives by producing a booklet, to give their perspective as women on the need for change in Guatemala and their own role in the process. In working on the booklet they cut across the isolation and fear of going mad that many refugee women experience. They worked to come to terms with the choice they had made — to flee from their own country and adapt to another culture.

> This booklet is the collective work of a group of us who are Guatemalan women refugees now living in Mexico...

> The army arrived at our house. We all left as a family and began to walk through the mountains without even grabbing a jacket to cover ourselves. That night we endured the cold. But all the chil-

dren were crying from the cold, and besides it was the rainy season and we couldn't do more for ourselves than just live through it. That was our first night...

...So long for now, my family. Good-bye my country. Some day we will return to help build a new society where we are all equal and where everyone's life will be respected...

When we were in our own country, we had our traditional dress, but because [of] the governments' manoeuvres... there was no other option left than to seek refuge in another country. But in order to do that we had to change our clothes. We felt it very deeply...Almost all the refugees cried a lot when they took off their traditional clothes and put on dresses, because it makes us feel strange, even to ourselves...We hope that some day our country will be liberated, and we will go back to wearing our traditional dress...we have to take advantage of our time here to study, to learn something new, to prepare ourselves for the return...

I feel depressed. I feel alone; sad. We should meet more often to talk about our problems and help one another. In order to begin to find mature solutions to our problems, we should try to meet with each other, talk about our problems, analyse them, look at our capabilities and begin to act positively...As capable, conscious, dignified people, we can contribute in making our country great.

The insights into the need for mental health provision that grew out of the process of producing the booklet encouraged the committee to set up a training scheme for mental health promoters, to work specifically with Guatemalan women refugees and their children. The idea was to train eight to ten refugee women who could then facilitate small groups of refugee women 'to deal in a healthful way' with their psychological and physical needs in the context of their past experiences — as victims of considerable trauma and terror — and in the light of their present needs in adapting to life in Mexico City.

The women refugees from Guatemala experienced specific difficulties on account of their gender roles; as mothers of traumatised children, as wives of partners who had been shot or had disappeared; as the pivotal person in the family struggling to keep the unit together. The mental health of these women, their anxiety, their trauma, their broken-heartedness, was a specific gender need that they alone were competent to judge and diagnose. As one report describes their lives: 'most of these women's life–plans spanned hardly more than a segment of 24 hours at any one time. Always their energies were suspended, awaiting the decisions for their lives to be made by the *companero*, the organisation, or an embassy.'[11] The women wanted space and time to deal with their mental and physical health, wanted and needed the space to work out for themselves the best way of caring for themselves as mothers and as women.

Gender and housing

Nearly one quarter of the world's population, some one billion people, is reckoned to be homeless or inadequately housed. Building houses and creating human settlements has consequently been an important part of development work in the last three decades, but work that has not kept pace with the urgency of the need.

Planning human settlements and developing low–cost housing is an area in which sensitivity to the different gender needs of women and men has been recognised as an important issue. The recognition that housing is 'much more than the buildings we see around us'[12] has focused attention on the different ways in which women and men use their dwelling space. Women's domestic responsibilities — maintaining and caring for members of a household — make the internal design, site and physical structure of a house matter to women in a way that they do not to the men of a household. In the growing number of female-headed households, women take on all the responsibility for household management, with added demands on the way they use their homes.

Until recently, few housing projects really considered the consequences of this, whether in the designing and building of new houses, or in the planning of infrastructural amenities such as water systems and sanitation. The dominant model followed by development planners and policy makers was of a married couple and two or three children sharing a single housing unit. As the social fabric of many countries change, and women head their own households, this model is no longer (if it ever was) appropriate. At the same time, the question of women's strategic gender needs — their long–term needs to gain access to and control over human settlements — raises another set of questions.

The documenting of inappropriate human settlements, which have not taken account even of women's practical gender needs, has produced a sizeable dossier of material, covering such things as the overall planning of settlements to the details of internal arrangements of houses. Moser cites an example of an upgrading project at George in

Lusaka, Zambia where the roads and plots were laid out in a grid pattern. The traditional layout of the settlements had been circular, and had enabled women to do their housework within sight of each other. The new layout forced them to work in more isolated conditions; they could no longer leave their houses unlocked if they went out, or trust that their playing children would be safe under the watchful eyes of neighbours. In an example of inappropriate sanitation design in a project in El Salvador, women were unable to use toilets designed by male engineers because the gap at the bottom of the door left their feet exposed and thus failed to guard their privacy. In countries where Muslim codes of practice restrict the movement of women, the amount of space available in the internal courtyard of the house may be of paramount importance to the happiness of the women. In two low-income settlements in Tunis, women were depressed and unhappy because of the small size of the inner courtyard; the projects had adopted the European ideal of space around the outside of the house.[13]

Women are seldom given the right of tenure, yet without tenure women are unable to protect themselves or their children from domestic violence or oppression. Without rights to property, women are vulnerable in the event of separation; they either end up homeless, or become dependent on another male relative, if one is available. When public facilities are being allocated, women may well be the last ones to be consulted, even on aspects which directly affect them, such as the siting of water and sanitation facilities.

Resettlement decisions may have extremely disruptive consequences for women's livelihoods. Moser cites a massive relocation of 700,000 people from Delhi squatter settlements into 17 new settlements on the outskirts of the city. In Dakshinpuri, one such settlement with over 60,000 people, the women were much more affected than the men, with over a quarter of the women losing their productive work compared to only 5 per cent of the men. Women found that the cost of public transport between their workplaces and their new homes was too great, and their work was no longer feasible. The pressures of organising childcare, transport, and continuing their domestic work, was just too much to cope with.[14]

The acute and growing shortage of housing has generated a number of debates as to the best way of dealing with the problem. The mushrooming of shanty towns the world over has produced a whole range of 'solutions'. One response has been to bulldoze shanty towns and clean up the 'slum' by simply destroying it. The short–sightedness of this policy is reflected in the fact that those who live in the shanty towns are central to the working of the urban economies, providing many of the services that make life tolerable for the middle classes. In the last decade, a growing recognition of the economic contribution made by shanty-town dwellers, and their right to adequate housing, has led to a switch in policy to upgrading existing housing, usually by providing security of tenure and assistance in improving properties. This approach can work well but, unless it is managed with a degree of gender sensitivity, tenancy may still automatically be offered to men; men may be employed to rebuildthe houses, rather than women being equipped with appropriate skills.

Many of the most successful housing projects have worked from the premise that women, because of the importance of their homes to them, and their role as community managers, make the best builders. At the same time, by involving women in the physical construction of housing, stereotyped ideas about women's work are challenged. The best of these projects can succeed in both meeting women's practical gender needs, and furthering their strategic gender interests by challenging the assumptions of what women can and cannot do.

The next case study illustrates the role that women can play and have played in creating new settlements for themselves, their families, and their communities.

CASE STUDY: Women and housing in El Salvador

Fundasal, 'the Low Cost Housing Foundation', is an NGO which has been working in El Salvador with community groups to provide low-cost, self-built housing, since the 1970s. Civil war and a major earthquake have added to an already enormous demand for housing. Fundasal facilitates the planning, organising and construction of the houses, and provides the building materials. The communities themselves do the building, with a member of each household becoming a member of the building team. It takes four months to build 25–35 houses, and the new residents gradually pay back to Fundasal the cost of materials, and when they have done so, the house is theirs.

Fundasal stresses that it had no specific brief to work with women, but has found that women have played a very active and important part in housebuilding. According to Celina Gomez, one of the engineers who works with Fundasal, women have been found to be adaptable, hard-working, capable, and more likely to pay back the loan for building materials.

An example of Fundasal self-help schemes is one in a community called El Jardin, of victims of the 1965 earthquake in El Salvador. Over time, what was supposed to be temporary housing became a typical shanty town community, with 140 families living in wooden shacks. In 1985, the government agency which owned the land started a process of eviction of the community of El Jardin, who turned to Fundasal for support. A legal process was begun to enable the community to become recognised, with judicial status, and a committee of 71 heads of families — 61 of whom were women — was set up. Women also took a major role in the community council. In May 1986, with support from Fundasal, a major rehousing project started; again, women assumed the leadership of the building activities, despite a myriad other duties. Six work groups were formed for building houses, each one with a co-ordinator, secretary, treasurer, and warehouse-keeper. Five of the groups were co-ordinated by women and three had women warehouse-keepers.

There was no part of the demolition and rebuilding processes that did not involve women. They were taught all the skills needed to enable them to build their own houses. According to Celina Gomez, women showed themselves to be the decisive element in the project, not only in physical terms, through that was crucial, but also in the social development of the community. Because women assumed the administrative, organisational, and co-ordinating functions, this helped to close the gender gap between women and men, and between planners and builders. Once the women were clear in their own minds that they were working for land tenure, and new, permanent houses, they overcame all the problems caused by childcare and other household tasks.

Fundasal now prefers to work with women, because of their effectiveness. It also recognises that education to raise women's awareness is a vital part of a successful project.[15]

Gender and health

Many women in the South are not in good health. But the reasons for ill–health are frequently to be found in the gender role women play, which leads to more sickness and less opportunity for recovery than the gender role of men. Health is determined by gender, class, and ethnicity, but many analyses of health and well-being fail to recognise the complex factors determining who will be well and who will not. The ill-health of women starts from birth, when son-preference and poverty may make a significant difference to the diet and opportunities for growth and development offered to little girls. Boys are, particularly in Asia, breastfed for longer and more frequently than their sisters. One study in Bangladesh found that boys received 16 per cent more energy–providing food than girls, and in the 5-14 age range, 11 per cent more. Studies in countries as diverse as Bolivia, Iran, and India have found that levels of malnutrition are significantly higher among girls, with the result that more girls than boys die between the ages of one and four. One study suggests that one in every six deaths of female infants in India, Pakistan and Bangladesh is due to discriminatory practices,[16] while a study carried out in the Punjab by three doctors in which they studied the progress of 1,500 infants found that the female child who was high priority was the first–born, so long as she was the only living child. They reported that in 'underprivileged' households the response to the nutritional and health needs of the third and fourth females was often 'let her die'.[17] Similarly, boys are invariably taken to doctors more rapidly than girls, while girls (and their mothers) tend to rely on local healers.

In many societies of the world it is customary for women and girls to eat after men and boys, so that even when women are pregnant and lactating, they may be inadequately fed, leading to anaemia and malnutrition. Chronic sickness is often regarded as a 'natural' part of being a woman; miscarriages caused by undernourishment, hard

JOHN OGLE/OXFAM

Cooking over a smoky open fire or stove is a health hazard for many Southern women.

work and frequent pregnancies, are seen as a 'normal' part of woman-hood. The hard physical work performed by Southern women brings health hazards; carrying water and wood can, over a life-time, lead to intensely painful strains and more serious problems such as prolapse of the uterus and damage to the spine. Old women bent double from the burden of their working days are a common sight in Third World villages. Women's traditional gender role involves cooking, usually over smoky fires in confined spaces, yet smoky stoves offer the same health hazards as heavy smoking — again a major problem for pregnant women who may produce lower birth-weight babies as a result. Women suffer health hazards in their productive work, ranging from exposure to pesticides and waterborne diseases in their farming work, to damaged eyesight and exposure to toxic chemicals in the electronic and microelectronic industries. Women who make their living through providing sexual services are exposed to violence and sexually transmitted diseases.[18]

Historically, developmental approaches to women's health have taken the primary health care route, with a focus on maternal–and–child–health, nutrition advice, and information and education on common health problems. While the need to prevent the half–million maternal deaths each year is obviously vital, it is not only as mothers that women need health care; women have needs for health care at times when they are not pregnant. The need not to become a mother (again and again) requires the provision of contraception, in a context which empowers rather than coerces. The treatment of diseases of the reproductive tract, including sexually transmitted diseases and AIDS, require comprehensive health care for women. A clinic in Bolivia found that 90 per cent of the women they tested were suffering from infections in their reproductive tract; the high rate of cervical cancer in India and other parts of the South is another example of a specifically woman's health issue that is as yet unaddressed.

Primary health care focuses on safe pregnancy and delivery, but worldwide perhaps as many as a third of all pregnancies are terminated; free, safe abortions are not available to many women in the South, with a resulting death toll which remains largely uncharted, although it is highly probable that a third or more of all maternal deaths recorded each year are the result of botched abortions.

In a paper on women and health, Claudia Garcia Moreno and Eugenia Piza Lopez argue that there is a link between women's reproductive role, their sexuality and their oppression.[19] They also suggest

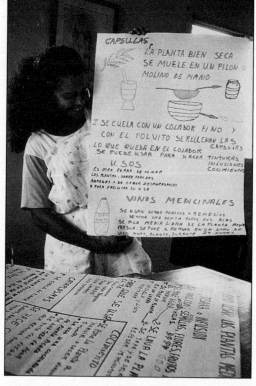

NEIL MACDONALD/OXFAM

Health as empowerment is the approach adopted by many women's groups. Simple, effective visual aid to illustrate nutrition issues, in a seminar organised by Casa de la Mujer, a women's health project in the Dominican Republic.

that it is only when women begin to increase control of their bodies and themselves that they 'begin to organise towards increasing controls over the structures that enslave them'.[20] This complex web of relationships — sexuality, reproduction, women's self-perception, and the oppression that they may feel, for many women experienced as routine violence — lies far outside the parameters of most primary health-care projects; silence surrounds sexuality, and many women never have the opportunity of learning about the processes of reproduction. Yet the connections between women taking control of their bodies, and the other areas of their lives, have been cogently argued by the women's health movement. Similarly, an understanding of the way in which ill-health is rooted in deprivation and poor working conditions, and in that sense, is socially constructed, enables women to begin to organise to change the circumstances that are making them sick. Women working in the microelectronic industry in Singapore, for example, have refused to carry out certain hazardous processes and, because of a shrinking labour pool, employers have responded by improving working conditions.[21] The Self Employed Women's Association in India encouraged women embroidery workers to organise themselves to have regular eye checks, and obtain spectacles if necessary.[22]

This broader, gender-sensitive analysis of ill-health and well-being is an illuminating example of feminist thinking in development. It argues that health is, above all, an issue in which the personal is political. It sees the connections between the most intimate experiences of a woman's life, her sexuality, her self-perceptions, and explains them in the context of a gender role in which she may be expected to accept violence, coercion, continuous childbearing; family relationships are then set in a broader social context of poverty, deprivation, class, ethnicity, but one in which gender still plays a pivotal part. The women's health movement has traced these connections backwards and forwards, and makes still broader connections between women's health and the environmental movement: 'The fertile body is at home in the fragile ecology of the earth; pollution can lay its finger on the purity of ova and sperm as well as the water we drink and the air we breathe.'[23] To begin to tackle health for women in a way that considers all these interconnections, and sees the act of becoming healthy as an act of empowerment, requires a very different project focus from that of traditional primary health care. However, it is an approach that is being used effectively in some of the projects that Oxfam supports, as the case-studies below explain.

CASE STUDY: Health for women in Bolivia: CIDEM

CIDEM, the Women's Information and Development Centre, is a programme for poor urban women in Bolivia which took as its starting point women's need to gain control over their own and their family's health. Its approach has been to integrate the different facets that determine an individual's health — from sexuality, and the role of women in their family's health care, to the need for improvements in the environment. At the same time, CIDEM is trying to respond to the growing demand of women for information and training on matters related to their own health. In order to address these issues CIDEM has set up a 'healthy woman' surgery, a small pharmacy, and a legal-aid programme, and produces a range of educational material, both for the women themselves and to provide gender education for professionals such as doctors and solicitors dealing with rape cases.

The surgery provides a range of services from traditional ones such as antenatal care and childbirth, to screening for cervical cancer, and less traditional services such as counselling for women facing marital problems and domestic violence. In carrying out smear tests for cancer, the centre found that a very high proportion of women were also suffering from infections of the reproductive tract, and by offering treatment for chronic and troublesome complaints have built up a very positive image of the clinic among local women. The clinic works with women both individually and in groups, and has a well-developed referral system so that cases needing specialist attention can be effectively dealt with.

CIDEM has developed ways of fostering 'horizontal' relationships between doctors and patients, in the clinic and in training courses for women in health education. These are run by a woman trainer, and are a weekly event; short courses are also run, and the work is complemented by the production of educational materials. The women choose the subjects for training themselves, and have included sexuality, contraception, pregnancy, birth, breast feeding, sexually transmitted diseases, nutrition, respiratory diseases, mental health, environmental health, and topics relating to women's social status. The meetings and courses have a high participation rate from women. The surgery is used as a meeting place for women to discuss their problems and to make friends.

CIDEM is making sure that it does not work in isolation. It is promoting integrated health policies for women and information exchanges on women's health needs; it is also sharing the results of its research on women's health in poor urban areas with other institutions, and is lobbying for changes in government policies and those of other NGOs. Indeed, the need to extend the services available for women, and make better use of state resources has led CIDEM to sign agreements with the Ministry of Health to coordinate women's health activities, such as cancer detection campaigns.

CASE STUDY: Exploring health, sexuality and control of our bodies: health workshops with women in North India

SUTRA is a women's organisation, based in the Himalayas. Over the last twelve years its work with local, village-level women's groups has developed in response to a growing demand from women for skills and information to empower them to address local and personal issues more effectively. Forest protection, and problems such as dowry payments, and violence against women, have been a focus of

SUTRA's activities. SUTRA has also developed a series of workshops dealing with women's control over their bodies and health; groups of village women came together in a women-only space, living and working together over a number of days. The workshops used a range of methods to explore the themes of bodies, health and sexuality. Storytelling gave all the women in the group a chance to share their own stories, and a chance to confront the fear and isolation many felt about issues such as menstrual taboos, infertility, violence and rape, in a supportive environment. Role play built on the personal stories, providing the group with an opportunity to explore how a particular issue such as first menstruation affected a woman, and those around her. Pictures, particularly those drawn by the women themselves of their bodies and internal anatomy, provided a wealth of new ideas, and a clearer understanding of the concepts women had about how their bodies work, events such as menstruation and conception, and the action of contraceptives. The drawings also stimulated discussion about relationships with men and how women perceived and experienced them. Dancing, body work, and traditional songs provided a chance for relaxation. The deepest exploration of women's sexuality, fertility, and creativity came when the workshops were joined by a researcher from Delhi who has worked on ancient Indian texts, temple architecture and sculpture, recording and interpreting its meaning for women. The workshops built up the women's trust and courage to the point at which they felt able to deal with the idea of self-examination, which again offered new insights and understandings about their bodies.

Janet Price, from whose account of the workshops these details come, sees the process initiated at the workshops as one which needs to continue in the future. In continuing, it will not only offer further support and healing to the workshop participants, but may serve to open new doors and create new avenues for talking about subjects in the community that are otherwise considered difficult, or taboo.[24]

CASE STUDY: SOS Meninas: The Passage House in Recife, Brazil

'Aunt, why can't we be born a second time?' This was the question of a 12-year-old street girl to a project worker in the Passage House (Casa de Passagem), a centre opened two years ago for the girls and young women of Recife. It reflects the vacuum inside children who survive on the street, abused, abandoned by society, living off their sexuality and casual work, surviving on drugs to take the edge off their pain. The project, started by SOS Meninas after two years of active research on the streets of Recife, is about the health of girls and women in the broadest sense of the term: it offers street girls their first experience of social limits, of the need to construct boundaries and develop independence and confidence.

> The girls arrive at the Passage House dirty, drugged and tired. They arrive and sleep. When they awake they ask for food, then sleep again. The work of the Project begins immediately. The girls want peace, food, and security and they show all the physical signs of having survived in a place where such things are not available to them....Working with these girls means working with permanent anguish. The project worker is never able to fill the vacuum inside these children.

Even if the Passage House project cannot heal all the pain that the girls bring with them, there is much that it can do. Project workers enable the girls to talk about their experiences, to work with them to exorcise their ghosts and fantasies, and in the process to begin to build a positive self-image. They help the girls deal with the guilt they feel about their sexuality, and offer them the opportunity to learn other forms of human communication and more appropriate ways of expressing their sexuality. Many of the girls need to come to terms with the pain of being abandoned by their mothers, before they themselves can learn to mother their own children. One 13-year-old stated that she now knew 'why my mother did the wrong things she did. When I was born she was only 13 years old and her father threw her out [of] the house because she was pregnant with me. I don't want to be a prostitute like my mother, I don't want to suffer like she suffered.'

The Passage House is the second stage of the overall programme of SOS Meninas, following on from work on the streets with the girls. In the third stage, girls either return to their families, or move into Community Homes where they take joint responsibility for running the homes, become fully independent, and start to live normal lives with friends and neighbours. Step four of SOS Meninas's programme embodies strategic gender needs: preventative work, working with poor communities in the City of Recife, and with female community leaders and teachers who, with girls and adolescents, discuss such subjects as violence, health, civil rights, children, work, housing, sexuality and discrimination. The hope is that, as time goes on, the young women will take responsibility for passing on what they have learnt and in this way play a part in changing the way of life for millions of Brazilian girls.[25]

Women in the Passage House, Recife, Brazil.

9

ACTORS IN SOCIAL CHANGE

The more I dissect and analyse and derive and pursue, the more I see hurdles ahead of any attempt to regenerate a just and peaceful society. The tunnel does not find an end through reason alone. But I believe — it is my real belief — that with faith in the ability of humans to change their destiny through their own will and collective determination, I see the potential of a united women's movement being a force in the world which can heal the division and thaw the confrontation and perhaps even the order — the economic and social order.

Devaki Jain, Founder of the DAWN network

Creating spaces

Social change needs a catalyst. The women's movement in the South is just such catalyst; new, oriented to justice between genders, between races, between classes, growing in confidence and organisational skills, and embracing those who have traditionally been left out of the political process: the world's poorest women. The resurgence of women as actors on the world stage is one of the most potent dynamics in the struggle against an unjust social order, both within and between nations. Disillusionment with traditional development solutions to the problems of poverty and deprivation, and all the ill-health, lack of education and opportunity that this entails, means that any alternative approach is rapidly seized on, hence the growing women-in-development 'industry'. But can the women's movement in the South, with its rhetoric of empowerment, its belief in putting the 'last first' do more than provide small, local-level solutions to individual, local-level problems? Can it, in the words of Devaki Jain be 'a force in the world that can heal the division and thaw the confrontation'?

In the last decade there has been a rapid growth of all types of NGOs in the South, including those focusing on aspects of gender and development. At the same time, Northern donor organisations have also expanded; collectively they now transfer more to the South than the World Bank group does. Far from being peripheral to the overall development plot, NGOs have now moved closer to the centre stage. As a result, there has been a growing interest in finding ways in which the NGO effort can be made more effective and more influential: the term 'scaling up' has become popular to describe the process. One of the key components of scaling up is the building of strong, grassroots movements in the South. This is also the concern of many of the women's groups whose stories have been included in this book. One of the most coherent accounts of this need to build a strong, grassroots movement has been written by the women of north-east Brazil, in their book *Why We Should Work with Women*. The following extract gives details of why this is seen as such a priority:

> The movement has various levels: grassroots, advisors, and, in the case of the union groupings, the executives. At the level of the grassroots, the women get together and mobilise. Advisers... help in developing strategies, producing materials, offer training programmes...Another level that is very rarely taken into account when looking at the structure of the women's movement is that of the donor agencies, who may or may not inject resources towards specific work.

> The widening of the impact of the work, as well as a deepening of awareness about women's situation, depends on constant and appropriate networking between the various levels. The grassroots has always been seen as a priority throughout the growth of the experiences that have been analysed here. It is here that women both exchange experiences and awake to the true nature of their situation, as well as gradually equipping themselves for political office in the public domain...For this reason strategies for networking and exchange of experiences are essential...In the same way as at the micro level of each group, meetings between women can break down personal isolation, networking between groups gets rid of the excessive personalisation of the work...'[1]

As women form networks, and small groups link up and work together, individual efforts become a movement. Gaining experience and confidence within this movement prepares women for another phase of scaling up, that of influencing public policy, particularly in areas which affect women gender needs. The work with domestic workers in Recife, mobilising them to take part in the struggle to widen the labour laws to guarantee them new rights, would be an example of this. How can Northern NGOs participate in the work of creating broad-based social movements around the world? Again, *Why We Should Work with Women* offers the perspective of a Southern NGO. Northern NGOs can 'prioritise gender' in their work, represented by the extent of funding, since '...the spread of the women's movement to include regional, national and international networking demands large sums of money...[such] occasions are very enriching and indeed necessary, so long as the objectives of the networking are thoroughly worked out especially in relation to a commitment to the grassroots.'[2]

The provision of financial support is only one aspect of the relationship. Oxfam's Gender and Development Unit have recently set up a new project in response to the perceived importance of this form of networking, called 'Women to Women: Worldwide linking on development', which is a South–North and South–South linking of women development practitioners and activists over a three-year period. The first part of the project took the form of a three-week visit by eight women to the UK and Ireland. They talked about their work to various groups, and each woman spent time with particular groups of UK women who were working in a similar field to her own. Part of their time during their visit was taken up in planning a conference, on gender and development issues, to be held the following year. The final part of the project will be a series of networking visits between women activists from different countries of the South.

The creation of 'spaces' for the discussion of gender and development is another way in which Northern NGOs can support the growth of the women's movement in the South:

> ...the relationship between funders and financed groups cannot be seen in terms of straight transfer of resources. It is more like a complex two-lane highway, where you find power, communications and different political stances. Given this, the agencies can carry out an important function of sensitising people to the issues, both within organisations and beyond, going much further than the

straight allocation of funds...We suggest a kind of 'positive discrimination', or in other words a real guarantee of 'spaces' for the debate on gender questions, which would in turn lead to more consistent support for specific work...This publication [*Why we should work with women*] is...[an] extremely positive example....[3]

This partnership between women in the South and the North, and the creation of spaces, whether in the media, in the agenda of development agencies, or in the form of international lobbying, can play a vital role in broadening the base of support for the work of women's organisations in the South, and contributes to the formation of the links which are a prerequisite for change.

A new partnership

Why We Should Work with Women raises questions about the sort of partnership that could exist between North and South. As development institutions increasingly make commitments to work with women and to prioritise gender in their programmes, it is important to ask questions about the kind of relationship donors have with those they fund, and how decisions are made. If there is a partnership, are the partners equal? Or is partnership a euphemism for a relationship that is hierarchical and which replicates the imbalances of power between the genders and between North and South?

One initiative between development agencies and women in the South to try and combat such imbalances and make cooperation a more democratic affair is a network known as 'Entre Mujeres' (Among Women). The network was started with the objectives of strengthening and consolidating ties between European development and Latin American organisations working with women, and contributing to knowledge in Europe about the social, economic, and political reality of Latin American women. Entre Mujeres also seeks to consolidate ties between Latin American NGOs working with women. The network was started in response to the difficulties that women's NGOs had in gaining access to funds that more general NGOs gain more generously. (It is worth remembering that, despite their rapid growth in the last 15 years, women's NGOs, particularly those with a specific gender perspective, are still hugely outnumbered by other NGOs. In India, for example, where the NGO sector is well developed, it has been estimated that less than 15 per cent of NGOs work with women, while the proportion of exclusive women's NGOs is likely to be much smaller.) As accessing funds became easier, the network then had to confront problems with the funding agencies' lack of understanding of both their programme work, and the autonomous perspective of the women's organisations: they 'had to consider accepting... recommendations and advice on what should be done with Latin American women', from Northern institutions that lacked a gender perspective.[4]

Five of the Latin America women involved in the network produced a document, 'Contribution to a new politics of women and development' in which they spelt out a range of gender issues involved in funding decisions, such as the nature of autonomy. Entre Mujeres defines autonomy as 'the process by which a group defines and decides its own needs and satisfactions, its own path to growth and development...We see autonomy as our capacity to define oppression for ourselves and to formulate our own proposals for transformation from our own interests as women.' It is through this growing autonomy that women's organisations are able to construct larger movements and networks, which in turn are able to act on a broader political canvas for social change. The challenge works both ways: for women's organisations to articulate their analysis and their proposals for change, assuming greater responsibility for both, and for donors to support or accompany them in this process.

The extract below comes from a summary of the document, produced by Carola Carbajal from the organisation CIDHAL. It offers a cogent rationale and a much broader agenda for further cooperation between Northern funders and Southern women's organisations:

> Black and white distinctions between the First and the Third World are neither useful not accurate any more. Interdependence reinforced by the advance of communications and rooted in the new international division of labour shows us a linked world where power and hierarchy is concentrated in just a few hands. Co-operation, within this context, cannot be a one-way process. It has to be a responsible and mutual activity which in addition must confront the need to preserve our world. It must also face its historic responsibility towards those countries which have supported at their own expense the progress of developed countries. Therefore, co-operation for development has to be a double way. We, in the Third World, have to assume responsibility for establishing a more equal exchange of relationship. We want to have a voice in the establishment of exchange terms. Up to now, we have accepted inequality, reduced to money terms; and have been part of the powerful-

donor/humble-receiver relationship. The interchange needs to be not only financial; human expressions could also be interchanged, such as: history, art, culture, faith and others. Power relations expressed in gender, race and age oppression are a problem for the whole world. The recognition of a common ground such as the search for a higher quality of life could be the basis for democratic cooperative relations.[5]

Making a fairer world

We have travelled a long way in this book, from the birth of a baby girl in the first chapter to the potential for social change and transformation offered by a united women's movement in the last. The thread that links the two is gender, the gender roles that women are born into, and which, while differing greatly for women in different parts of the world, tend to offer women less opportunity for achievement in all spheres of life — only half a chance: less opportunity for ownership of property and other assets, for political power, education, good health, and even, as we have seen, for earning a decent living. We looked at the ways in which gender roles are constructed from the basic biological building bricks with which we are all born, but that class, ethnicity, colour, religion, caste, and nationality have a vital role to play in deciding exactly what life chances women will have, in relation to men from the same background. Only women can become mothers, and suckle their children, but this biological or 'natural' ability has often meant that all of women's work in maintaining life — from nurturing children, to collecting fuel and water, growing the family food, marketing the surplus, and caring for those who are sick or elderly — is also seen as 'natural' rather than 'work', which is what men do. This false perspective on the importance of what women do has meant that, in the development process, women have often lost out. It is also an untrue picture, since millions of women in the South are engaged in work for financial gain to support their families in conditions of profound poverty; because of the family responsibilities with which they are charged, they tend to work part time, and in the informal sector.

Development as practised in the 1950s and 1960s tended to use the model of modernisation in the belief that industrialisation, capitalism and modernised agriculture would bring expansion and growth that would trickle down to all sectors of society. Few if any of the initiatives were targeted at women, largely because of ignorance about their economic roles, and in the belief that if men benefited from development, so too would the women related to them. Much of the development of the first two 'development decades' was not neutral to the world's poorest women, but significantly destructive: environmental depletion, national debt, and structural adjustment, a crisis in food production, and the growing militarisation of the South have made life harder for millions of Southern women, even while others have benefited from national development agendas. By the 1970s, the serious omission of the majority of poor women from most planned development began to be recognised; the last 20 years have seen a variety of different initiatives to redress the development balance with varying degrees of success. In the last decade, the women's movement in the South has become sufficiently self-confident and clear in its analysis to begin to suggest alternative development paradigms, in which it is seeking partnership with donor organisations and other women's groups in the North.

This book has told two stories; the story of the enormous odds against which millions of women struggle, and the story of some of the solutions that are daily produced out of this hardship and struggle. As community managers, as farmers, as water collectors, as caretakers of fragile ecologies, and as mothers, women daily produce and reproduce life. Only when, and if, their energies and expertise are valued and released for the well-being and growth of societies along peaceful and equitable lines will any other development initiatives have half a chance of succeeding.

'As community managers, as farmers, as water collectors, as care–takers of fragile ecologies, and as mothers, women daily produce and reproduce life.'

NOTES AND REFERENCES

Chapter 1

1   Cited in Archer, A. and Lloyd, B. (1985) *Sex and Gender*,
    Cambridge: Cambridge University Press, p. 220.

2   Reeves Sanday, P. (1981) *Female Power and Male Dominance*,
    Cambridge: Cambridge University Press, pp.76-90.

3   ibid. p. 11.

Chapter 2

1   Comment, *Guardian*, 1 June 1992.

2   Oakley, P. and Marsden, D. (1984) *Approaches to Participation in
    Rural Development*, Geneva: I.L.O., p. 5

3   ibid. pp.6-7.

4   ibid. p.6

5   See for example the discussion in Kitching,G., (1982), *Development
    and Underdevelopment in Historical Perspective*, Milton Keynes: Open
    University.

6   AAWORD, (1985) 'AAWORD in Nairobi', *Occasional Papers, Series
    3*, pp. 1-3

7   Shiva, V. (1988) *Staying Alive*, London: Zed Books, New Delhi: Kali
    for Women, pp. 12, 220.

8   O'Connell, H. (1990) *Just Ordinary Feminists*, London: War on Want, p.27

9   Hulme, D. and Turner, M. (1990) *Sociology and Development: Theories, policies and practices*, New York and London: Harvester Wheatsheaf, pp. 49-50.

10 Oakley and Marsden, op. cit. p. 9.

11 World Commission on Environment and Development (1989), *Our Common Future*, Oxford: Oxford University Press, p. 71.

12 Timberlake, L. (1988) *Africa in Crisis*, London: Earthscan, p. 4.

13 I am grateful to Eugenia Piza Lopez for clarification on this point.

14 I am grateful to Neil Macdonald for discussion on these points.

15 Oakley and Marsden, op. cit. p. 10.

16 *New Internationalist*, 214, December 1990, p. 15.

17 Sen, G. and Grown, C. (1988) *Development, Crises and Alternative Visions*, London: Earthscan, p. 18.

18 Nash, J. (1991) 'The World Capitalist Crisis', in *Gender and Society*, 4; 3, p. 341.

19 Bhatt, E. (1989) *The Grind of Work*, Ahmedabad: Self Employed Women's Association, p.iii.

20 Bleier, R. (1984) *Science and Gender*, Oxford: Pergamon Press, pp. 139-140.

21 Folbre, N. (1988) 'Patriarchal social formations in Zimbabwe' in Stichter, S.B. and Parpant, J.L. (Eds) *Patriarchy and Class: African women in the home and workforce*, Colorado: Westview Press, p.63.

22 War on Want (1987) 'Women, food and famine', in *Women for a Change*, London: War on Want.

23 'Does the British Aid Programme want development for women?' in *Women for a Change*, op. cit.

24 Robinson, M. (1992) 'NGOs and rural poverty alleviation: results of an empirical investigation and implications for scaling up'. Paper for conference on 'Scaling up NGO Impact: Learning from Experience', IDPM, Manchester, January 1991, p.10.

Chapter 3

1 Young, K. (1989) *Serving Two Masters*, Ahmedabad: Allied Publishers Ltd, p.xiv.

2 'Song of Ocol', by Okot B'Pitek, Uganda, in Advocates for African Food Security, Lessening the Burden for Women, A Task Force, (1987) *Case Studies from Africa: Towards Food Security*, p.3.

3 Moser, C.O.N. and Levy, C. (1986) *A Theory and Methodology of Gender*, University of London: DPU Gender and Planning Working Paper 11, p.3.

4 Piza-Lopez, E. 'Overcoming the barriers; women and participa tion', *GADU Newspack* 4, reprinted in Wallis T. and March C. *(eds)* (1991) *Changing Perceptions: Writings on gender and development*, Oxford: Oxfam, pp. 115–116.

5 See discussion in Jeffrey, P., Jeffrey R. and Lyon, A. (1989) *Labour Pains and Labour Power*, London: Zed Books, pp. 71–95.

6 Change (undated) *Daughters of the Nightmare: Caribbean women*, London: Change International Reports, p.8.

7 Watson, C. (1988) 'The development needs of Turkana Women', a report prepared for Oxfam and the Public Law Institute.

8 Bhatt, E. op. cit. p.iii.

9 Census of India (1971), *Centenary Monograph*, p.693.

10 Quoted in Jeffrey, P et al, op. cit. p.43.

11 Mosse D., field research 1991, personal communication.

12 Momsen, J. Henshall (1991) *Women and Development in the Third World*, London: Routledge, p.26.

13 Ivan-Smith, E. et al (undated) *Women in Sub–Saharan Africa, Report 77*, London: The Minority Rights Group, p.9.

14 ibid. p.9.

15 Momsen, op. cit. p.26.

16 ibid. p.26.

Chapter 4

1   Momsen, op. cit. preliminary pages p.i.

2   Dumont, L. (1972) *Homo Hierarchicus* (English edition) London: Paladin, p. 40.

3   Jeffrey, P. et al., op cit. pp. 9ff.

4   Charlton, S.E.M. (1984) *Women in Third World Development*, Boulder and London: Westview Press, p. 50.

5   Patel, V. (1987) 'Campaign against amniocentesis', in *In Search of Our Bodies: A feminist view on women, health and reproduction in India*, Bombay: Shakti, pp.70-74.

6   Plummer, K. (1984) 'Sexual diversity; a sociological perspective', in Howells, K. (ed) *Sexual Diversity*, Oxford: Basil Blackwell, and cited by J Weeks in *Sexuality*, London: Tavistock Publications, p. 108.

7   Cartledge, S. and Ryan, J. (eds) (1983) *Sex and Love: New thoughts on old contradictions*, London: The Women's Press, p.1, and quoted in Weeks, op. cit. p.23.

8   Brydon, L. and Chant, S.L. (1989) *Women in the Third World: Gender issues in rural and urban areas*, Aldershot: Edward Elgar, p. 50.

9   Cited in ibid. pp. 84–85.

10 Ivan–Smith et al, op. cit. p.8.

11 ibid. pp.8,9.

12 ibid. p.8

13 ibid. p.8.

14 May, N. 'Women, law and development workshop', *GADU Newspack 11* and internal Oxfam documents.

15 Bunch, C. (1990) 'Towards a revision of women's rights', in *Women's Health Journal*, 19, p. 6.

16 Womankind Worldwide (undated) 'The Elimination of violence against women', *Women's Lives 5*, London: Womankind Worldwide, p. 3.

17 Mies, M. (1988) 'Class struggles and women's struggles in rural India', in Mies, M., Bennholdt-Thomsen, V. and Von Werlhof, C. *Women: The Last Colony*, London: Zed Books, p. 138.

18 Kappeler, S. (1986) *The Pornography of Representation*, Cambridge: Polity Press.

19 Internal Oxfam document.

20 Bourdieu, P. (1977) *Outline of a Theory of Practice*, Cambridge: Cambridge University Press, pp. 89-95.

21 Women Living Under Muslim Laws (1988) *Dossier 3*, p.3.

22 *Women's World* (1989) 21-22, p.6.

23 Menchu, R. (1984) *I, Rigoberta Menchu*, London: Verso Books, pp. 120, 122, 131, 134.

24 Rios, P.N. (1990) 'Export-oriented industrialization and the demand for female labour', in *Gender and Society*, op cit. pp. 321-337.

25 Leon, M. and Viveros, M. (undated) 'Rural women in Colombia: invisible labour and the double day', in Harris, O. (ed) *Latin American Women, Report 57*, London: Minority Rights Group, p.9.

26 World Bank (1991) *Gender and Poverty in India*, Washington: World Bank, p. xxii.

27 ibid. p. xxii.

28 Lorfing, I. (1989) 'The work of women in Lebanon from 1970–1985; realities and perspectives', *GADU Newspack 10*.

29 Thanh-Dam, T. (1990) *Sex, Money and Morality*, London: Zed Books, p. 129.

30 ibid. p. 189.

31 Details taken from Institute for Religious Studies, *Area Activities Report*, 1990, 'Self–esteem in outcast groups'.

32 Women Living Under Muslim Laws (1988) *Dossier 3*, pp.33-35.

33 The Tribune (1990) 'Women and Law', *Newsletter 45*.

34 Clark, L. and Lewis, D. (1977) *Rape: The price of coercive sexuality*, Toronto: The Women's Press, p.119.

35 Internal Oxfam documents.

36 Young, K. (1987) 'Women's Education and Training', in *Women's Education and the British Aid Programme*, London: War on Want and World University Service (UK), p. 3.

37 Quoted in Womankind Worldwide (undated) 'Women and Education', *Women's Lives 4*, p. 10.

38 Young, K., op cit. p. 3.

39 Womankind Worldwide, 'Women and Education', pp. 6-8.

40 Adapted from Mwau, A. (1990) 'Production of adult literacy material', *GADU Pack 12*.

Chapter 5

1 DAWN, op cit. p. 54.

2 Acosta-Belén, E. and Bose, C.E. (1990) 'From structural subordination to empowerment', *Gender and Society*, op cit. pp. 316-317.

3 Quoted in Grossholtz, J. (1984) *Forging Capitalist Patriarchy: The economic and social transformation of feudal Sri Lanka and its impact on women*, Durham: Duke University Press.

4 ibid. p. 76.

5 Von Werlhof C. (1988) 'On the concept of nature and society in capitalism', in Mies, M. et al., op cit. p. 104.

6 Grossholtz, op. cit. pp. 59–61.

7 Timberlake, L., op cit. p.4.

8 ibid. p.5.

9 Mies, M. 'Capitalist development and subsistence production: rural women in India', in Mies, M. et al, op cit. p. 28.

10 ibid, p.31.

11 Oxfam internal documents.

12 Griffiths, I. (1984) *An Atlas of African Affairs*, London and New York: Methuen, and cited by Timberlake, op cit. p. 23.

13 David Edgar, cited by Gonzalez, L. (1988) 'For an Afro–Latin

American feminism', in *Women Organizing for Change*, Rome and Santiago: ISIS and DAWN, p.96.

14 Feijoo, del C.M. (1989) 'The challenge of constructing civilian peace: women and democracy in Argentina', in Jaquette, J.S. (ed) *The Women's Movement in Latin America*, London: Unwin Hyman, p. 91.

15 Alvarez, S.E. (1989) 'Women's movements and gender politics in the Brazilian transition', in Jaquette, J.S., op. cit. p. 23.

16 ibid. p. 30.

17 Case study compiled from internal Oxfam documents.

18 Thiam, A. (1986) *Black Sisters, Speak Out: Feminism and oppression in Black Africa*, London: Pluto Press, p. 13.

19 *Speak*, 27, p. 7.

20 African National Congress (1987) *Women's March to Freedom*, Lusaka: ANC, p. 1.

21 *Speak*, 27, p. 7.

22 *Women's March to Freedom*, op cit. p.6.

23 Internal Oxfam document.

24 *Speak*, 27, p. 7.

25 ibid.

26 Burger J. (1987) *Report from the Frontier: The state of the world's indigenous peoples*, London: Zed Books and Cambridge, Mass: Cultural Survival, p.1.

27 ibid. p.9.

28 Piza-Lopez, E. and Wooding, B. (1987) 'Latin American/Caribbean Gender Seminar', Oxfam internal document, pp. 16–17.

29 Burger, op. cit. p.9.

30 ibid. p. 23.

31 Rocha, J (1992) 'Hopes 2: Brazil' in *Earth*, London: The Guardian in Association with Oxfam, p.11.

32 Mies, M. et al., op. cit. p. 138.

Chapter 6

1   World Bank (1990) *Poverty: World Development Report*, Oxford:
    Oxford University Press, p. 1.

2   Piza-Lopez, E. (1990) 'Beyond the debt crisis: structural transfor
    mation', Oxford, Oxfam, p. 1.

3   Clark, J. (1986) *For Richer For Poorer*, Oxford: Oxfam, p. 64.

4   Quoted by John Clark, Oxfam, UK, at UN/NGO Workshop,
    Oxford, September 1987.

5   Ahooja-Patel, K. (1989) *Women and the World Economic Crisis,
    Women and Development Kit, 6*, Geneva: United Nations
    Information Committee/Non-Governmental Organisation
    Programme Group on Women and Development, Part 1, pp. 10-11.

6   *Our Common Future*, op cit. p. 74.

7   Elson, D. (1987) 'How is structural adjustment affecting women?',
    GADU Newspack 4, p. 2., and reprinted in *Changing Perceptions*, op.
    cit.

8   World Bank, op cit. p. 103.

9   *Our Common Future*, op cit. p. 124.

10 Grigg D (1985) *The World Food Problem 1950–1980*, Oxford: Basil
    Blackwell, pp. 135–136.

11 State of the World's Women (1985), World Conference to Review
    and Appraise the Achievements of the United Nations Decade for
    Women, Nairobi, and cited in Change (undated), *Farmers, Food and
    Famine: Women's role in ending hunger*, London, Change, (no page
    numbers).

12 Barrett, H.R. and Browne, A. W. (1989) 'Time for development?
    The case of women's horticultural schemes in rural Gambia',
    Scottish Geographical Magazine, 105; 1, pp. 4-11.

13 FAO (1984) *Women in Agriculture; No. 1: Women in Agricultural
    Production*, Rome: FAO, p. 6.

14 Whitehead, A. (1991) 'Food crisis and gender conflict in the
    African countryside', in Bernstein, H., Crow, B. and Mackintosh,
    M. (eds.) *The Food Question*, London: Earthscan Publications, p. 59.

15 Advocates for African Food Security/Lessening the Burden for Women: A Task force (1987) *Case Studies from Africa: Towards food security*, p. 69; and (undated) *Women: Key to African food security*, p. 4.

16 ibid.

17 Whitehead, A. op. cit. p.63.

18 ibid. p. 63.

19 ibid. p. 55.

20 ibid. p. 57.

21 ibid p. 57.

22 Change, *Farmers, Food and Famine*, op. cit.

23 Population Crisis Committee (1991), data sheet: 'Cities: Life in the World's 100 Largest Metropolitican Areas'.

24 *Our Common Future*, op cit. pp. 237-238.

25 IUNC (1987) 'Women and the World Conservation Strategy: Report of the first strategy workshop', and quoted in Womankind Worldwide (undated), *Women and the Environment, Women's Lives 6*, p. 5.

26 D'Monte, D. (1989) 'India: The pavement dwellers of Bombay', in *Against All Odds*, London: The Panos Institute, p. 11.

27 Ramirez, S. (1988) 'Women confront the economic crisis and demand participation', in DAWN and ISIS International, *Women Organising for Change: Confronting the crisis in Latin America*, p. 29.

28 Compiled from internal Oxfam documents.

29 For example, the sterilisation drive during the Indian Emergency is documented in Cassen, R. H. (1978) *India: Population, economy, society*, Basingstoke: Macmillan, pp. 181–193.

30 Bruce, J. (1990) 'Fundamental elements of the quality of care: a simple framework', *Studies in Family Planning*, 21; 2, pp. 61–91.

31 Davidson, J. and Myers, D. (1992) *No Time To Waste: Poverty and the Global Environment*, Oxford: Oxfam.

32 Shiva, V., op. cit. pp. 179-180.

33 Graham, O. (1988) 'Pastoral women and drought: Social dislocation in Central Somalia', *GADU Newspack* 6, pp. 2-3.

34 Brett, A. (1987) 'Changing the Approach? The Wello Water Experience', *GADU Newspack* 3, pp. 1-5.

35 Shiva, V., op. cit. p. 189.

36 Timberlake, L., op. cit. pp. 87-88.

37 McCracken, J. (1989) 'Women, environment and development in India: a collection of quotes and anecdotes', Women's Environmental Network and War on Want, *Women, Environment and Development: Report of a Conference*, London: War on Want, p. 19.

38 Shiva, V., op. cit. p.60.

39 ibid. p. 94.

40 'Women contract-workers in the Iraq-Kuwait conflict', *GADU Newspack 13*, 1991; Valentin, P. (1991) 'Some reflections on gender issues in situations of conflict', internal Oxfam document; Piza-Lopez, E. and Sollis, P. (1988) 'War, women and development', internal Oxfam document.

Chapter 7

1 Boserup, E. (1970) *Women's Role in Economic Development*, New York, St. Martins, p. 5.

2 Sen, A. (1987) *'Gender and Cooperative Conflicts'*, World Institute for Development Economics Research, *Working Paper 18*, Helsinki: World Institute for Development Economics Research, p. 4.

3 *Gender and Society*, op. cit. p. 307.

4 Moser, C.O.N. (1989) 'Gender planning in the Third World: Meeting practical and strategic gender needs', *World Development*, 17; 11, p. 1807.

5 World Bank (1990) op. cit. p. 2.

6 Moser, C.O.N., op. cit. p. 1810.

7 Lycklama a Nijenolt, G. (1989) 'Women as Producers of Development', in Vronweneraad nederlandse ontwikkelingsin

stanties, *Women, Producers of Development*, p. 16.

8 Rathgeber, E.M. (1990) 'WID, WAD, GAD: Trends in research and practice', *The Journal of Developing Areas*, 24, p. 490.

9 World Bank (1987) 'The World Bank New Approach to Women in Development', F.Y. 87.

10 Overseas Development Administration (1989) *Women, Development and the British Aid Programme: A progress report*, London: Overseas Development Administration.

11 Moser, C.O.N., op. cit. p. 1813.

12 ibid. p. 1814.

13 Bentley, E. (1988) *Struggle for Survival: Organizing the paper pickers of Ahmedabad*, Ahmedabad: Mahila Sewa Trust, p. 36.

14 DAWN, op. cit. p. 16.

15 Antrobus, P. (1990) in Wallace, T. and March, C. (eds) *Changing Perceptions*, Oxford, Oxfam, p. 312.

16 Molyneux, M. (1985) 'Mobilization without Emancipation? Women's interests, state and revolution in Nicaragua', *Feminist Studies*, 11; 2.

17 Moser and Levy (1986), op cit. pp. 8-9.

18 Young, K. (1989) *Serving Two Masters*, op. cit. pp. xix-xx.

19 Longwe, S.H. (1989) 'Supporting women's development in the Third World: distinguishing between intervention and interference', paper presented at FINNIDA, Helsinki.

20 DAWN, op. cit. pp. 80-82.

21 Antrobus, op. cit. pp. 314-316.

Chapter 8

1 Piza-Lopez, E. (1987) 'Overcoming the barriers: women and participation', *GADU Newspack 4*, p. 5.

2 Adapted from Eade, D. (1991) 'If I don't know who I am...': women's awareness training in Honduras, Central America', *GADU Newspack 14*.

3 Womankind Worldwide (undated) 'Women Organizing', *Women's Lives 1*, p. 1.

4 DAWN, op. cit. pp 90-93.

5 I am grateful to Bridget Walker for information on this point.

6 I am grateful to Eugenia Piza-Lopez for discussion on this point.

7 *Why We Should Work with Women*, pp. 71-77.

8 Kelley, N. (1989) 'Working with refugee women: A report of the international consultation on refugee women', Geneva: UNHCR, p. 85.

9 Wallace, T. (1990) 'Refugee women: their perspectives and our responses', *GADU Newspack* , p. 1.

10 Ball, C. (1987) 'When broken–heartedness becomes a political issue', *GADU Newspack 2*, and reprinted in *Changing Perceptions*, op. cit. pp. 263-267.

11 Oxfam internal memo.

12 'Declaration of the national campaign for housing rights in India', in *Our Homes: Ourselves, National Conference of women and housing, 1987*, London: Shelter, p. 15.

13 Moser, C.O.N. (1987) 'Women, human settlements and housing: a conceptual framework for analysis and policy-making', in Moser, C.O.N. and Peake, L., *Women, Human Settlements and Housing*, London: Tavistock Publications, pp. 18-19.

14 ibid. p. 20.

15 Compiled from Oxfam internal documents.

16 Both studies quoted in Womankind Worldwide (undated), 'Women and Health', *Women's Lives 3*, London, Womankind, pp. 1-2.

17 Cleves Mosse, J.C. (1991) 'The risks of being female', in *Changing Perceptions*, op. cit. p. 85.

18 Women and Health, *Women's Lives 3*, op. cit. p. 5.

19 Garcia-Moreno, C. and Piza-Lopez, E. (1991) 'Gender and health', Oxfam internal document.

20 ibid. p. 6.

21 'Women and Health', *Women's Lives 3*, op. cit. p. 6.

22 Chaterjee, M. (1987) 'The double burden: occupational health and self-employed women', in *In Search of our Bodies: A feminist view on women, health and reproduction in India*, Bombay: Shakti, p. 46.

23 Mosse, J.C. and Heaton, J., (1991) *The Fertility and Contraception Book*, London: Faber and Faber, p. 373.

24 Adapted from Price, J. (1991) 'Notes on workshops conducted with women in North India', *GADU Newspack 14*.

25 Adapted from Vasconcelos, A. (1991) 'SOS Meninas', *GADU Newspack 13*.

Chapter 9

1 'What we want from funding agencies', *Why We Should Work with Women*, p. 89.

2 ibid. p. 91.

3 'The part funders should play', *Why We Should Work with Women*, p. 92.

4 Carbajal, C. (unpublished paper) 'A women's approach to North and South co–operation for development', p. 1.

5 ibid. p. 4.

INDEX